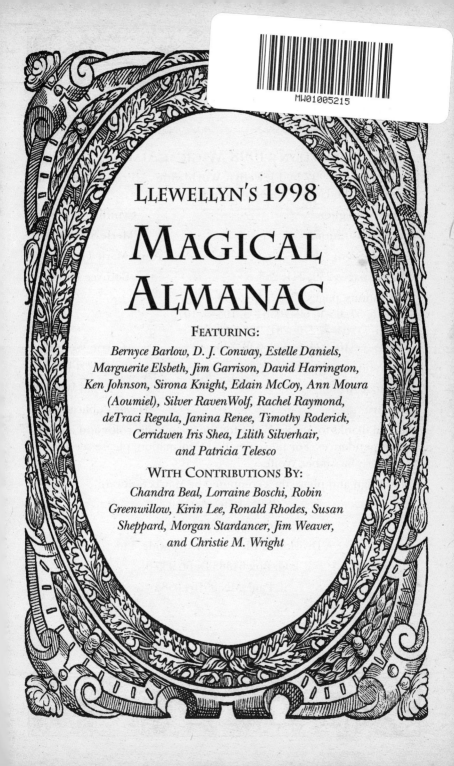

Llewellyn's 1998

Magical Almanac

Featuring:

*Bernyce Barlow, D. J. Conway, Estelle Daniels,
Marguerite Elsbeth, Jim Garrison, David Harrington,
Ken Johnson, Sirona Knight, Edain McCoy, Ann Moura
(Aoumiel), Silver RavenWolf, Rachel Raymond,
deTraci Regula, Janina Renee, Timothy Roderick,
Cerridwen Iris Shea, Lilith Silverhair,
and Patricia Telesco*

With Contributions By:

*Chandra Beal, Lorraine Boschi, Robin
Greenwillow, Kirin Lee, Ronald Rhodes, Susan
Sheppard, Morgan Stardancer, Jim Weaver,
and Christie M. Wright*

LLEWELLYN'S 1998 MAGICAL ALMANAC

Editor/Designer:	Cynthia Ahlquist
Cover Illustration:	Merle S. Insinga
Cover Design:	Anne Marie Garrison
Photos, pages 239, 241, 283:	Bernyce Barlow
Illustrations, pages 22, 32, 35–6, 38, 46, 54–5, 57, 65–6, 69–70, 84–5, 104–5, 107, 246–7, 264–7, 279, 281, 286, 288–90 302–3, 310, 324–6, 328, 338, 340:	Carrie Westfall
Illustrations, pages 236–8:	Jim Garrison
Calendar Art:	Robin Wood
Clip Art:	Dover Publications

Special thanks to Amber Wolfe for the use of daily color and incense correspondences. For more detailed information, please see *Personal Alchemy* by Amber Wolfe.

Moon sign and phase data computed by Matrix Software.

ISBN 1-56718-935-0

Llewellyn Publications

A Division of Llewellyn Worldwide, Ltd.

P.O. Box 64383 Dept. 935-0

St. Paul, MN 55164-0383

Welcome to the *1998 Magical Almanac!* Far be it from me to keep you from diving immediately into the smorgasbord of magical advice, spells, recipes, and tidbits our authors have cooked up for you, but as my mother used to say, it's not polite to dig in to the feast without a nod the chefs. Bearing that in mind, I extend a big thank you to our authors: Bernyce Barlow, D. J. Conway, Estelle Daniels, Marguerite Elsbeth, Jim Garrison, David Harrington, Ken Johnson, Sirona Knight, Edain McCoy, Ann Moura (Aoumiel), Silver RavenWolf, Rachel Raymond, deTraci Regula, Janina Renee, Timothy Roderick, Cerridwen Iris Shea, Lilith Silverhair, and Patricia Telesco. Their creativity and willingness to share their insights are an inspiration from which we all benefit, and it is a privilege to work with them.

I also thank our contributors, whose work rounds out the feast (we have to make sure all of those magical food groups are represented, after all): Chandra Beal, Lorraine Boschi, Robin Greenwillow, Kirin Lee, Ronald Rhodes, Susan Sheppard, Morgan Stardancer, Jim Weaver, and Christie M. Wright. These are the brave people who sent in their work "on speculation," or without any promise of publication. Many of them responded to an ad for new writers that I ran in Llewellyn's *New Worlds Magazine.*

If the articles in the *Magical Almanac* are the feast, then the artwork is the dessert. Thank you to Carrie Westfall, whose delightful illustrations are scattered throughout the book. If you've ever tried to find a picture of an aura, a Slavic shaman, or a sheila-na-gig in a standard clip art collection, then you have some appreciation for the regard in which I hold Carrie. Thank you also to Merle Insinga for a fabulous and truly magical cover illustration, Jim Garrison for the stang illustrations, and Bernyce Barlow for the sacred site photos. Each of you has greatly enhanced this book. Now, a brief word about the creators of this fabulous feast!

BERNYCE BARLOW is the author of *Sacred Sites of the West,* from Llewellyn. She researches and leads seminars on sacred sites of the ten western states. In addition to excavating sites in the Great Basin, Bernyce is involved in in-depth research on the Peter Pan ride at Disneyland, and insists that Never Never Land is her favorite sacred site.

D. J. CONWAY has been involved in many aspects of New Age religion from the teachings of Yogananda to study of the Qabala, healing,

herbs, and Wicca. Although she is an ordained minister in two New Age churches and holder of a Doctorate of Divinity degree, Conway claims that her heart lies within the Pagan cultures. No longer actively lecturing and teaching, she has centered her energies on writing. She is the author of the Llewellyn books *Celtic Magick; Norse Magick; The Ancient and Shining Ones; Maiden, Mother, Crone; Dancing with Dragons; Animal Magick; Moon Magick; Flying Without a Broom; By Falcon Feather and Valkyrie Sword; Astral Love; Magickal, Mythical, Mystical Beasts; Dream Warrior* (fiction), and *Soothslayer* (fiction).

ESTELLE DANIELS is a professional, part-time astrologer and author of *Astrologickal Magick,* a book about astrology written for people who are interested in using astrology, but aren't interested in becoming astrologers themselves, and astrologers who are interested in exploring psychic and magical topics. She has been contributing to Llewellyn's annuals since 1997. Her work appears irregularly in the pages of *The Mountain Astrologer,* and she is available for lectures and book signings with advance planning. Estelle is also an initiate into Eclectic Wicca and teaches the Craft with her High Priest. She is still writing, and hopes to have another book coming soon.

MARGUERITE ELSBETH (Raven Hawk) is a professional diviner, and a student of Native American and European folk healing. She has published numerous articles in *Dell Horoscope, The Mountain Astrologer,* and other publications since 1984, is co-author of *The Grail Castle: Male Myths and Mysteries in the Celtic Tradition* and *The Silver Wheel: Women's Myths and Mysteries in the Celtic Tradition* with Ken Johnson, and is the author of *Crystal Medicine: Working with Crystals, Gems, and Minerals.* Marguerite is a hereditary Sicilian Strega, and is proud of her Delaware Indian ancestry. She resides on a Pueblo Indian reservation in the desert Southwest.

JIM GARRISON is a writer, artist, and consulting occultist, as well as a husband and father who is very proud of his magical little girl Zoe. A dedicated student of a wide variety of magical systems and techniques, he teaches subjects from scrying, tarot, sigil magic, and basic ritual. His primary affiliations are modern/eclectic Wicca and post-industrial shamanism. During the day he works as one of the editors of Llewellyn's *New Worlds Magazine.* He contends that his cat Maya

has just recently converted to an obscure form of Kashmir Shaivism known only to a highly evolved group of six other cats, four of whom have already transcended this plane of existence.

DAVID HARRINGTON has been a chronicler of the magical arts for the past fifteen years. He is the co-author with Scott Cunningham of *The Magical Household* and *Spellcrafts*. He is also the co-author of *Whispers of the Moon* and the forthcoming *Body Magic: The Art and Craft of Adornment and Transformation* with deTraci Regula. David has traveled extensively in the Yucatan and recently returned from the wilds of Greece. He is currently studying traditional folk harp.

KEN JOHNSON holds a degree in comparative religions with an emphasis in the study of mythology. He has been a professional astrologer since 1975, and is co-author of *The Grail Castle: Male Myths and Mysteries in the Celtic Tradition,* and *The Silver Wheel: Women's Myths and Mysteries in the Celtic Tradition* with Marguerite Elsbeth; and co-author of *Mythic Astrology* with Ariel Guttman. He is also the author of *North Star Road* and *Jaguar Wisdom.*

SIRONA KNIGHT, M.S., C.H.T., is author of *Greenfire* and *Moonflower,* and the forthcoming *Shapeshifter Tarot* (Llewellyn) with D. J. Conway. She also serves as a contributing editor for *Magical Blend Magazine.* E-mail her at oneknight@juno.com.

EDAIN McCOY is part of the Wittan Irish Pagan Tradition and is a Priestess of Brighid and an elder within that tradition. She occasionally presents Pagan spirituality workshops and works with students who wish to study Wiccan and Celtic Witchcraft. She is a member of the Authors Guild and the Wiccan/Pagan Press Alliance. Edain is the author of *Witta: An Irish Pagan Tradition; A Witch's Guide to Faery Folk; The Sabbats; How to Do Automatic Writing; Celtic Myth and Magick, Mountain Magick; Lady of the Night; Entering the Summerland; Inside A Witches' Coven;* and two forthcoming titles, *Making Magick* and *The Bottomless Cauldron.*

ANN MOURA (AOUMIEL) has been a solitary Witch for over thirty years. She is the author of the Llewellyn books *Dancing Shadows* and *Green Witchcraft,* and has recently completed work on a book about the dark aspects of the Lady and the Lord. She conducts seminars on Green Witchcraft and enjoys working in her herb garden.

SILVER RAVENWOLF is the Director of the International Wiccan/Pagan Press Alliance, a network of Pagan newsletters, publishers, and writers, and the editor of the organization's mouthpiece *The Mid-Night Drive*. She is also the National Director of WADL (the Witches Anti-Discrimination League). Silver is a degreed Witch, receiving her eldering from Lord Serphant from the Serphant Stone Family (Gardnerian lineage), and is Clan Head for the Black Forest Traditional Witches. Silver is the author of the books *To Ride a Silver Broomstick, HexCraft, Beneath A Mountain Moon, To Stir a Magick Cauldron,* and *Angels: Companions in Magick.*

RACHEL RAYMOND is a writer, astrologer, herbalist, artist, bookkeeper, Pagan priestess, wife, and mommy. She lives in Northern California with her husband, two children, a dog, a cat, two gecko lizards, countless spiders, and many, many books.

DETRACI REGULA is the author of *The Mysteries of Isis* and co-author with David Harrington of *Whispers of the Moon,* a biography of Scott Cunningham. She has recently returned from Greece, where she led a Goddess tour to various Isis sites. With David, she is currently working on *Body Magic: The Art and Craft of Adornment and Transformation,* exploring the magic of jewelry, tattooing, and other forms of adornment. When not writing, she can be found refining her fencing skills.

JANINA RENEE holds a degree in anthropology and is a scholar of such diverse subjects as folklore, ancient religions, mythology, magic, and Jungian psychology. She is currently exploring the ways that practicing in the presence of Deity relates to the myriad names and forms of the old gods and goddesses, because she believes that they reveal themselves to us in every moment of our waking and dreaming lives. Her other interests include geomancy and genealogy. Janina is the author of *Playful Magic* and *Tarot Spells.*

TIMOTHY RODERICK is the author of the Llewellyn books *The Once Unknown Familiar* and *Dark Moon Mysteries.* He holds a Master's degree in clinical psychology, and is an interning psychotherapist in Los Angeles. He is a Wiccan Priest and founder of the Earthdance Collective.

CERRIDWEN IRIS SHEA writes in several genres under several different names. Her play *Roadkill* had successful runs in London, Edinburgh, and Australia. *Scrying* received four-star reviews in Edinburgh. *Plateau*

is being adapted for the screen. She is currently working on a play based on the Iphigenia myth, and a feminist comedy for several of her priestesses in Circle of Muses called *Rock Chicks Rule*. She has been published in *Circle Network News* and *Llewellyn's 1997 Magical Almanac.*

LILITH SILVERHAIR is a solitary practitioner of an eclectic Pagan Path, living in what has been dubbed "weird central" with her husband and two children. She is co-editor of the newsletter *Coll of the Goddess.* Her articles have appeared in several newsletters including *Silver Chalice.* She is currently putting the finishing touches on her first novel, *Miranda's Children,* about reincarnation and Goddess worship.

PATRICIA TELESCO has written fifteen new age/metaphysical/self-help books, including *Victorian Grimoire, Victorian Flower Oracle, Urban Pagan, Kitchen Witch's Cookbook, Witch's Brew,* and *Folkways* for Llewellyn. Trish travels regularly for lectures, workshops, book signings, and readings, and is available to consider future engagements. She is currently working on a tarot deck and enjoys hearing from her readers.

CHANDRA BEAL is a freelance writer whose first name is Sanskrit for "the Moon." She attributes her fascination with that celestial object to this fact. She credits her mother for teaching her many magical ways, and for sharing her Llewellyn books with her as she grew up. She is currently writing a book about recreation and swimming.

LORRAINE BOSCHI is a playwright, former teacher of literature, philosophy, and women's studies, and enthusiastic collector of mythology and folklore who lives her New Age lifestyle. A world traveler who lived in Italy for several years, she likes to do her research "on the spot," and it was a recent trip to Ireland that inspired her article on the Irish harp.

ROBIN GREENWILLOW has been a practicing Witch and astrologer for ten years. Robin finds meaning and truth in all faces of the Goddess, and seeks to share that knowledge with anyone who also heeds the call of the Divine. A "transplant" to the state of Minnesota, Robin has chosen to reside where all the seasons of the year can be fully experienced. Like the many faces of the Goddess, each season teaches different lessons, and each should be appreciated for what it is.

KIRIN LEE writes and does graphic design for a science fiction magazine, and is the managing editor for a rock and roll magazine. When she is not writing articles she is writing science fiction, and she is

currently working on a Star Trek novel. She is also beginning a Pagan parents' handbook. Her other interests are horses and cats.

RONALD RHODES is an eclectic practitioner, blending Wicca, shamanism, and dragon magic in his religious practice. His hobbies include jewerly making and herbal wildcrafting. He can see auras, and uses gemstones and crystals in his healing work.

SUSAN SHEPPARD is the author of the *Phoenix Cards,* published in 1990 from Destiny Books. She writes articles for *Dell Horoscope* and *American Astrology* magazines. She also has a novel forthcoming in 1997 from Caramoor called *The Gallows Tree.*

MORGAN STARDANCER is a Wiccan and Pagan activist living in Texas. She tries to juggle three kids, a wolf, a dog, and several cats with multiple careers in freelance writing, graphic design, and internet website design. She also grows herbs, collects stones, and avidly studies the healing arts.

JIM WEAVER writes articles on folk traditions of Greece and the near east, combined with elements of Christianity and modern culture. These traditions were passed on to him by his grandparents. When he is not writing, he enjoys working in his herb garden.

CHRISTIE M. WRIGHT sent us the following bio: "I am sixteen years old and a sophomore in high school. I am an Aquarian—creative, special, wonderful, beautiful, and slightly conceited (at times)! Although I'm a creative writer, would you believe I make Cs on my essays in English 2 Honors? This is my first publication ever, and I would like to thank Jim Garrison, a writer for Llewellyn's *New Worlds Magazine,* and Cynthia Ahlquist, Senior Annuals Editor. I would also like to give special thanks to Silver RavenWolf, an angel in disguise. Mom, luv ya. Oh yeah. I'm still 'playing' and haven't decided what tradition I'll follow. But then, I've got a while."

Now that you know the chefs, it's time to grab a chair, tie a napkin around your neck, stick your elbows on the table, and dig into this magical smorgasbord. Have a wonderful 1998!

—Cynthia Ahlquist, Editor

TABLE OF CONTENTS

The Maiden, The Mother, The Crone *by Christie M. Wright.* 1

A Mayan Creation Story *by Ken Johnson* 4

Personal Spirituality *by D. J. Conway* 6

Spirit Dreaming *by Marguerite Elsbeth* 9

Rite in Honor of the Goddess of the Dawn *by Janina Renee* . . . 10

Shamanism: The Non-Religion *by D. J. Conway* 12

The Knights Templar *by Jim Garrison* 14

Cretan Goddesses *by deTraci Regula* 18

Curanderismo: Mexican-American Folk Healing
    by Marguerite Elsbeth. 22

Chantways *by Lilith Silverhair* 24

Psychic Shielding for Your Home *by Estelle Daniels* 26

Home as Sacred Space *by Cerridwen Iris Shea* 29

The Rainbow Harmony Candle *by Silver RavenWolf* 32

Witch Bottles *by Jim Garrison* 36

The Magical Art of Pacific Rim Tattoo *by Bernyce Barlow* . . . 39

Magical Tattooing in the Ancient World *by David Harrington* . . 42

Unleashing the Magic of Your Aura *by Edain McCoy.* 46

Will *by Jim Garrison* 48

The Irish Harp *by Lorraine Boschi* 52

Plumb-Bobs and Y-Rods: Divination by Dowsing
    by Lilith Silverhair. 54

Native American Giveaways *by Marguerite Elsbeth* 57

The Washoe Seeress *by Bernyce Barlow.* 58

The Law of Threefold Return *by Jim Garrison* 60

Seeing Through Justica's Eyes *by Edain McCoy* 61

Hawiian Magical Symbology *by Bernyce Barlow.* 62

Charm Jar *by Silver RavenWolf* 65

A Children's Story for the Spring Equinox *by D. J. Conway* . . . 66

Maximon: The Earth Father *by Ken Johnson* 70

Animal Spirit Teachers *by Timothy Roderick* 72

Languages of Healing and Light *by Bernyce Barlow* 74

The Power of Words *by Jim Garrison* 79

The Power of Almonds *by Jim Weaver* 80

Income Tax Magic *by Silver RavenWolf* 82

The Angel Bottle *by Silver RavenWolf* 84

Magical Tools *by Jim Garrison* 86

Cord Magic *by Estelle Daniels*. 90

Magic Fingers *by Rachel Raymond* 93

Elemental Specifics *by Cerridwen Iris Shea* 96

Places of Power *by Ken Johnson* 98

Temples of Isis in Greece *by deTraci Regula*. 100

The Legend of Lost Lemuria *by Ken Johnson* 104

Fairies *by Silver RavenWolf* 105

The Fey Folk *by Lilith Silverhair*. 108

Lord of the Wild Hunt *by D. J. Conway*. 110

A Ride with the Wild Hunt *by Ann Moura (Aoumiel)* 112

BBS, Cyberspace, and Privacy *by Estelle Daniels*. 114

Almanac Section **117**

Almanac Listings **118**

Time Changes **120**

1998 Sabbats and Full Moons. **121**

The Planetary Hours **122**

Calendar Pages **128**

The Summer Solstice: A Garden of Delights
    by Sirona Knight 187

Planting an Enchanting Sun Flower Circle
    by Silver RavenWolf. 190

The Buffalo Dance *by Marguerite Elsbeth* 192

Rockhounding *by Marguerite Elsbeth* 194

Crystal Enchantment *by D. J. Conway* 196

Greek Oracle Sites *by deTraci Regula* 199

Tattwas *by Jim Garrison* 204

Ancestral Paths *by Ken Johnson* 206

Tree Medicine *by Marguerite Elsbeth* 208

Tree Magic *by Ken Johnson* 210

Blessed Bug Repellent *by Patricia Telesco* 212

Bug Magic *by Rachel Raymond* 214

Make a Portable Altar! *by Edain McCoy* 217

Mobile Magic *by Cerridwen Iris Shea* 220

Working with Herbs and the Moon *by Chandra Beal* 223

Taming the Wild Dandilion *by Edain McCoy* 228

Sea Shell Secrets *by Marguerite Elsbeth* 230

Cosmic Camping *by Ken Johnson* 232

The Sacred Pipe *by Marguerite Elsbeth* 234

Making a Stang *by Jim Garrison* 236

Iao Valley, Maui *by Bernyce Barlow* 239

Remote Viewing *by Silver RavenWolf* 242

Worry Bead Spells *by David Harrington* 246

The Rocking Chair Meditation for Success
by Silver RavenWolf 248

Sacred Mountains *by Ken Johnson* 252

Mixing Pantheons *by Cerridwen Iris Shea* 253

Lady Sheba *by Jim Garrison* 256

ABCs of Pagan Parenting *by Kirin Lee* 260

Rainy Day Crafts for Kids *by D. J. Conway* 263

Rituals for Pets *by Cerridwen Iris Shea* 268

Incense for Cats *by Bernyce Barlow* 272

10/31/96 *by Susan Sheppard* 273

The Evil Eye *by Marguerite Elsbeth* 274

A Folk Cure for the Evil Eye *by Jim Weaver* 276

The Vrykolakes of Santorini *by deTraci Regula* 279

The Watchers *by Bernyce Barlow* 282

The Raven *by Marguerite Elsbeth* 284

Green Hecate, The Dark Phase of the Moon
   by Estelle Daniels 286

The Charge of the Crone *by Jim Garrison* 289

Accepting the Passage *by Robin Greenwillow* 290

Shapeshifting: Reflections of Ourselves *by Sirona Knight* 292

Ritual and Magical Masks *by Patricia Telesco* 295

Mysterious, Magical Masks *by Silver RavenWolf* 298

Creating Chinese Lanterns
   to Honor the Dead *by Edain McCoy* 301

Otherworld Mist *by Ken Johnson* 304

Mr. Crowley *by Jim Garrison* 305

Past Lives Meditation *by Ann Moura (Aoumiel)* 308

A Wizard's Prayer *by Ken Johnson* 310

Dressing Kabbalistically *by Estelle Daniels* 312

Teaching a Circle *by Cerridwen Iris Shea* 316

Jewitchery *by Edain McCoy* 320

Sheila-na-Gig *by Edain McCoy* 324

The Basics of Stone Work *by Morgan Stardancer* 326

Magical Correspondences? What Do I Use Them For?
   by Silver RavenWolf 329

Common Scents Incense *by Ronald Rhodes* 332

St. Nicholas the Pilgrim *by Ken Johnson* 336

Making Your Own Magic Kits from Scratch
   by Silver RavenWolf 338

Directory of Products and Services 341

THE MAIDEN, THE MOTHER, THE CRONE

BY CHRISTIE M. WRIGHT

The room begins to darken,
No, it is not the dusk.
For even now, I hear the cock stirring atop his post.
They tell me the candles burn bright as the Sun at high noon;
Yet, their light seems to me as dull as my hair that once shone like gold,
and is now gray as the storm clouds of the sea.
Faces fade in and out of my weakening vision:
faces of my childhood,
faces of those I loved.
My clawlike hand grips another's tightly,
a hand smooth and soft as mine once was.

Flickerflickerflickerflicker

I blink.
And see a beautiful girl-child holding my hand.
Her skin is smooth to the touch,
and laughter sparkles in Her emerald eyes.

Her long, silky hair cascades down Her back in loose waves,
and a wreath spun of spring buds adorns Her untroubled brow,
Her slim form, barely beginning to ripen into womanhood,
reminds me of my youth.
She smiles gently
and whispers a word.
Maiden.

Flickerflickerflickerflicker

I blink,
and see a woman.
Her steady hazel eyes comfort me.
The laugh lines around Her eyes and mouth are clear and beautiful.
Her thick hair is bound in a braid
and a circlet of gold rests upon Her brow.
Her rounded belly reveals the life nestled inside.
She bends close to me,
and places Her smooth lips on my withered cheek.
She whispers.
Mother.

Flickerflickerflickerflicker

I blink,
and see a face all too like my own:
Her cheeks are hollow and Her skin withered.
She leans upon a great staff,
Her clawlike hands grasping it as if it were life itself.
Her eyes burn with a gentle intensity,
and as I gaze into them,
I see the WiseWoman,
She gestures
and whispers.
Crone.

Flickerflickerflickerflicker

I blink.
And see Them.

The Three.
Maiden.
Mother.
Crone.
The Three who are One.
As one, They beckon me;
and I feel my spirit stir in response.
The Maiden whispers
Come with us, Mother.
The Mother whispers
Join your companions, sister.
The Crone whispers
Do not be afraid, my daughter.
I sigh and close my eyes.
My soul rises and greets the Three.
And upon each of Their brows
the crescent blazes,
and I know that it burns upon my brow as well.

Flickerflickerflickerflicker

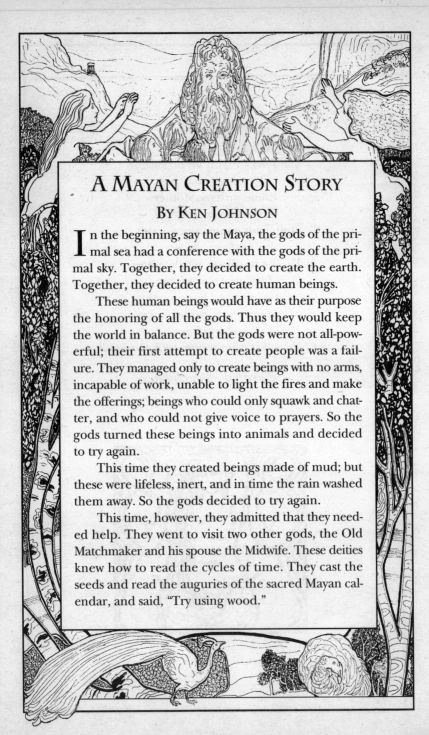

A Mayan Creation Story

By Ken Johnson

In the beginning, say the Maya, the gods of the primal sea had a conference with the gods of the primal sky. Together, they decided to create the earth. Together, they decided to create human beings.

These human beings would have as their purpose the honoring of all the gods. Thus they would keep the world in balance. But the gods were not all-powerful; their first attempt to create people was a failure. They managed only to create beings with no arms, incapable of work, unable to light the fires and make the offerings; beings who could only squawk and chatter, and who could not give voice to prayers. So the gods turned these beings into animals and decided to try again.

This time they created beings made of mud; but these were lifeless, inert, and in time the rain washed them away. So the gods decided to try again.

This time, however, they admitted that they needed help. They went to visit two other gods, the Old Matchmaker and his spouse the Midwife. These deities knew how to read the cycles of time. They cast the seeds and read the auguries of the sacred Mayan calendar, and said, "Try using wood."

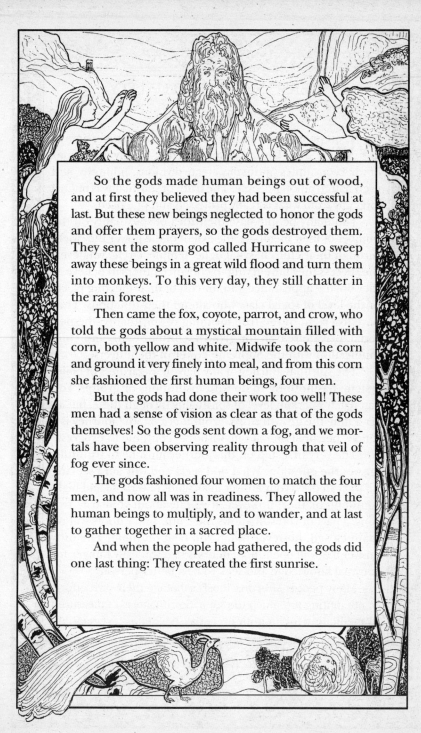

So the gods made human beings out of wood, and at first they believed they had been successful at last. But these new beings neglected to honor the gods and offer them prayers, so the gods destroyed them. They sent the storm god called Hurricane to sweep away these beings in a great wild flood and turn them into monkeys. To this very day, they still chatter in the rain forest.

Then came the fox, coyote, parrot, and crow, who told the gods about a mystical mountain filled with corn, both yellow and white. Midwife took the corn and ground it very finely into meal, and from this corn she fashioned the first human beings, four men.

But the gods had done their work too well! These men had a sense of vision as clear as that of the gods themselves! So the gods sent down a fog, and we mortals have been observing reality through that veil of fog ever since.

The gods fashioned four women to match the four men, and now all was in readiness. They allowed the human beings to multiply, and to wander, and at last to gather together in a sacred place.

And when the people had gathered, the gods did one last thing: They created the first sunrise.

Personal Spirituality

By D. J. Conway

Most people give thought to spirituality at some time in their lives. Unfortunately, often the many definitions of what constitutes spirituality create divisions, animosity, and even hatred among people. The truth of spirituality is often a long way from what is really professed and practiced.

Too many people base their idea of spirituality on the number of their members, the extent of the power they wield through their church, synagogue, temple, circle, whatever, the success they have trying to convince others to believe as they do, the appearance and/or cost of their meeting place, or the level of social class who attend their functions. They have lost sight of the true meaning of spirituality: the personal, private search for growth, contentment, and communication with the Supreme Power of the universe.

The spiritual journey of any person, regardless of belief system, has nothing to do with institutions or groups. You can reach a certain level of spirituality through these, but after a time the growth stops. From there on, the journey is a lonely, personal one, if one wishes to continue to progress.

The very first step on this journey must be to truthfully answer the question: What do I seek, and why am I seeking it? You can dress your answer in all kinds of verbose and high-sounding blather; however, if you lie about your true reasons, a part of you still knows the truth. Inner doors will remain closed, however much you beat on them. The only answer that will open those doors is that you truly hunger for spiritual knowledge and seek to be a better person.

Many people subconsciously sabotage their own efforts by attempting too much too soon. Spirituality isn't measured by meditating for an hour every day, becoming a vegetarian, practicing strange (and sometimes painful) yoga positions, giving away all your money and possessions, letting some high mucky-muck tell you how to live your life, dressing in strange garb, or refusing to speak to anyone who isn't of your faith. The true spiritual level of a person is seen only through actions, words, contentment, and the way he or she generally lives life.

You do need to have a fairly consistent routine for spiritual endeavors, however. Start your morning by silently saying, "Thank you for what I have. Help me do good things today." Meditating once or twice a week is good, if you are into meditation. If not, substitute a prayer session. If you are Pagan, do a little candle ritual for yourself or someone else who needs a boost. If you aren't Pagan, just light a candle and say a prayer. Don't tell anyone what you did, however. This teaches you humility.

Treat your body like the marvelous machine it is by not overexercising, overeating, putting anything harmful into it, and basically not overindulging. Keep it clean and healthy without becoming a fanatic. Like the Chinese say, live and eat eighty percent healthy eighty percent of the time.

Set aside time each week for an hour or so of study in a spiritual subject that interests you. Read something uplifting and inspiring. If you do this just before you go to bed, the subject will sink into your subconscious mind and have the best effect.

Try to be understanding and patient with those with whom you come in contact. If you're having a bad day, watch carefully what you say; you could be sabotaging yourself with negative words. If others are rambling on in a negative matter, excuse yourself (if possible) and refuse to take part. Words, positive or negative, build the envelope of energy that surrounds us, and that we carry with us everywhere we go. This energy can have positive or negative effects on all of your life. Don't be a doormat, however.

Whatever spiritual path you have chosen, don't proselytize. Proselytizing means that you actively seek to make others convert to your belief in order to gain followers to your cause. This is actually only a membership drive for an institution and has absolutely nothing to do with spirituality. Don't be shoving your religious material in anyone's face, and don't allow others to do it to you.

The religion or belief system you choose to follow has nothing to do with your personal search for spiritual growth. This journey is all done within the mind and heart and soul of each individual in private. The judgment and opinion of others on our progress is not important. Deep within, we each know how well we've made the effort.

When we've stretched ourselves to a new spiritual level, we discover an amazing result. We deeply desire to continue with the spiritual journey. There are so many positive side effects that we enjoy the journey, even when it becomes difficult, which it does at times.

Although we are temporarily living in finite, physical bodies, we won't always do so. The part of us that is spirit will some day release that body and try to find its way back to the source. Through our personal, private efforts of taking a daily spiritual journey, we will find we already know the way home.

Spirit Dreaming

By Marguerite Elsbeth

Every evening, after you have settled yourself in bed, talk to your ancestors, guardian spirits, and animal totems, whoever or whatever they may be, asking them to reveal themselves to you. Say to yourself, "Tonight I remember my dreams." Then, go to sleep—and dream. If the dreams don't come right away (many of us are blocked in the department of dream memory), keep saying the affirmation right before you go to sleep each night. Eventually, the dream spirits will come.

Some dreams will wake you up in the middle of the night, especially if they are nightmares. If this happens, stay with the dream for as long as possible, and try to change the outcome in your favor. Then, wake up. Some nightmares are good things—the scarier, the better. They are your shadows, your allies, your friends, your power.

When you wake, write down the vision you have seen. Do not analyze the images. Simply describe them. When you are finished, make a note of what you felt as you dreamt. Were you afraid, bold, happy, tired, bored, or confused? Write it down. Your feelings are the essence of the dream symbols and spirits you have envisioned. They are your own personal interpretation of the meaning of your dream. In this way, you will learn what is good or bad for you. You will discover who your guardians, allies, and helping spirits are as well as those from which you may require protection.

When you are finished, thank the spirits that visited you in dream. Now go back to sleep, and dream on.

Rite in Honor of the Goddess of the Dawn

By Janina Renee

Every morning we unconsciously perform Aurora's rites in the simple act of awakening and quickening. For those who wish to know this Goddess better, the simplest way to honor Her is to take a moment to greet Her. Following is a small rite you can perform to seek inspiration from this Goddess. She can help you to get off to a good start on the daily job of personal transformation, become more focused in pulling your life together, and bring art and beauty into your life.

Arise while the sky is still dark and go to an eastward facing view, if possible, where you can stand ready to greet the goddess. Outdoors is best, but an eastern window is also appropriate. The area should be fairly private and quiet, so that you can compose yourself and focus on the rite. Have on hand a glass of orange, apricot, or papaya juice, or some other fruit beverage with the naturally warm tones of dawn's palette—a tangible way of drinking in her power.

Stand for a while in quiet contemplation as you watch the transformation of the morning sky. Then, raise your glass in salute and say:

Graceful Lady,
As you bring me the gift of this new day,
I honor you in this, my new beginning.

Take a few sips of your juice, thinking about the liquid energy contained therein, then set your glass aside for later. Now, stretch your arms out in an invoking position or any other position of greeting and welcome that you prefer, and say:

Lady in the form of light,
I honor you in the names of Eos, Aurora,
Hemera, and Mother Matuta,
Ausca, Aushrine, Ausekelis, and Auszra,
Ushas, Anpao, Princessa D'Alva,
And by all other names
By which the world has known you.
I praise your radiant and ethereal beauty.
I open my being to you,
Even as you open the gates of morning.
Your vibrant colors energize my body
And purify my spirit,
As they penetrate the morning sky.
You teach me to love life and welcome change,
And I seek harmony with you
By filling life with art and color.

Stand for a while in contemplation. As you watch the rosy light spread through the morning sky, allow Aurora's palette of colors to suffuse your being—a mystical penetration that caresses your soul. Visualize your every atom being stirred and renewed with the energy of vibrant color, as the Goddesses' fingertips of light reach in to illumine the corners of your soul.

If you wish, you may then invoke Aurora's quickening effect by doing a dance or some graceful stretching exercises to get your body in motion and stoke your metabolism. You can borrow movements from ballet, Tai Chi, etc., or improvise your own. Your motions should especially include bowed arm movements to symbolize reaching out to the Goddess and welcoming her into your home and being, as well as to emulate her own action of opening the gates of morning and spreading light. (These exercises need not be too complicated or strenuous for those of us whose life juices are slow to circulate in the morning.)

Drink the rest of your juice. When you are ready to turn away, send a kiss to the rising Sun (or in that direction if conditions don't permit you to see the Sun), then proceed with your daily business.

SHAMANISM: THE NON-RELIGION

BY D. J. CONWAY

There is a resurgence of interest in shamanism today, but not everyone is interested in its most commonly known form, Native American shamanism. It may surprise people to learn that at one time nearly every other part of the world had a form of shamanism.

Shamanism, however, is not a religion, but a supplement to any religion. It is an ideal way to begin a spiritual search for the true inner self and to establish once more the vital link with the deity or deities in which one believes.

Shamans originally used their abilities to heal, find food for the clans, and predict the future. They knew that shamanism enabled them to merge the spiritual and physical without sacrificing either. The greatest personal quest on the shamanic path was, however, to find the spiritual center of the individual.

Shamanic excursions (a form of deep, meditative astral travel) into the Otherworlds were a vital part of the practice. The names applied to the Otherworlds differed from culture to culture. For example, many Europeans called it the Land of the Mothers, a term used much later by the Celts to describe the worlds of faery and the gods. Others simply divided it into the Upperworld and the Underworld, with no other specific name.

Shamanism is really a solitary path toward spirituality. Shamans seldom work together, not because of professional jealousy, but rather because shamanic journeys can only be experienced by the person making them. Each journey is intensely personal. The shaman encounters deities, entities, and experiences tailored to his/her own spiritual needs. No shamanic journey is ever duplicated by another shaman.

Once individuals become serious about practicing shamanism, they begin to understand the importance of the spiritual stories of their personal religion and their spiritual symbols. These stories come alive while on shamanic journeys. One encounters the deities, other entities, and symbolic events mentioned in them. The shaman discovers that the God/Goddess mentioned by one spiritual path are the same as those held in reverence by other paths. Only the names have changed. Shamans of all religions have a common ground in that they become messengers from the All to all people.

The practice of shamanism can benefit anyone. It provides each person with a personal method of contact with the God/Goddess and the human subconscious and superconscious minds. It requires no special equipment, although many shamans gradually gather what they feel they need. It can be done at any time, in almost any place. All you need is your resolve to journey and a quiet place in which to do it.

Although you may use shamanism to help others, you can easily use it to help yourself. Its practice brings a deeper understanding of the self, the chosen religion, and the interconnectedness of the universe and everything in it.

There are no absolutely set ways of taking a shamanic journey. Each person can tailor the method to suit their beliefs. Because shamanism is not a religion, it conflicts with no other religion. Each intense prayer or meditation can lead you into a shamanic journey. In fact, you may be unaware that you are taking such journeys already in your daily devotions.

THE KNIGHTS TEMPLAR

BY JIM GARRISON

The Order of the Knights Templar—The Poor Knights of the Temple of Solomon—is commonly believed to have been created in 1118 C.E., although there is evidence that it was already in existence as early as 1114. Ostensibly formed to protect pilgrims in the Holy Land, the Knights Templar were given a monastic rule, the equivalent of a constitution, at the Council of Troyes, conducted under St. Bernard. This represented a radical new phenomenon; for the first time in Christian history, soldiers would live as monks.

From 1128 C.E., under Grand Master Hughues de Payens, the Templar Order expanded at a tremendous rate—both in terms of recruits and through immense donations of land and money. In only a year's time the Templars held property in France, England, Scotland, Spain, and Portugal. Within a decade they had spread to Italy, Germany, Austria, Hungary, and even Constantinople. In 1131 the King of Aragon bequeathed a third of his domains to the Templars.

Richard the Lion-Hearted was on such good terms with the Templars that he is considered something of an honorary Templar. He often traveled in the company of Templar Knights, sailed on their ships, and stayed in their preceptories and castles. When he had to flee the Holy Land, he did so disguised as a Templar, and an entourage of authentic Templars accompanied him. Richard sold the island of Cyprus to the Templars, and there is evidence that he may have been involved in their dealings with the Hashishim—the Muslim sect also known as the Assassins.

At the same time, the Templars had become strong enough that Richard's brother King John had to respect them. He often stayed at their London preceptory, making it his part-time residence during the last four years of his reign. The Master of

England, also the premier baron of the realm, Aymeric de St. Maur, was King John's closest advisor, and it is very likely that Aymeric helped to influence King John to sign the Magna Carta in 1215.

By the mid 1300s the Templars established themselves as the second most wealthy and powerful institution in Christendom, second only to the Papacy itself. Officially, the Templars' primary sphere of activity was supposed to be the Latin Kingdom of Jerusalem. Europe was supposed to be their source of men and material, and their clearinghouse for travel to the Holy Land.

As a religious order, the Templars were exempt from taxes. They exported their own wool, granted sanctuary as any other church might, convened their own courts, and ran their own markets and fairs. Templars were free from tolls on roads, bridges, and rivers, making it easy for them to move about the countryside.

Western Europe's economic institutions were founded on the machinery and procedures developed by the Templars, as adopted by the Italian merchant houses. The origins of modern banking can be attributed to the Templars. Even though canon law forbade Christians from engaging in usury—the collection of interest on loans—the Templars lent money and collected interest on a massive scale. In one proven case the rate was 60 percent a year, which was 17 percent more than Jewish moneylenders were allowed to collect by law.

One of the most important financial developments attributed to the Templars was the arranging of payments at a distance, without the actual transfer of funds. One could deposit a sum at a Templar preceptory and receive a chit or letter of credit that could be converted into cash in any currency desired at any other Templar facility. Theft, as well as fraud, was precluded by a system of codes that only the Templars knew. Additionally, the Templars provided the service of safe deposits; in France the Templars Paris Temple was also the royal treasury, housing the state's wealth as well as the Order's. All the finances of the French King were thus dependent on the Templars.

In England, the Templars also acted as tax collectors, collecting papal taxes, tithes, and donations, as well as taxes and revenues for the crown. Templars mediated in disputes involving ransom payments, dowries, pensions, and a multitude of other transactions. They maintained a number of long-term trust funds for the dead or dispossessed.

In 1291, the last bastion of the crusaders in the Holy Land, Acre, fell to the Saracens. The Latin Kingdom of Jerusalem was lost. The Templars no longer had any official reason to be there. The best-trained, best-equipped, and most professional military power in the West was suddenly left without a home.

Cyprus served as a provisional base for the Templars, but they had bigger plans. Inspired by the Ordenstadt of the Teutonic Knights in Prussia and the Baltic, the Templars wanted to establish their own "Ordenstadt." However, unlike the Teutonic Knights, who were out on the fringes of Christendom, the Templars wanted to build their Ordenstadt in the very heart of Europe, in the region of Languedoc, which had been annexed by France less than a century before. The possibility of a Templar state on his southern border did not please King Philippe IV of France.

Philippe IV of France had tried to join the Templars in an honorary status, as Richard had done, but he had been insultingly refused. In 1306, Philippe was chased into the Paris temple by a rioting mob, and it was there that he learned of the Templars' vast wealth. The Templars' refusal to admit Philippe into their ranks led to a bitter grudge that bore fruit years later.

At dawn, on Friday, October 13, 1307, all Templars in France were seized, their preceptories placed under sequester, and all their goods confiscated. Bold and thorough, Philippe's plan should have caught the Templars by surprise. It didn't quite work out that way. Just prior to the crackdown, Jacques De Molay, Grandmaster of the Order, had commanded many of the Order's books and rules to be gathered and burned. An official edict was circulated to all the French preceptories, stressing that no information about the Order's rites or rituals was to be released.

Many of the Templar Knights fled France. Those who were captured submitted peacefully, as though under orders to do so. There is no record of a Templar resisting arrest. One particular group of Knights did manage to escape the grasp of Philippe. The Order's treasurer was able to smuggle the Order's entire treasury out of France on a group of eighteen galleys, which were never seen again. There is no report of the Templars' ships ever being found.

On March 22, 1312, the Templars were formally dissolved by Papal decree—without a definitive verdict of guilt or innocence ever being pronounced. In March of the following year, Jacques De Molay and Geoffri de Charnay, the Preceptor of Normandy, were roasted to death over a slow fire by Philippe's soldiers. The fabulous wealth of the Order was never recovered.

As events unfolded in France, many Templars saw the proverbial writing on the wall and joined other Orders. German Templars entered the Order of St. John or the Teutonic Order. Spanish Templars joined the Order of the Calatreve, or helped to found the new Order of Montesa, which was almost entirely made up of former Templars. In Portugal, the Templars were cleared by an inquiry, and simply changed their name, becoming the Knights of Christ. This branch of the Templars survived well into the sixteenth century. Vasco da Gamma was a Knight of Christ, and Prince Henry The Navigator was a Grand Master of the Order. Their ships sailed under the Templars' distinctive red cross. Christopher Columbus was married to the daughter of a former Grand Master of the Order, and it may well have been through his father-in-law that Columbus gained his maps and diaries.

Of all the Orders of Knighthood, no other group has captured the imaginations of so many or played so instrumental a role in shaping the world of today. Mysterious as always, the Templars stand as a symbol of the Crusader spirit. Once the proud defenders of Christianity, their fall from grace has also made them synonymous with the occult, heresies, and secret rituals. What more could you want from a legend?

CRETAN GODDESSES

BY deTRACI REGULA

Home of Minoan civilization, Crete was the cradle of many of the gods and goddesses later worshipped in the rest of Greece. Zeus, Hera, Demeter, Hercules, and others seem to have first known the rough mountains of Crete before ascending to the loftier peak of Mount Olympus in Greece. Following are some of the goddesses of Crete.

THE SNAKE GODDESSES OF KNOSSOS

Probably one of the best-known images of the Goddess is the little faience snake goddess found at the palace of Knossos. With a cat perched on her head, two snakes writhing in her outstretched hands, large eyes staring defiantly at the viewer, this nameless goddess exerts a powerful fascination over us. Who was she? What was her name, what were her titles and functions? We can only guess.

She was not alone. Two other statues, similar but not identical, were found with her. One, broken into bits, leaving only the bell of her skirt and separate, severed limbs, seems lost to us forever. The other, taller, revealing less youthful breasts behind the frontless bolero jacket which was a common article of Minoan women's clothing, is sometimes dubbed "The Mother," while the narrower-waisted, smaller figure is called "The Daughter." Others associate the two with Demeter and Persephone, again forgetting the third shattered divinity. Making any assumption of a clear relationship between these figures is impossible. If they are

not goddesses themselves, they may represent priestesses of an unrevealed deity to whom snakes and other animals were sacred. The intent gaze of the eyes of both figures indicates a trancelike state. Perhaps these women were "pythonesses," specially designated and trained oracle priestesses who delivered prophecies.

In an attitude of either blessing or adoration, a nameless poppy-crowned goddess waits, safely encased in glass. With the clear, yet blankly unrevealing, lines of much of Aegean and Cycladic art, this figure too seems caught between the human and the divine. Does she worship, or does she call for worship, or both? The clay opium poppy flowers adorning her head speak of divine intoxication and oracle dreams. Surrounded by similar figures, the observer seems to be illicitly watching a ritual trapped in clay. (Apparently this sacred spying was not unknown in Crete. Nearby, a clay model of a tomb or temple holds a sacred statue. On the roof, peering through an opening, a stealthy figure clings, observing the sacred rites.)

BRITOMARTIS

Though the museums hold many divine figures, some are too elusive to be captured. One of the favorite goddesses of Crete is a swift mermaid maiden called Britomartis or Vritomartis, ancient Minoan for "sweet virgin." In Eastern Crete, one of her havens and haunts was the bay at present-day Elounda, just opposite Spinalonga Peninsula, which until recently was a leper colony. In ancient times, the merchant city of Olous dominated this bay, and Britomartis

comfortably shared her site and her status with the Egyptian visitor, Isis, among others. Coins from Olous show the head of Britomartis or bear an eight-pointed star, which may have also been a symbol of Britomartis.

A later legend describes how Britomartis fled the embrace of Minos, ultimately traveling to the island of Aegina. Here a beautiful temple was built to her high among the pines, overlooking the Aegean far below. On Aegina, Britomartis was called Aphaia, the hidden or invisible one, since she was believed to have arrived on the island and immediately concealed herself in a cave among the pines around her temple site.

On clear, still days the remains of Olous are visible beneath the waters of the bay, and local merchants and restauranteurs will be happy to point out the walls. When the city was on the shore, Britomartis must have contented herself with swimming past it. Now every rock and stone beneath the waves of this curiously soothing bay is hers. One expects mermaids, of the cheerful kind, to break the surface of the water and wave a graceful, if slightly finny, hand.

DicLynna

Crete is a rough land, with high mountains, difficult trails, hidden caves, and sharp shorelines. Game is abundant, and a goddess, DicLynna, decides which hunter will be granted a full table that night. In later times, she was often called Diana DicLynna, recognizing her similarity with that goddess of the hunt. Western Crete was her own territory, and her name comes from Mount Dikte, the highest peak. Like

Britomartis, she could also take a sea-going form, and some believe the goddesses to be identical, one receiving worship in the east of Crete, the other in the west.

Eileithyia

Another Cretan goddess who retained prominence in later times was Eileithyia, whose worship centered on caves. Eileithyia, or Eleutheria, as she is sometimes called, eventually served the Olympian deities as divine midwife. On Crete, she tended to the needs of purely human women. Her caves are filled with votive objects and were probably used as havens for women about to give birth. Eileithyia's rough form is carved into the rocks, and pillar-like stalagmites bearing her image may have been clutched by women for support as they gave birth within her sacred enclosure.

At least two of Eileithyia's birth caves still exist, and one can be visited near Heraklion. Though once remote, modern civilization has intruded to within a few feet of the entrance. It's not a well-visited site, and a barred doorway keeps the site safe from the profane. Like most goddesses, Eileithyia is only reached at the end of a maze of initiation. Access to the cave is controlled by a keykeeper living nearby, who must be found by persistent questioning. She does not reveal herself easily to the casual seeker, but for those seeking aid in either physical birth or spiritual rebirth, she will always be in attendance.

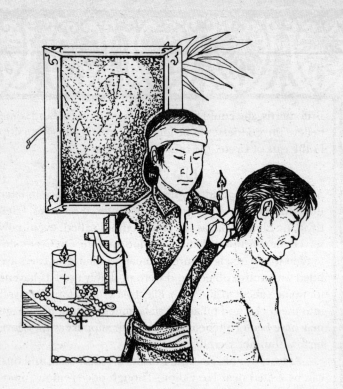

Curanderismo:
Mexican-American Folk Healing

By Marguerite Elsbeth

The practice of *curanderismo* comes from a union of Spanish folk healing traditions with those of the Aztec, Maya, and other Indian groups. The practitioner, or *curandero*, puts great faith in fate, personal gods, spirits, and the saints, and he or she will worship these deities with presents, prayers, and ritual magic.

Some curanderos are poor and illiterate, born with the power to heal. Others are well-to-do and educated. All are deeply spiritual individuals; this one factor is the most crucial indicator of their authenticity and success.

Rattles, drums, masks, and fetishes are not used by the Mexican-American healer, who prefers to rely on religious paraphernalia such as crosses and pictures of the saints. His or her home is usually filled with these items as well as an altar, replete with religious icons, candles, incense, flowers, and holy water. Offerings are made to the saints and spirits on a regular basis.

Aside from relieving physical symptoms, it is the curandero's job to help a patient accept suffering, because illness is believed to be part of a universal purpose on earth, affecting the individual, the family, and the entire community. Many people consult the curandero for otherworldly problems also. Evil *brujos* (Witches) and *hechiceros* (sorcerers) are said to derive their powers from the devil and often plague the pious and the good through use of *mal ojo* (the evil eye), *envidia* (envy), *susto* (soul loss) or even the threat of *muerte* (death). Then the curandero becomes an ardent *arbulario* (Witch-fighter), removing harmful objects shot into the victim's body by illicit magical means, or retrieving the heart of the victim, stolen to bring loss or ruin to the victim.

Patients are treated in the room where the healer keeps his or her altar; they are safe there. The healer may use a decoction or infusion made of leaves, bark, roots, and flowers, or an herbal cure, such as *agua piedra* (mineral water) for kidney stones, *ajo* (garlic) for bowel and stomach trouble, toothache, and dog bites, *albaca* (sweet basil) for bee stings, colic, and adulterous mates, *alhucema* (lavender) for vomiting and menopause, *yerba del lobo* (licorice) for blood clots, and *anis* (parsley) for shoulder pain. Massage eases sore muscles and limbs; cupping (a candle applied to the site of the pain with the lit end placed under a glass) sucks out the illness. Along with these cures the healer also uses liberal doses of Vicks Vaporub™, Ben Gay™, and prayer.

Day after day, the curandero selflessly brings ailing bodies, minds, and souls back into balance with the spirit of nature and life itself. The practice of curanderismo continues to prevail throughout Mexico and the American Southwest because it works.

BIBLIOGRAPHY

Kiev, Ari. *Curanderismo: Mexican-American Folk Psychiatry*. New York: Macmillan, 1968.

CHANTWAYS

BY LILITH SILVERHAIR

The Navajo believe that diseases result from an imbalance in the harmony of the cosmos. These imbalances are only caused by human beings and can only be restored by ceremonial chantways.

WHAT IS A CHANTWAY?

Chantways are curing ceremonies that invoke supernatural powers to heal physical and psychic ailments. They last from one to nine days, and involve very long and precise chants, purification, prayer, dancing, the use of herbs, and sand paintings. To this day, chantways are still of utmost importance to the Native Americans of the Southwest. There are many Navajo who will not go to conventional medical doctors until they are assured that treatment will be accompanied by the chantway.

According to Navajo tradition, instructions for the chantways were given to the People by the Holy Ones, through intermediary spirits. The first practitioners spent seven days and nights in purification and instruction. They were told that the sand paintings that accompanied the chantway were very important, and must be done on Mother Earth to be seen and felt by all who needed the sacred knowledge.

THE HEALING PROCEDURE

A nine-day chantway (most last for more than one day) begins with four days of purification and invitations for the Supernaturals to appear. The next four days involve the Supernaturals appearing, and the final day involves the healing. The chant itself is a long retelling of the story of the hero or god who first received the ceremony. The chant must be done without error or else it is invalid, and serious errors can result in the chanter himself falling prey to the sickness he is trying to heal. This man, the *hatathli*, or chanter, has spent many

years learning the chants before he is allowed to perform them. In one lifetime, a chanter usually learns only one great rite and perhaps a few lesser ones, and the Blessing Way, which ends each ceremony.

Sand Paintings

The coming of the Supernaturals is marked by the sand painting, which must also be done exactly right and must be done in one day. One chantway may have a hundred or more illustrations, out of which the chanter or patient chooses four. They are done in sand of the five sacred colors: white, red, black, yellow, and blue. The Supernaturals themselves are done in elongated figures to show their power and otherworldly origins. These figures are arranged at the cardinal points and can be accompanied by sacred plants and animals. Paintings may also show Mother Earth and Father Sky, and depict the Sun and the Moon.

After the sand painting is empowered by the placing of sacred feathers, a sprinkling of pollen, and use of items from a medicine bundle, the patient sits on the painting. The earth is pressed against the sick person's body, especially the ailing parts, which makes the patient one with the Supernaturals, sharing their power. As the earth falls back to the ground the sickness falls from the patient's body. At the end of the ceremony, before the setting of the Sun, the sand painting is erased with a sacred feather staff. The sand is then carried away and disposed of.

Reproductions of sand paintings sold to tourists are deliberately made with errors so that the power of the paintings and the chantway are preserved for the actual ceremonies. There are no permanent copies of sand paintings.

Psychic Shielding for Your Home

By Estelle Daniels

Nowadays, the world seems to be more psychically and spiritually "active" than ever. The level of psychic noise has risen in the past years, and many people find it helpful to psychically shield their living spaces, especially the room where they sleep.

Some people can shield an area with just energy and intent, but others find it easier to anchor the shielding to objects. Some objects in themselves help provide shielding and protection, without additional energy.

What area you shield is up to you. The most basic is to just shield around your bed, so when you sleep you will not be bothered by extraneous "noises" from the other planes. You can also shield your bedroom, your entire living space (the most practical), or your entire house. If you live in an apartment or share space with others, it is best to shield only those areas that are yours alone, unless you have permission from the others sharing your space. If you live in a house, you can extend your shields to the edges of your property. You can build the shields any way you need to make them fit your requirements.

The basic idea of shielding is to somehow create a "force field" of energy that blocks out unwanted etheric noise, like a sound barrier. Visualize a golden translucent curtain that allows air to pass through, but that will block any energies from other planes. Once in place, these shields will be there, but probably won't be apparent to guests or others living in your space. You should be able to notice them if you "look," for you put them in place. It is easiest to shield if you use actual objects to "tie" the shields into, and also as a memory aid of their presence. The objects can be open or hidden, and what you use and how you place the objects is up to you.

Gather the objects to be used for shielding, and then pray over them, or otherwise put protective energy into them. Maybe light a candle and meditate over the objects, thinking about how strong and effective they will be in keeping unwanted influences out of your home. Ask your guardian angel or spirit guides to help keep your space shielded and clear of unwanted energies. Ask the deity to help keep you secure from outside influences. Any or all of these techniques can be effective. Once you have somehow put energy into the objects, place them wherever you have decided they will go, and know they are there doing the job you have intended them to do.

The objects you use can be varied. Place a small quartz crystal on every opening in your living space (door and window), and it will block unwelcome disturbances. Add a clove of garlic, and you have more protection. Check the garlic often; weekly is best. If a clove has shriveled or turned black, replace it with a fresh one and discard the old one. Other pleasant aromatic herbs (sage, mint, etc.) can also be used. Rocks work well for shielding, including tourmaline, jade, granite, fossils, and agate. Any sturdy black stone can be absorptive of unwelcome energies. Stones gathered from a river or stream (water washed), as well as stones from deep in the Earth, like from a mine or quarry, also work.

Some people use plants to shield, either inside or outside the space. Use existing trees or bushes, or plant some for the purpose. If you use plants, check them often. If they become distressed, replace them or change your anchors. Make sure the plant is strong and healthy. Don't start a small new plant and attach your shields. Wait until it has grown and matured and is strong before using it as a shield anchor. Keep the plants properly fed, watered, and healthy, and they will shield very effectively.

Made, bought, or found objects also can work for helping anchor shields. Generally, plastic is not a good material as it does not absorb energy well. Metal conducts energy well, but

may not block unwanted influences, so it is best to experiment. Natural materials work well as they are good energy conductors. You want something that is solid enough to take the energy, and will stand up to the elements if you put it outside.

Religious objects have been used for centuries as a form of shielding. Religious statues, pictures, or icons can be very effective.

Experiment with various materials and placements. If something doesn't work, try changing the placement or use something else. Some place objects over doors and windows, some use the corners, some use the four walls. Don't forget the ceiling and floor. You can place objects inside your space, or outside. Do whatever is most convenient and practical.

Once you put up shields, monitor them every so often. Take a feel and see if they are working and still there. If they seem to be weaker in one direction, reinforce that direction. Energies change with the seasons, so you may have to change and adapt throughout the year. You can incorporate your shields into seasonal decorations. If you move your furniture around, you should also check your shields and see if they need readjusting. If you hold a party, you will want to reinforce the shields afterward as part of the cleanup.

Make checking your shields part of your cleaning routine. You can make sure your space is psychically as well as physically clean. If you do yard work, or household repairs, check your shields then also. If you have nightmares or trouble sleeping, check the shields. You may need temporary or more permanent reinforcement. You may have to change your shields; whatever you chose may not be working.

Shielding your living space can aid in keeping your equilibrium in a psychically active world. You want your own little corner to be as peaceful and quiet as possible. If your living space is shielded, then it is safe for you to drop your own barriers and relax at home. Blessed Be.

HOME AS SACRED SPACE

BY CERRIDWEN IRIS SHEA

My home and hearth are the physical centers of my strength. If my home is stable, no matter what is going on with the rest of my life, I feel confident about handling it. If my home is in turmoil, so is the rest of my life.

I live in Manhattan, which is a wonderfully wacky place to live in general. There is energy careening around twenty-four hours a day, both good and bad. There is constant stimulation. You never know what or who you will run into at any given moment, and need to literally be ready for anything. It's exhilarating and exhausting. It makes it even more important that my home be a sanctuary. How does one do that? I have a few ideas that I would like to share.

ORGANIZING YOUR SPACE

Set your home up the way you want it. My desk used to be in the bedroom, because that is where there was room for it. However, I don't like to write in my bedroom. I like to sleep, read, make love, play with the cats, and do ritual work in the bedroom. Having my computer in there was distressing. I like to write in the kitchen. I like to be near the phone and fax machine, the food, the coffee, and the cats. So, I now write on my kitchen table, and I am in the process of converting my bedroom desk into a sewing table. I don't have television or telephone in my bedroom. I realize that if one has children, one must have a telephone in the bedroom, but I don't yet, and I'm taking advantage of it. I have an answering machine and my fax machine in the living room, and that's the way I like it.

There are, of course, practical considerations to organizing your living space. Feng shui is great, but one can't always

make it work. If you live in a studio apartment, you do everything in one room; if you live with other people, you have to take them into consideration. Within those considerations, however, you can keep shifting your objects around until they feel right. You'll feel it when you've hit it. The entire room will feel lighter.

ALTARS AND SHRINES

I consider my working spaces "altars," although some of them could be considered shrines, I suppose. I have one for each direction, set on the farthest outer wall of each direction in the apartment: north, east, south, and west. The north, east, and south happen to be in my living room. The west altar doubles as my Moon altar and is in the bedroom. I also have an altar to Hestia over my stove (which is in the exact center of my home), an altar to Iris under construction, an altar to Kuan Yin filled with small, beautiful objects with special meaning to me in the bedroom, and my main working altar also in my bedroom. Yes, it's a lot of sacred spaces in one small apartment, but it makes it possible for me to look up from whatever I'm working on and look into a special place.

The altars are not large—most of them are simply a shelf attached to the wall, or the top of a bureau or table with a few special objects that to me embody the energy of the direction or the goddess.

ATMOSPHERE

Candles and statues are scattered throughout the apartment. I try to keep fresh flowers in the living room and the bedroom. My bathroom is decorated to be part undersea grotto and part garden. I have enough scented bath oils and powders to make a great fruit salad in the tub. Although I am not the world's greatest housekeeper, I try to keep the place at least vacuumed and the floors mopped with a scented floor wash. I burn incense. I do monthly protection, purification, and thanks rituals.

Sadness, grief, and unpleasant emotions are a part of life, and we will all experience them. However, if the atmosphere in the home is sacred and balanced, it gives one room to experience the negative emotions without becoming overwhelmed by them. It is easier to regain perspective and to start finding active solutions to what is not working in one's life.

BLESSINGS AND CONSECRATIONS

The entire apartment has been blessed and consecrated. I do regular purifications, protections, and, if necessary, banishments on the appropriate Moon cycle. I like to wash my doorway and threshold with a tea-like brew made of steeped rosemary and lavender leaves. I like to wipe my chrome, shelves, and metal lampshades with peppermint oil diluted in hot water. I pour vinegar down my drains each New Moon. Most importantly, I enjoy performing each of these acts, and as I work, I visualize how I want the apartment to look and feel.

Often, when I'm doing ritual work within a cast circle at home, I cast to include my entire apartment. There will be those who disagree and believe that energy needs to be contained within the nine-foot circle in order to be effective. If that is what you believe, that is what is true for you. However, I found that by using my entire apartment as the place between the worlds, once the circle is opened, the energy still permeates the entire apartment and it feels wonderful for several days.

When I have had a hard day out in the world, I want to step over my threshold and enter a sacred place where I am safe, happy, and in close contact with the spirits. By making my entire home a sacred space, I feel like I walk into a loving embrace whenever I walk through the door. Inside my home, I find strength and renewal and joy to face whatever needs to be faced in work and life.

The Rainbow Harmony Candle

By Silver RavenWolf

This enchantment uses the simple application of candle magic, yet can help to resolve some of your most difficult problems. The premise lies in the technique of the "built candle," where through simple ritual, you will build one candle color on top of another to achieve the goal of harmony in your life. This magical technique takes seven days to complete. Thereafter, you can continue to use the power candle by adding new candles, for as long as you feel it is appropriate. You do not have to choose the colors used in the example. Feel free to match other colors with your specific desires.

Supplies

One white pillar candle (unscented preferred)

Seven votive candles in the colors red, orange, yellow, green, blue, violet, and white

Your favorite oil or holy water

A fireproof ceramic tile

Procedure

Step One

On a piece of paper make a list matching your desires with the candle colors you chose. In this example I used the following correspondences:

Red: Lineage of my ancestors

Orange: Stability in my career

Yellow: Continued good health

Green: Financial stability

Blue: Continued transformation of self to higher levels

Violet: Wisdom

White: Continued connection with spirit

Step Two

Choose the magical timing that corresponds with your list. For this project, I could use the New Moon, crescent moon, or Full Moon when picking a Moon phase. Under magical days, I could use Sunday (success in any endeavor) or Wednesday (communication with spirit). For the planetary hour, I might choose between the Sun (success) or Mercury (communication). Because this application lasts seven days, I would begin at the New Moon and work through the crescent Moon phase. If my main thrust involved levels of banishing, I would begin at the Full Moon and work through the waning cycle.

Step Three

If I'm into herbs, I might set aside some vervain (to make the spell go) and dragon's blood (more power) to sprinkle around the base of the pillar candle. Magical practice often calls for multiples of three, so I might choose angelica to ward off any negativity. Don't forget to consecrate and empower the herbs you use.

Another choice involves deity. Do you wish to work only with Spirit, with the Lord and Lady, or with an archetype? To make this spell universal, I'm going to use Spirit.

Step Four

Cleanse, consecrate, and empower the eight candles with your favorite oil. Hold each candle in your hand (one at a time), concentrating on what that candle color stands for. The base pillar candle corresponds with awakening your desires.

Step Five

Cast your magic circle and call the quarters in the manner most comfortable to you. Call Spirit into your circle.

Step Six

Hold the white pillar candle in your hand and say:

This white candle represents the base of my power.

Set the candle down. Sprinkle the herbs you chose earlier around the base of the candle. Light the candle, and say:

As I light this candle, I call upon Spirit to assist me in my magical working, and help me build positive magic to reach my goals.

Allow the candle to burn until the top is soft enough to place the next candle on top. While the candle burns you can focus on the flame, and ask for a message from Spirit, or meditate on your overall goal.

Step Seven

Take the first colored candle in your hands. In this case, we will be working with the red candle. I might say something like:

I empower this red candle to connect with my ancestral lineage. Great Ancestors, may your wisdom and strength continue to guide my path in life as I work toward harmony in my life.

Light the red candle from the flame of the white candle, saying:

From the strength and power of Spirit, I bring the energies of my ancestors into my life, so that they may provide me with wisdom and strength in my goal of harmony.

Set the red candle on top of the white candle. Allow to burn for seven seconds, then put out the red candle.

Step Eight

Thank Spirit and your ancestors. Close the quarters. Close the circle.

Step Nine

Twenty-four hours later, cast your magic circle, call the quarters, and invite Spirit into the circle. Light the red candle, saying:

Great Ancestors, may your wisdom and strength continue to guide my path in life as I work toward harmony in my life.

Allow the candle to burn until the top softens. During this time you may listen for a message from your ancestors, or meditate on your goal.

Pick up the next candle, which in this project would be the orange votive candle. Say something like:

> *With the assistance of Spirit and my ancestors, I ask for stability in my career, which will affect my desired goal of harmony in my life.*

Place the orange candle on top of the red candle. Light the orange candle. Burn for seven seconds. Put out the candle, thank Spirit, thank your ancestors, close the quarters, and take up the magic circle.

Continue the pattern shown each evening, building your rainbow power candle with the assistance of Spirit and your ancestors. On the last evening, after you have concentrated on the goal, ask Spirit once again to bless your work and to assist you in your overall goal of harmony in your life.

You can continue to use the harmony candle whenever you wish. For example, you may use it as an illuminator candle for other workings, as a need-fire candle to acknowledge the beginning or ending of each season, or to signify the opening and closing of a Full or New Moon ritual. To keep the candle from getting too high, you can allow the votives to burn longer than twenty minutes.

WITCH BOTTLES

BY JIM GARRISON

Witch Bottles were originally sold by Matthew Hopkins and other such self-proclaimed "witchfinders" who promised that their bottles would protect their customers from all of the hysterical nonsense and ickiness they tried to blame on Witchcraft. These enterprising ecclesiastical extortionists had a captive clientele, because if you didn't buy one of these creations from them, you might just get accused of being a witch yourself. Where these guys got the idea from in the first place is still a matter of dispute. It's quite possible that the idea originated with the Witches in the first place, and Hopkins and company stole it from folk magic they grew up with or discovered as they traveled through Europe decimating villages.

Witch hunting was nasty stuff, but the technique of using a Witch bottle is still magically useful, and if some good can be brought out of the sorrow and pain of the past, perhaps we should do so. The Witch bottle has bogus beginnings, but it is fertile with potential applications nonetheless—the idea of working magic with a bottle as the primary medium of expression is just too good to let languish because of some some ill-mannered louts.

Using bottles for magic pre-dates the Inquisition by a considerable stretch. The whole process of blowing glass to make a bottle was an alchemical art in and of itself. Old bottles seem to have a charm to them, a quality or character that makes them somehow special. Perhaps there was something to the notion of the glassblower emulating the gods by blowing life-breath into the glass in order to form it. There are all manner of romantic notions you can draw on to add color to this particular practice of folk magic.

To make a Witch bottle, first select a bottle you want to work with. Your bottle may be clear or tinted. If it is colored, select a color that suits your purpose. If you want to see the contents, obviously you'll want to avoid using brown bottles. Tinted bottles are wonderful for spells that make use of color correspondences.

Once you have a bottle, wash it with warm soapy water, then magically cleanse it, and bathe it in the light of the Full Moon. If you want to be more finicky, choose a time when the Full Moon is in a favorable zodiacal sign—check your ephemeris or Llewellyn's *Moon Sign Book* for more information about the Moon's signs.

When the bottle is clean, it's time to to fill it. There are a lot of options when it comes to the contents. Some suggestions are:

✪ To make a Witch bottle to aid in grounding, such as in a training group, fill your bottle with sand, small rocks, granite dust, or other such materials. Seal it with colored wax or a cork, and place the bottle in view when it is to be available for use. If made for a training group, upon graduation/initiation you might consider pouring out a share of the charged material for each student to make his or her own bottle.

✪ For protection from unfriendly forces, you can fill a bottle with sharp objects such as pins, needles, and nails. You can find ideas for this sort of Witch bottle in the book *Magical Household* by Scott Cunningham and David Harrington

✪ By collecting appropriate herbs, resins, leaves, and spices and filling a bottle with them, you can concoct a wide variety of wards, spells, or talismans. Add vegetable oil or cider vinegar, and you have wonderful gifts for your friends that not only can enhance their lives with magic, but can enhance their food as well.

✪ Colored sand can be sifted into a bottle in order to create patterns of rough symbols like a rune or planetary sigil. This takes a bit of patience and care. You need a thin stick, like a tongue depressor, to move the sand around in order to build the symbol from the bottom up. It takes some practice, but once you get the hang of it, this looks very impressive, especially if you use your color correspondences or the more advanced flashing colors of the Golden Dawn.

✪ You can use iron or other metal filings to create a magical battery or repository for specific sorts of workings. Let the filings acquire a good charge from various rituals, then use them in divination or spellwork as desired.

✪ Fill your bottle with different sorts of sawdust from various trees, according to their magical properties. This is a bottle that can be charged during the particular month, season, or sabbat appropriate to the wood(s) used. You may even want to use this sawdust to start ritual fires for specific sabbats or rites in order to add something special to the proceedings.

✪ A bottle filled with ashes from special campfires, or pinches of soil from campsites you've stayed at, makes a powerful memory catalyst and allows you to carry some of that energy with you, or to bring it to another ritual or sacred space like a talisman.

✪ You can also fill a bottle with a variety of flower petals selected for their healing properties, attributes, or correspondences to planetary or other forces. You may want to include a bit of alcohol, vinegar, or olive oil to preserve the flowers.

Witch bottles are versatile, eminently useful, and can be a lot of fun to make and share. Once you start playing around with this idea, you'll come up with your own unique uses and applications.

THE MAGICAL ART OF
PACIFIC RIM TATTOO

BY BERNYCE BARLOW

B ody tattoo has been used as an adornment by cultures around the world. In ancient times the tattoo meant a lot more than the word *mother* inked onto someone's chest. Throughout the Pacific Rim, tattoo was considered a sacred form of art. It was a symbolic visual display of lineage, name, rank, family gods, ancestors of power, birth date, birth time, birth place, personal symbols of power, society initiations, occupation, residency, and spiritual history (and that was just on the face).

Some cultures took tattoo to great extremes, adorning the entire body with it. Because the ordeal of receiving a full-body tattoo was quite traumatic, the tattoo priest was held in high esteem. It was not unusual that patients died due to infection, blood loss, or shock. For this reason, some island groups elected to use tattoo moderately, or pass on the art form altogether.

Trying to trace the origins of tattoo through the Pacific gets tricky. I personally feel the art goes back a lot further than the hardcore evidence suggests. Tattoo instruments have been found dating back a few thousand years to the Lapita culture, but in view of recent archaeological discoveries made in Australia, the human family has been around for at least 176,000 years. The Lapita culture had its roots buried deep in Austronesia, and since tattoo was also a part of the aboriginal culture of Australia, it makes sense that sacred tattoo was not originated by the Lapita, but passed on to them. Nevertheless, the official history of Pacific tattoo begins with the Lapita culture, who in turn influenced Tonga and later Samoa, who in turn carried the art eastward among the islands of the Rim, including Hawaii.

A typical tattoo ceremony performed 3,000 years ago on the son of a chief might have transpired like this. The tattoo priest would first make the instruments to perform the operation, then prepare fresh inks to be used in the tattoo dye. The tattoo instruments usually consisted of a myriad of tools used for various purposes. Different sizes of puncture combs were attached to a hardwood dowel. They had three

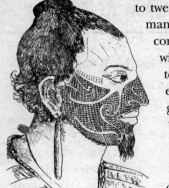

to twenty teeth, and were fashioned from human, bird (albatross), or whale bone. The combs were vigorously tapped into the skin with a bamboo or wood baton about eighteen inches long and an inch thick. Other combs carried bone blades of different grades that were used for incisions and usually reserved for the facial area. Single pointed puncture tools were also created from bone.

Another tool of the trade was a food funnel that the patient would have to eat and drink from for approximately two weeks after the tattoo ceremony. Elaborate ink pots to hold the dyes would also be created from the finest pieces of wood. Both the ink pots and the funnels were lavishly carved and decorated with magical designs and symbols of healing. Bowls to hold the medicines to be applied to the body throughout the procedure were likewise made according to prescription.

The medicines to be used during the rite of tattoo were gathered by the practitioner before the ritual. Herbs and sea life thought to have curative and anesthetic constituents were harvested and ceremonially prepared for application during the ordeal. Offering bundles for the gods and the family ancestors were prepared not only by the priest but by the family of whoever was being adorned. Pigments for the tattoo dyes were also gathered before the ceremony. The blue-black ashes and soot from the candlenut, mixed with sea turtle or whale oil, were usually used as pigment. Certain caterpillars provided a dark blue dye that was used for specific symbols. If a brighter dye was necessary, roots from "dye" plants were prepared. Sometimes red, yellow, or white-pigmented earth clay was added to the dye mixture, but as a rule Pacific Rim tattoos were colored blue-black.

A day or two before the ceremony, a community feast was prepared in honor of the patient, where songs, chants, and dances were performed. At the closing of the feast the priest, one or two of his apprentices, the patient, and the patient's family would retire to the tattoo hut in order to begin the tattoo process, which often took as much as a week to complete. Another ceremony would take place a day after the tattoo had been completed. This ceremony was a purification sprinkling, with prayers directed toward the healing of the patient.

The family remained in the tattoo hut to encourage the patient with songs, prayer, instrumental music, and drum beating. They built his confidence with exuberant exclamations of his bravery. The family helped to hold the patient in place during "tapping," and calmed his screams and whimpers. Suffice it to say, tattoo was a family affair.

Most men experienced tattoo around fifteen years of age. It was a way to identify comrades on the battlefield, so before a male went into battle for the first time his tattoo was at least partially in place. As men grew older, tattoo touch-ups were sometimes needed or special events were later recorded. When princes became kings, more tattoo was added, heralding their accomplishments on the battlefield or in politics. As members of societies climbed in status and rank, their success was also recorded on the skin. Secret societies also used the tattoo as a means of identification. The evil One Tooth Shark Society members sported a single-toothed shark on their backs. Of course, if this tattoo was discovered by the priesthood, it meant instant death to its wearer. If a commoner accidentally discovered the One Tooth's secret tattoo, a code of silence was observed. If the code was broken by the commoner, the One Tooth would be immediately killed, but the snitch would also get it in the neck at the revengeful hands of another One Tooth.

Women were also tattooed, but not to the extent men were. Women's tattoo did not cover the entire body. It was generally restricted to the legs and arms. Facial and neck tattoos were also moderately worn by women. Women wore their tattoos proudly and considered them a beautiful adornment as well as a sign of status. On some islands a woman could not marry a partially tattooed warrior, nor could the warrior marry an unmarked wife. These facts alone show two very good reasons thay the tattoo priest was so popular.

There is a revival of sacred tattoo happening in the Pacific. Men and women are once again celebrating this ancient art form. Tribal chiefs, priests of rank, and women of power are experiencing the tapping baton and puncture comb with the hope of becoming an example to a new generation who might otherwise lose this sacred tradition altogether. In Samoa and Hawaii, body tattoo rites are regularly being celebrated, and other islands are also in the process of reviving the art.

MAGICAL TATTOOING IN THE ANCIENT WORLD

BY DAVID HARRINGTON

Ancient people the world over marked their bodies to indicate initiation, the protection of a deity, or the power of a totem animal. Unfortunately, unless the bodies of tattooed people are preserved through extraordinary circumstances, such as mummification, freezing, or natural drying, tattoos and other body markings are lost forever after the person dies. Some descriptions of tattooing and other body marking methods have been preserved, however. Here are some examples of ancient magical tattooing in the Western world.

RITUAL TATTOOING IN ANCIENT EGYPT

The lands that bordered the long flow of the Nile River were rich in varied customs of body adornment. Tattooing appears to have been practiced in predynastic times. Clay figurines from burial sites bear marks indicating tattoos or scarification patterns. The clearest evidence comes from a period that Egyptologists call "late" in Egyptian history, approximately 3,500 years ago. During the New Kingdom (1567–1085 B.C.E.), some Egyptians tattooed their chests and arms with the symbol of a favored deity.

The Eleventh Dynasty funeral temple complex of King Nebhepetra Mentuhotep at Deir el-Bahri includes several tattooed women. At least one of them, Amunet, was a priestess dedicated to the Goddess Hathor. These three women bore tattooed dots and lines on their lower abdomens. In an excavation at Aksha in Nubia, mummified women from about the fourth century B.C.E. bore marks that duplicated those on Amunet. This indicates the possibility of an unbroken tradition of at least fifteen hundred years.

During the New Kingdom, images of the lion-headed dwarf god Bes were tattooed on the upper thighs of women, particularly women musicians. While some authorities believe that this was a sexual symbol, indicating the bearer's delight in sexuality, it seems more likely that the Bes-images were protective. Bes was, in addition to being a god of sexuality, a protective deity particularly invoked during the trials of childbirth.

An intriguing mummy of a dancer was bound so that her limbs, while covered with linen, were not bound against her body as is the case with most mummified bodies. Perhaps because she had been so lithe and graceful in life, the overseers of her embalming and wrapping made certain that she was still ready to move at the first notes of a thrilling melody. Great effort has been taken to preserve the natural appearance of this mummy. Two images painted on the wrappings at her knees probably represent tattoos. If so, this may be the earliest appearance of a custom later known almost worldwide: the tattooing of joints to keep them limber. The images on her knees appear to be lotuses or fruit. Tiny black dots encircle her nipples, which are treated as if they are bare of covering.

A bronze statuette of a seventh century B.C.E. official named Khonirdis bears a profile image of Osiris on his bared right upper chest. It's obvious this design was on the man's skin, and does not represent any item of jewelry, but it's impossible to determine whether this represents a permanent tattoo or brand rather than a less permanent, drawn image. Since the statue itself is designed to be permanent, it seems likely that no "temporary" marks would be included.

One of the Greek rulers of Egypt, Ptolemy IV Philopater, was tattooed with leaves of ivy, probably as a way of showing reverence to his deity, Dionysus, the God of the Vine, and of ecstatic revels. This design recalls an even more ancient mark used among the Thracians. The Thracians employed tattooing as a mark of status and rank, with shamans bearing the most tattoos of all. In other sources, the ecstatic maenads who were the entourage of Dionysus instead bore snakes tattooed on their bodies.

Some temples placed tattoos on the bodies of those seeking sanctuary within their walls, possibly as a method of protecting these persons from attack. When Paris was in Egypt with Helen of Troy, some of his servants rebelled against him and fled to an Egyptian temple for sanctuary. Herodotus, the major historical writer of the time, identifies the temple as one of Heracles, which would probably mean it was devoted to Horus in one of his more war-like aspects. Herodotus says "...there is a very ancient custom, which has remained unaltered to the present day. If a runaway slave takes refuge in this shrine and allows the sacred marks, which are the sign of his submission to the service of the god, to be set upon his body, his master, no matter who he is, cannot lay hands on him. Some of Paris' servants found out about this and, wishing to get him into trouble, deserted and fled as suppliants to the temple..." where they presumably underwent the "marking" process that replaced secular slavery with sacred service.

SHAMANIC TATTOOING IN THE GREEK WORLD

EPIMENIDES OF KNOSSUS

Epimenides was a renowned shaman who began his career by falling asleep in a cave sacred to a Cretan mystery-god, probably Zeus. He woke up fifteen years later, with magical skills acquired while asleep. Among his many abilities were that of appearing in two places at once and being a master of herbal remedies and magic. When the renowned Delphic Oracle informed the Athenians that it was necessary to purify the city, Epimenides was requested to come and make the appropriate offerings and sacrifices. In exchange, the Athenians tried to pay him, but he refused payment and hoped that his services would foster unity between the Athenians and the Cretans. After his death, it was discovered that his body was covered with mystical tattoos. The various designs may have represented his particular powers, totem animals, or deity figures. Epimenides was also a believer in reincarnation, and he was especially prized for his insights into periods when he had lived other lives. Some of his tattoos may have marked his past-life memories.

ZALMOXIS OF THRACE

One tattooed shaman of Thrace, Zalmoxis, gave his name to a form of ecstatic dancing and singing and, like Epimenides, spent a long time in an underground retreat, and apparently helped spread the doctrine of transmigration, or reincarnation of souls. He was noted by the Greeks for a tattoo he bore upon his forehead, though what it indicated was not understood by them. Greek writers assumed that he had at one time been captured by pirates and marked as a preparation for being sold into slavery. His forehead might have been marked with a triangle, since Greeks used the triangle-shaped delta letter tattoo to mark their own slaves. If this symbol was the one borne by Zalmoxis on his forehead, it may have been an early representation of the mystical sign of "The Eye in the Triangle," since the tattooed triangle would have been placed over the region of his third eye.

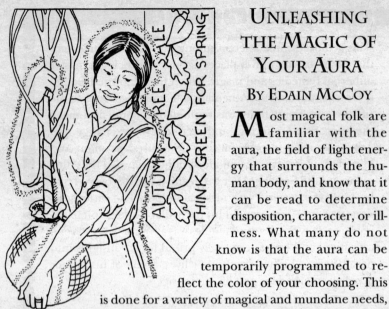

AUTUMN TREE SALE

THINK GREEN FOR SPRING

Unleashing the Magic of Your Aura

By Edain McCoy

Most magical folk are familiar with the aura, the field of light energy that surrounds the human body, and know that it can be read to determine disposition, character, or illness. What many do not know is that the aura can be temporarily programmed to reflect the color of your choosing. This is done for a variety of magical and mundane needs, such as helping alter your mood, giving you a boost of energy, or projecting a desired image to others. Even people who are not psychic, and who vehemently do not believe in the existence of the aura, unconsciously pick up on the color changes if you project them strongly enough.

To alter your auric color, close your eyes, relax, and allow yourself to feel grounded and centered. As you do this, focus on the color you want to project, then begin to feel the core of energy at the center of your being expanding as this color. Keep up this visualization for about five minutes, or until you feel that you have sufficiently colored the light field around you. The results will be temporary and, depending on how much energy you put into the act, how good you are at projecting energy, and how far you are deviating from your natural auric color, the effect should last between twenty and sixty minutes.

RED: Project red when you need a boost of energy, when you want to let off steam, or are preparing for an athletic event. Keep in mind that others may perceive a red aura as stress or anger.

ORANGE: Project orange to attract attention to yourself, or when you need a boost of energy but do not feel you can handle the intensity of red.

YELLOW: Project yellow when you need to bolster your creative self or when you are deep into intellectual pursuits, such as studying for an exam. Others who sense the yellow aura will likely view you as being very smart.

GREEN: Project green when you need a calming influence. The color sense will be picked up by others around you, and you may find that you not only calm yourself, but your entire environment as well. Try on a green aura when you are gardening to help you merge with the energies of the plants.

BLUE: Project blue when you are attempting any spiritual pursuit or when you suffer from insomnia. Those with blue auras are preceived by others as being balanced and selfless people, impressions that make this is a good color to work with when applying for a job in a service-oriented industry.

INDIGO: Project this blue-violet color when attempting any psychic work. Others who perceive this color will see you as being dreamy and not completely "with it." Avoid indigo when on the job hunt or any other time when you need to appear competent.

VIOLET: Project violet when attempting to heal yourself or others, or when you are working with visualization to ward off a bad habit. Those who pick up on your violet aura think of you as a person of intense emotion—ever hear of a purple passion?

PINK: Project pink for peacefulness, when trying to stir up a romance, or when you wish to appear non-threatening.

PEACH: Project peach when you want to turn your attention outward to other matters. This can be useful to help overcome depression or when you need to put aside an issue for a while and let things work themselves out. Peach auras are perceived by others as being compassionate, making this a good color for health care professionals to use when dealing with difficult patients.

BROWN: Project a brown aura when you are working earth magic or magic for animals. Be aware that others sense brown as being dull-witted and even untrustworthy, so avoid carrying them into the workplace or anywhere else where first impressions matter.

WHITE: Project white when you want to go unnoticed. White appears very neutral to the psychic eye as it tends to camouflage itself against the other energy fields that surround us. It is sometimes even hard for trained psychics to pick up on white auras.

WILL

By Jim Garrison

Do what thou wilt
Shall be the whole of the law
Love is the law
Love under will

Powerful, beautiful, dangerous words. This is the law of Thelema as established by Aleister Crowley. Thelema is Greek for will. Mr. Crowley was of the opinion that each of us possesses a true will, and it is our task in this life to manifest or fulfill this true will. All sorrow comes from working in opposition to our will. He even went so far as to define magic as being the "...act of causing change in conformity with the will." To practice magic, then, one needs to have a strongly developed will.

An It Harm None, Do as You Will

The Wiccan Rede also mentions will, and the context is essentially the same as in Thelema—we all have a true will and it is our purpose in life. Magic is one means to discover the nature of our true will and to fulfill this inner purpose. At the center of nearly all forms of magical practice is the concept of "true will." What is this "will," and how do we know if we're doing it?

You can read a thousand books, or talk to a hundred teachers, or attend as many seminars and workshops as you care to, but if you never apply what you've learned, it doesn't do anyone a bit of good. That need for action is essential in life, in spirituality, and in magic. The driving, motivating force behind all actions is will. We all make choices. We all make decisions. We all have our own, unique will that makes us who and what we are. Your will is an intrinsic part of you. Your will is the one thing that is truly yours in this life, or rather you are its expression, your life is the direct consequence of your true will.

Destiny, fate, and karma are all reflections of the true will. Destiny is the acceptance that the will is predestined, but in truth it is more open-ended than that. Will is a direction, but we remain free to choose how we accommodate this direction.

At the center of each of us is our true will, the essential core of who and what we really are. It is this true will that shapes our direction in life. Will is the force from within that determines our course. It is like a sun at the center of our being that sends out rays of light that become our words, our actions, and the foundation of our personalities. All the high-faluting words and bad poetry aside, your true will is your most basic, deepest drive. It is the essential force that gives you direction and it is the core around which your personality is built up like rock candy on a string. The true will is the motivating force behind all our actions, words, or thoughts—whether we are aware of our true will, ignorant of it, or in constant involuntary reaction to it.

WORKING YOUR WILL

Acting in accordance with our true wills brings us into harmony with the universe. If we lose track of our true will, the universe acts to restore equilibrium. That's when we get those wonderful little reminders to get with the program, you know; zits, bad TV reception, illness, junk mail, and opportunities to spend money or time fixing or replacing stuff. The more you go against your true will, the more this universal response escalates. The key is in responding to the challenge, not reacting to the attachments of the false layers of your outer personality or the ego. Modern magic is heavily based on visualization, for better or worse, and this visual bias creates a subtle trap for many who seek to practice magic. We tend to accumulate false images and layers to our personalities and identities that are further and further removed from the true will deep inside. These false layers build up as we interact with others. We build up psychic masks, and ego accumulates like lint in a dryer screen. Removing or cutting through these layers so that we can reconnect with the source of our being, the true will, is the goal of many of the sometimes odd-seeming techniques of ceremonial magic, as well as the simple, but by no means easy practice of meditation or prayer.

The most basic practices of ceremonial magic such as the Lesser Banishing Ritual of the Pentagram were developed precisely as a means to clean out the aura, to purge the magician of excess ego, and to scrape off the accumulated gunk of false images, etc. We need to clear away the debris of our day-to-day lives and get back to the reality within each of us. It is from this interior reality, this inner plane, that we can form a clear image of who and what we truly are, and what we're all about. When we return to our center, we realign ourselves with the true will. This is essential to any sort of real magical practice or spiritual pursuit. You need to see where you're going if you want to ever get there. In order to fulfill our innermost natures, and to realize our potential, we need to discover, understand, and express our true will, and that, in a nutshell, is what magic is all about.

WILL VERSUS WANT

Doing your true will is not always doing what you want. In fact, often it can be quite the opposite. Whether you prefer to express it in terms of "thy will be done," "as ye will," or "do what thou wilt," it all boils down to acting in accordance with the true will—but whose will? The true will is the essential motion of your being, the intrinsic direction of your life that is immutable and inevitable. In many ways the true will can be likened to the Tao, or "way"—the intrinsic eternal direction of the universe that everything needs to follow to be in harmony. Crowley likened the true will to the orbit of a star; every man and every woman being a star in their own right. As Crowley saw it, we have no right but to do our true will.

It is the nature of the true will to express itself in our lives. It is only natural that we realize our potential. The true will is like a beautiful gem swaddled in layers of gauze that we must shed, like old skin. The techniques of magic provide ways to cut through or to get rid of all the stuff we have accumulated so that we might get down to the core of who and what we truly are. The will is the innermost self, the center point of our consciousness that is like a star from which our personalities and lives ripple outward. At the center of each of us is the essential core of who and what we really are; this is sometimes referred to as the Holy Guardian Angel. It is from this superconsciousness that the true will emanates. It is this true will that shapes our direction in life. It is the force from within that determines our course. Whenever you use the Lesser Banishing Ritual of the Pentagram and vibrate the Hebrew word *Ateh*, you are calling on this divine spark within you, for it is this inner deity whose will shall be done. You could say that the true will is the point of consciousness deep within each of us around which we are all wrapped like onions or Russian nesting dolls.

Any form of magic or spirituality worth the name will teach you how to discover your true will, and enable you to act on it. Whether you prefer the dynamic approach of Thelemic magic or the passive path of contemplative prayer; the wild, ecstatic frenzy of shamanism; the more sensual rites of Wicca, or the silent meditation of Zen, there are many, many ways to the center, and it's all a matter of finding the right one for you. Do as you will, and you harm none, blessed be.

THE IRISH HARP

BY LORRAINE BOSCHI

No one knows when or where the harp was invented, but this much is certain: when it arrived in Ireland, the people claimed it for their own and put it in the hands of their gods.

The first divine harper was Lugh, God of Light, who played it so skillfully for his sleeping lady-love that she dreamed of the Sidhe, dancing under the Moon.

After Lugh came the Dagda, a god of the Tuatha de Danaan, who enchanted his harp, called "Uaitne," to keep it from playing for anyone else. One night a band of Fomorian warriors stole it for use at a banquet, but when it wouldn't play they hung it on the wall. The Dagda strode into the hall and cried, "Uaitne!" and the harp sprang down with such enthusiasm it killed nine Fomorians at a stroke before leaping into its master's arms. Afterward, the Dagda charmed the banqueters with three kinds of music: the laugh-strain that made the children smile; the woe-strain that made the women weep, and the sleep-strain that carried the men to dreamland.

Of course there was the unknown harper of Tara, whose instrument has been immortalized in a famous song:

> *The harp that once through Tara's halls*
> *The soul of music shed,*
> *Now hangs as mute on Tara's walls*
> *As if that soul were dead.*

The soul of the Irish harp did not die at Tara. It has survived most wonderfully, thanks both to craftsmen and harpers of great skill.

Ireland's most famous "real" harper, and perhaps the greatest harper the world has known, was Carolan Turlogh (1670–1738), called Carolan the Blind.

Sightless from birth, Carolan traveled from manor to manor entertaining nobles and their families. No one ever spoke of him, wrote Oliver Goldsmith, "without rapture."

Carolan was more than a harper, however; he was a bard in the classic tradition, for he composed poems extemporaneously, singing them to his harp—light poems that flattered his patrons and their families, and serious ones that have been compared to the odes of Pindar.

Carolan had a phenomenal ear and memory. Once, while entertaining a nobleman and his family, he challenged a visiting violinist to a trial of skill. "Play anything you want," he said, "and I'll play it afterward, note for note." The violinist chose Vivaldi's *Fifth Concerto,* which Carolan had never heard. As soon as he finished, Carolan picked up his harp and not only repeated the concerto faultlessly, but went on to compose one of his own, "with such spirit and elegance," wrote Swift, "that it may compare (for we have it still) with the finest compositions of Italy."

George Frederick Handel, composer of *The Messiah* and Carolan's contemporary, said he would rather have written the harper's *Eiblin a Run* (Eileen Aroon) than all the fugues, oratorios, and cantatas he had composed for kings.

Fortunately, many of Carolan's tunes were written down by his patrons and are now available on sheet music.

Also available—and at a reasonable price—are harps like the one he plucked and strummed with such elegance. An authentic Irish lap harp, thirty-one inches high, carved from a single slab of wood—cherry, maple, or walnut—with twenty-five strings, costs around $1,200. Kits, with choice of wire or nylon strings, are available for around $375. There is even a foot-tall, eight-note mini-harp for children, capable of playing most nursery rhymes.

PLUMB-BOBS AND Y-RODS: DIVINATION BY DOWSING

BY LILITH SILVERHAIR

Have you ever used a plumb-bob to find your lost keys? Have you ever seen a doodlebug use his bobber to answer yes or no questions? Do you think I've fallen into a Lewis Carroll book and can't find my way out? The above questions (except maybe the last one) really do make sense. They just need a little translation.

A plumb-bob is simply a pendulum. A doodlebug is an oil dowser, and a bobber is the instrument that a dowser would use. The subject we are talking about here is dowsing: the use of both tools and intuition to locate numerous types of objects, people, and even to diagnose illness.

It is uncertain when and where dowsing began. It is known, from evidence found in Egyptian art and pictoglyphs in the Sahara Desert that could be upwards of 8,000 years old, that dowsing is an extremely ancient practice. Several different deities and mythological figures are said to have invented and brought dowsing to humans. The Egyptian God Thoth, and Daedalus, the Greek inventor, were both said to have invented the plumb-bob, or pendulum.

DOWSING TOOLS

Y-RODS

There are four different types of dowsing tools: y-rods, pendulums, l-rods, and the bobber. The best known is the y-rod, and is used by those people popularly known as "water witches." The y-rod is a forked stick, traditionally cut from an apple or willow tree, although today's modern water witch is more likely to use plastic, because it doesn't break under the continual twisting of the rod as it bends down. The ends of the y are held in each hand with the thumbs pointing outward. The tip of the y is held in an upright position, called the search position. When the tip of the rod moves down in a sharp motion, it's time to dig.

PLUMB-BOBS

The plumb-bob, or pendulum, can be any well-balanced weight on the end of a string or light chain. Pendulums can be made of just about anything: chrome, brass, copper, wood, or crystal, which is becoming more and more popular. What is important is that the pendulum is well balanced and weighs enough to work well even in the wind, and that the person using it is attuned to it. The dowser using a particular pendulum tunes it by concentration and visual images. They also set up their own codes as to what the motion of the pendulum means. Some people take back and forth to mean "yes" and side to side to mean "no," while others use a clockwise rotation and counterclockwise for opposite answers. There are many possible combinations of answer movements, so it is up to the dowser to work with the pendulum to find the right combination. Divination by pendulum is especially useful for finding lost objects and missing persons. This is done by holding the pendulum over a layout of a house or a map and asking the appropriate questions.

BOBBERS

Last, but not least, is the bobber, used by the aforementioned "doodlebugs." Bobbers can be made of stripped tree branches, wires, or even the ends of fishing rods, which have been weighted on the end. These instruments bob up and down for yes and bob side to side for no, hence the name.

L-RODS

Bent coat hangers or pieces of welding rod held in the hands are called "l-rods." Held much like y-rods (except the dowser uses two at

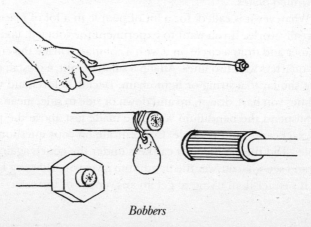

Bobbers

a time instead of one y-rod), when the rods are over the specified target they either swing inward, crossing over each other, or outward, depending on how the rods have been programmed beforehand.

DOWSING HISTORY

Exactly why dowsing works is still a mystery. That it does work can be attested to by oil, gas, and mineral companies throughout the United States. Some of these companies will freely admit that they believe dowsers to be more accurate than any "scientific" method used by geologists. Dowsing was widely used until the eighteenth century, when it was rejected by scientists as superstition. It made a comeback in the twentieth century, specifically in Great Britain and Europe. In the United States, water companies use dowsers to locate buried cables, pipes, and damaged areas. According to the American Society of Dowsers, there are more than 25,000 dowsers in the United States.

Though prohibited in the United States, dowsing is used in Europe and Great Britain as a diagnostic tool in alternative medicine. By using a pendulum suspended over the patient's body, the dowser attunes to the healthy parts of the body being worked on. When the pendulum is passed over unhealthy parts of the body, its movements change. More information is then acquired by asking yes or no questions and divining the answers by the clockwise or counterclockwise movements of the pendulum.

In the 1930s, a French priest, Abbe Alex Bouly, in an attempt to make dowsing more acceptable to the scientific community, coined the term "radiesthesia," which basically means radiation perception. The term is used throughout Europe, but never really caught on in the United States.

Whatever it is called, for a lot of people in a lot of places, dowsing really works. If you want to experiment for yourself, take a piece of paper and draw a circle on it with a compass. Divide the circle into four quarters with two lines. Attach a small weight, a crystal, or something similar to a string or light chain. Decide beforehand which of the lines you have drawn, up and down or side to side, means yes and no. Suspend the pendulum you have made just above the paper in the exact center of the circle. Concentrate on your question, for example: "Did the cat hide my car keys under the couch again?" Then wait and see what answer the pendulum gives you. Dowsing is simple, and it's easier than trying to get an answer out of the cat.

Native American Giveaways

By Marguerite Elsbeth

A throng of people gather in the plaza of a small Pueblo Indian village for the special feast day. Chosen families stand on the roof tops of their homes, waiting to throw many presents to the people assembled below. This is a traditional Southwest Indian giveaway or *gallo,* where the object is to dodge soda cans, boxes of laundry detergent, candy bars, and fruit, including whole watermelons, while trying to catch as many goodies as possible.

Offerings and giveaways demonstrate prosperity and bounty among many different Indian tribes. These displays provide a way to acknowledge medicine work, generosity, or a particular communal experience. This is the Indian way of saying "thank you" to the Creator, the community, and to special individuals. Next time you receive teaching, healing, or an act of kindness, or participate in a dance, sweat lodge ceremony, or vision quest, keep the following ideas in mind when it comes time to show your gratitude.

Smoke opens the mind, clears the environment, carries your prayers up to the Creator, and is a blessing for all our relations. Dried cedar, sage, copal, bearberry, red willow, and tobacco are some of the most common herbs used for smoke offerings.

Money offerings help the medicine healer, because often he or she has a family to feed and bills to pay, just like you. A money offering given to Mother Earth is a way of asking for her assistance and/or thanking her for the abundance you enjoy on a daily basis.

Fasting, singing, sweating, dancing, or drumming can be used as an offering to cleanse the body, heart and mind, or to help those who are suffering for whatever reason.

Genuine Caring is always appreciated at any gathering, Indian or otherwise. Bring along a kind and helpful attitude.

THE WASHOE SEERESS

BY BERNYCE BARLOW

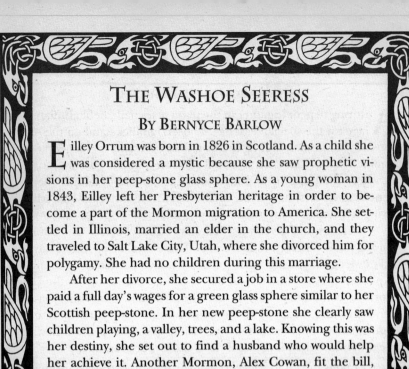

Eilley Orrum was born in 1826 in Scotland. As a child she was considered a mystic because she saw prophetic visions in her peep-stone glass sphere. As a young woman in 1843, Eilley left her Presbyterian heritage in order to become a part of the Mormon migration to America. She settled in Illinois, married an elder in the church, and they traveled to Salt Lake City, Utah, where she divorced him for polygamy. She had no children during this marriage.

After her divorce, she secured a job in a store where she paid a full day's wages for a green glass sphere similar to her Scottish peep-stone. In her new peep-stone she clearly saw children playing, a valley, trees, and a lake. Knowing this was her destiny, she set out to find a husband who would help her achieve it. Another Mormon, Alex Cowan, fit the bill, and together they found the site of Eilley's vision in the Carson Valley. Alex built a cabin and Eilley took on boarders, and for a short duration things went well. During this time Eilley's peepstone was showing gold, miners, and wagons. When Alex was called back to Salt Lake City by Brigham Young, he left Eilley to run the boarding house on her own. Eilley finally divorced him for desertion. Eilley was now thirty-two, and had no children by her second marriage.

Eilley's peep-stone began to show her visions of black streaks of sand. When the kind-hearted Eilley allowed a miner to pay his boarding house tab with his mining claim, the claim turned out to be one of the richest silver veins in the area of Gold Hill, Nevada. Eilley then married Sandy Bowers, whose claim was next to hers, and he struck it rich as well. Together, they built the magnificent Bowers Mansion.

Stories of the Bowers European spending spree to furnish the mansion are well known. Thousands of dollars were spent on ornate wood furniture, art, and silks. At the end of their expensive journey, Eilley wanted to meet Queen Victoria, but was denied an audience due to her divorced status. Shamed and disappointed, she sailed immediately for the U.S. However, during the trip back on a luxury liner called the Persia, a woman died, leaving an infant. The woman was buried at sea, and Eilley and Sandy adopted the child and named her Margaret Persia Bowers. Persia filled the mansion with her laughter and friends, completing Eilley's vision. Eilley was blissfully content and put her peep-stone away. Perhaps this is why she did not see beyond her riches and fame.

In 1867, the unraveling of Eilley's vision began. Sandy died of miner's disease (silicosis). He had grossly mishandled their funds, leaving Eilley to deal with the heartless creditors. Even though she turned the mansion into a hotel, she still couldn't meet the debt owed. Then, her beloved Persia died at age twelve in July of 1874. By 1875, Eilley had lost everything, including the mansion, by default. Penniless, Eilley started telling fortunes with her peep-stone and became known as the Washoe seeress. In 1903, she died at age seventy-seven and was buried next to Sandy and Persia on a hill overlooking the mansion.

Today, the Bowers Mansion rests on forty-six acres of pine-forested land. It was built in 1864 by stonecutters out of granite brought from Scotland. The cost of building the mansion is estimated to be over $200,000. It has two stories with sixteen rooms. In 1966, the mansion was bought by Washoe County as a playground for the children of Nevada.

There is a daguerreotype of Eilley taken in the late 1870s. There is a spirit picture of a child looking over Eilley's shoulder in the photograph. The child is said to be Persia. Since trick photography was not possible then, the shadowy figure looking over Eilley's shoulder is most captivating. A crystal ball sits next to the photo, which is in the parlor of the mansion.

The Law of Threefold Return

By Jim Garrison

Ever mind the Rule of Three, that whatsoever you do
Be it for good or for harm, shall come back to you threefold

Intent without action is worthless, and action without intent is worse than useless—it can be harmful. When our actions are true expressions of our intentions—our wills—we are doing magic.

The Rule of Three illustrates the power underlying our intentions. Everything we do is returned unto us threefold. The ethical directive of the Wiccan Rede is balanced by the moral guide of the Rule of Three, without lengthy lists of prohibitions and "sins." Our intent determines the approach we take to life. Our actions determine the response life takes to us.

While the Rede is an ethical statement, the Law of Three is a moral one. We cannot ask for what we do not ourselves offer to others. Think of it as applied common sense; our actions and words ripple outward from us, touching countless other lives in one way or another. Every good deed we do, every helping hand we lend, and every time we act responsibly, we improve our society by fostering an environment in which positive actions begin to outnumber negative ones.

The Rule of Three is not a mandate to become a pacifist. Rather, it's a challenge to find a constructive, positive way to deal with the situations we all face in the course of our lives. We all are still part of the world, and our relationships with other people are still very much our own matter to deal with. We all have to live with the results and consequences of our actions and the fruit of our intentions.

The Rule of Three demonstrates the importance of right intent, and reveals the secret to bringing about real prosperity. Every little thing we do comes back to us, so it behooves us to send out the sorts of things we really want to have come back to us. When applied alongside the Rede, we are given a goal to work toward, that of doing good, of helping others, and of making the world a better place. Wicca is a lifestyle as much as it is a religion. Its lessons are best appreciated by experiencing them.

Seeing Through Justica's Eyes

By Edain McCoy

As her name implies, Justica was a goddess of justice, fairness, and truth. It was in her name that witnesses in Roman courts swore the truth of their testimonies. They believed that under her influence, the eye, mind, and tongue would become impartial, and that no lie could be uttered.

We have since discovered that impartiality is not always enough, and that the word "truth" carries many shades of meaning, as evidenced by events from which witnesses walk away with a very different opinion of just what occurred. We also know that many people's ideas of justice vacillate depending on what outcome most benefits them. This is a common human failing, which is why Pagans have so many admirable deities of wisdom and fairness.

If you are unsure of your ability to get to the truth or to remain impartial in a given situation, place a drop of truth and impartiality oil, blessed and dedicated to Justica, on each temple and allow her sense of fairness to guide you.

Justica's Truth and Impartiality Oil

Dedicate this oil to Justica before using it, asking that she will impart her wisdom, fairness, and clear thinking to you. Mix all ritual/magical oils in a dark eyedropper glass bottle, which can be purchased at a pharmacy. In a base of ½ ounce olive or safflower oil blend the following:

4 drops lavender oil

9 drops magnolia oil

2 drops rosemary oil

1 drop clove or cedar oil

¼ teaspoon peach cooking extract

Hawaiian Magical Symbology

By Bernyce Barlow

All tribal systems, regardless of race or culture, understood the power of symbology. The Pacific islanders were no exception. The language of the Hawaiian Islands became one of the most symbolic languages to evolve among the Pacific islands. Birds, fish, clouds, mountains, caves, streams, plants, foods, and different types of rain and wind all had specific titles, meanings, gods, and symbols assigned to them, and were used in ceremony and ritual. In other words, everything that existed had a purpose and some sort of spiritual symbolism attached to it. The confusing part is that some islands, even districts on the same island, called things by different names.

As an example, let's look at some of the symbols, both literal and figurative, that might be used in a Hawaiian rite of passion. Before the ritual, or perhaps as a part of the ritual, leaves from the ti (*ki*) plant would be gathered in a certain way by a kahuna, then cleaned. Some of the ti would be arranged in a circle large enough for an altar and people or a single person to sit in. Offerings would be wrapped in more ti leaves. Ti was thought to ward off evil spirits. A bowl of sea water symbolizing purification, and the root of the turmeric (*olena*), which was thought to fight evil, might also be included as part of the altar setup. The turmeric was added to the salty water, then sprinkled around the circle with a ti leaf, sanctifying the area. Sometimes an offering of *awa* was prepared and placed in a coconut half (*nui*), preferably a species with a dark shell. Awa (*kava*) is a narcotic drink. If the awa swirled in the nui bowl it meant the gods were participating in the ritual.

For the ceremony, offerings would correspond to the petitioner's request. A ritual of passion might include a banana (*mai'a*). Its phallic shape speaks for itself, and in one form the symbol of the banana represents the word *lele*, which means to fly. To use a banana in an offering would assure the request would fly to the gods.

Another offering might include a packet of fish wrapped in ti. The type of fish would depend on the goal of the rite. If the petitioner wanted to strip away the affection one person had for another, the *ahole* fish was used, *hole* meaning to strip away. Apathy could also be stripped away if a chosen companion showed indifference toward mating. Of course, a little sugar cane (*ko*) is always nice to offer to sweeten things up a bit. Another offering that would be appropriate in a Hawaiian passion spell would be the *makahiki* shrimp, because the name represents the ability to "cast out." At times, the chakras are blocked with spiritual residue left over from previous relationships. The makahiki is said to symbolically exorcise this kind of residue. If your love has found satisfaction in the arms of another, the sea cucumber, called *loli,* might be offered, because loli means "to change." The *kamole* plant, whose name means "to return," would also make an appropriate altar offering under these circumstances.

There are also fish offerings one would want to avoid in passion rituals, like the octopus, whose name means to flee, unless of course you are attempting to cover your tracks! If that is the case, toss a little seaweed into the ritual bundle too, because one form of its names (*li pe'epe'e*) means "to hide." If these offerings cannot protect you, I suggest you buy a one-way plane ticket to *Kahiki,* whose name means "land far away."

At this point, the site of the ceremony was purified and well protected, petition offerings were in order, and the altar was set up. More offerings were added according to personal deity (*'aumakua*) and family ancestor spirit (*akua*) preferences. Specific lineage colors, flowers, plants, and fish were prepared for these types of offerings. For instance, if an akua was a part of the Lono lineage, a dark pig or the *amu* fish might be offered. If the goddess Hina or her akua ancestors were being addressed, herbs gathered with the left hand, like *limu kala* (a type of seaweed), or the mountain apple (*'ohi'a-'ai*) might be included instead of fish or meat.

Once the offerings were ready, the petition was made. If all went well, the petitioner's desire was fulfilled. The kahuna might

 require the petitioner to eat portions of the bundles while other bundles were taken to secret places favored by the gods and left, perhaps in a cave or near a sacred spring. A bundle may have been placed in the sea or burnt crisp until blackened ashes were the only reminder of its existence. A woman might be sent to pray and leave an offering bundle at the base of Maui's Iao Needle, a phallic-shaped rock formation. Under certain circumstances, men were required to take their offerings to a *heiau* (spiritual temple), then fast, purge, and pray for a day or two.

The period after the ceremony was just as important as the time during a ceremony. This was a time for the petitioner to integrate the ceremonial symbols into his/her daily life, to project symbolic power in thought, spoken word, and action. It was a time to keep the favor of the gods and not break *kapus* (tabu laws). In other words, good behavior influenced the decisions authored by the gods. More often than not, after the ceremony, the petitioner wore a lei of ti leaves around the neck for protection. It was usually knotted five times, five being a dominant number in some types of Hawaiian symbology, specifically within the healing and spirit kahuna societies.

As you can see, Hawaiian symbology runs deep. A simple ritual of passion encompasses so many levels that the offering of fish invariably seems appropriate. True passion does tend to make one's head swim, after all. Nevertheless, symbolic offerings should be chosen wisely, or the petitioner may wind up offering a spiny fish (*i'a kuku*) that symbolizes protection or armor against the passion he or she just asked for. The phrase "Oops, sorry, I used the wrong fish" is not a part of the kahuna language, nor will it ever be, because these folks really do know their stuff! Remember that a little symbology can pack a lot of power, so use it carefully as you enjoy its magic. Aloha.

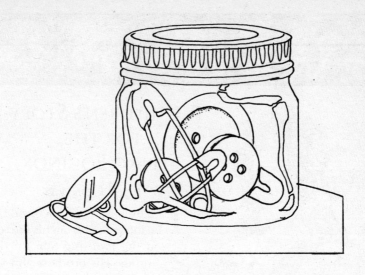

Charm Jar

By Silver RavenWolf

I don't know what your house is like, but over the years I've managed to have a constant stream of visitors, from the curious to the downright needy. Often you would find me burrowing my nose in my magical cabinet, trying to come up with the right stone, herb, or "thingie" to assist a guest with whatever difficulty they might have. As I have taken an oath not to charge for magical services, I found myself putting out a large amount of cash to meet these needs. After a while the proverbial till ran out and I faced a nasty decision—stop helping people to save my family budget from disaster or start eating hash every night. I didn't like either choice.

It took me a few weeks, but I finally came up with a solution—buttons and pins. I took a canning jar and filled it with assorted buttons and safety pins. In Pow-Wow, practioners use safety pins to ward off negativity (worn on the left sleeve), and buttons for charming various purposes. When there is a minor magic to perform, I bring out my trusty jar and let the visitor choose which button or pin they would like to have. Together we cleanse, consecrate and empower the object.

They leave happy and we can eat baked chicken for dinner with mincemeat pie for dessert.

A Children's Story
for the
Spring Equinox

By D. J. Conway

The little rabbit yawned wide as he looked out from his burrow at the morning Sun on the grass. His brothers and sisters crowded behind him, twitching their whiskers, impatient for him to go outside.

"Oh, do get out of the way, Fluff," said one of his sisters, pushing against him. "You always just sit around and look at everything. We're hungry."

As Fluff hopped out into the spring sunshine, his brothers and sisters rushed past him and began to scamper about, eating the tender new grass. Fluff nibbled a few leaves, but he was more interested in the strange bright colors he saw among the grass stems over by the edge of the meadow. No one saw him hop away to find out what grass grew in such wonderful colors near the trees.

"What strange grass is this?" Fluff said as he smelled the brightly colored plants. "And why doesn't my family eat it?"

"It isn't grass, little rabbit, but flowers." The soft, gentle voice startled Fluff, and he jumped back, then looked to see who was speaking.

A beautiful young woman stood smiling at him. Around her head was a crown made of flowers. Her eyes were the deep blue of the sky just after the sun went down, her hair a rich brown like the leaves left on the oak trees. Fluff could see her bare toes under the edge of her long white gown. In one hand she carried a basket woven out of willow limbs.

"Who are you?" he asked. "You aren't a rabbit."

The lady laughed, and the laughter made Fluff feel safe and warm. "No, Fluff, I am not a rabbit. I am the Spring Maiden. At this time of year I walk through the forests and meadows, calling to the flowers and plants and trees to drink in the rich sunshine and grow faster. The birds and animals hear me also and begin to plan their nests and soft burrows for the babies who will soon be born." The lady smiled again. "Do you like my flowers?" She pointed at the bright plants peeping through the grass.

"So these are flowers," Fluff said as he smelled them. "They are very beautiful, but not as beautiful as you are, Spring Maiden."

The rabbit jumped back as a small boy timidly peeked out from behind the Spring Maiden. A bright light shone around the boy, so bright that Fluff blinked his eyes.

The Spring Maiden put her hand on the boy's shoulder. "This is the little Sun King," she told Fluff. "I am teaching him about the plants and animals, and the turning seasons of the year, so he will be a wise ruler of the Earth and all its inhabitants."

"Can we take Fluff with us, Lady?" the boy asked, looking up at the Spring Maiden.

"Yes," she answered with a smile. "Fluff will help humans remember the importance of this season."

"Why do we have to remind humans?" the Sun King asked as he knelt down to pet Fluff. "They should remember."

"The grownups get too busy with other things," answered the Spring Maiden, "So we leave special gifts for the children. When the grownups see the gifts, they remember and celebrate this season of the year. They remember that the Goddess loves all Her creatures and creations and cares for them."

Fluff left the meadow with the Spring Maiden and the Sun King, hopping along through the new grass and spring flowers. Everywhere they went in the forests and meadows and along the streams, they blessed all the animals and plants and the Earth herself. At last they came to the first houses Fluff had ever seen. There were children playing around the houses.

The Spring Maiden reached into her willow basket and took out a bright red egg. "This egg is a symbol of hope and new life," she said as she placed it into the Sun King's hand. "Animals and plants always know that the Goddess cares for them, that She always makes spring follow winter and good times follow the bad times. Humans forget and need to be reminded."

"I remember," the Sun King said softly. "No life ever really ends. It is always reborn, just as I was."

The Spring Maiden took the Sun King's hand and, with Fluff hopping beside them, went out to greet the children. They gave each child a red egg and a spring flower from the Lady's basket. The children all petted Fluff and called him a messenger from the Goddess. As they walked away, Fluff heard the children calling to their parents.

"Mother! Father! Look what the beautiful Lady and a shining boy gave us! And we got to pet the Goddess' special rabbit messenger!"

"Is it Spring Equinox already?" The father looked toward the forest where the Lady stood with Fluff at her feet. He took off his hat and bowed his head for a moment. "Thank you, Spring Maiden," he called. "Bless this house and all those who live here. We remember the ancient symbol of renewing life and hope."

The Spring Maiden smiled, and all the colors of the plants and trees and even the little house seemed brighter to Fluff. The Sun King waved to the children, and the Sun shone warmer and everything seemed to grow a little more.

All day the Spring Maiden and the Sun King went about the world, leaving the red eggs and spring flowers. They blessed everything and everyone, and Fluff went with them. As the Sun began to set, and the sky darken with the coming night, Fluff realized he was very tired and sleepy.

"Dear little rabbit, you have been so wonderful to help us," the Lady said, as she knelt to rub Fluff's ears. I will take you back to your meadow now, if you wish."

"I would rather stay with you, Lady, and with the Sun King," Fluff answered. "But I am only a rabbit and really not important, I know. Even though the children all called me a messenger of the Goddess."

"But you are special, Fluff," said the Sun King as he gathered the rabbit into his arms. "Don't you know that everything in this world is important to me and to my Mother? And you are very special because you have so much yet to do. I will keep you with me always, Fluff." Fluff snuggled down in the Sun King's arms and yawned. "Some people don't believe in the Goddess or in me anymore. But even though their minds say it is all superstition and nonsense, their hearts and souls will remember the truth. And every spring when they see you, they will remember to celebrate the joy of renewing life and the ancient truth that my Mother and I will always love and care for them."

"Dear Fluff, come and live with us in the Sacred Grove." The Spring Maiden smiled when Fluff nodded that he would.

The Goddess gave a special blessing to the rabbit, so that he could remain the friend and companion of Her son, the Sun King. Fluff and the Sun King are born together, grow up together, die at the same time, and are reborn together.

Fluff still lives in the Sacred Grove, and each spring he goes through the world with the Spring Maiden and the Sun King, reminding the people and animals and plants that there is always hope and new life. They carry their gifts of the special colored eggs and spring flowers to all the children. The children still love Fluff and call him the messenger of the Goddess.

MAXIMON: THE EARTH FATHER

BY KEN JOHNSON

Much has been written about the Earth Mother, but the Quiche Maya of Guatemala worship an Earth Father. In the village of Santiago Atitlan the Earth Father goes by the name of Maximon. He is a somewhat tricky and treacherous character, as unpredictable as an earthquake or volcano, and as deep as the interior of a cave; yet he is also a lord of worldly abundance who gives us all the good things of this world. Maximon is nature in the raw. He is a wanderer who travels on foot, and may strike a man with madness or snakebite. He is worshipped at the mouths of caves, which is where the underworld gods of the Maya have always been worshipped.

Maximon is an idol, almost life-sized, who sports a black coat and hat, a black beard, a bottle of booze, and a big cigar. Just before Lent, the young men of Santiago Atitlan go into the mountains to gather flowers and fruits for Maximon. They go without their wives, but indulge in wild sexual activity when they return, for Maximon is a powerful sexual force who will lend vigor and potency to the young men. The flowers and fruits they gather are stored next to Maximon in his special "dawn house."

During Lent, Maximon is brought down from his home in the rafters of the dawn house. The mountain offerings are presented to him, the people dance and sing, and Maximon is taken to the church. A pole symbolizing the Tree of Life is raised in a side chapel, and Maximon is hung from the pole.

On Good Friday, an effigy of Christ is carried to the same church, and hanged on yet another Tree of Life, which is raised in a small pit of earth called "the center of the world." Within the cloak of this Mayan Christ are fruits and small animals. In time, he is taken down and placed in a glass-covered casket covered with flowers and decorated with Christmas tree lights. Christ and Maximon will both exit the church at the same time, and will engage in a kind of ritual confrontation, during which Christ is "impregnated" by Maximon in a blasphemous homosexual union so that the New Year may begin.

To the Maya, this dynamic tension between Christ and Maximon is a balanced cosmic dance. In 1950 a Catholic priest, convinced that Maximon was actually Judas, stole the idol from the dawn house. Somehow it ended up in the Museum of Man in Paris, where it was enshrined for many years! Then, in 1978, two Americans negotiated the return of Maximon to Santiago Atitlan.

Sadly enough, though, the trouble has continued. The growing strength of both Catholics and Evangelicals in the Guatemalan highlands presents an ongoing danger to the devotees of Maximon. But, for the moment, the Earth Father continues to survive.

Animal Spirit Teachers

By Timothy Roderick

Did you know that you have animal spirits that guide and empower your life? Everyone has these magical helpers, but many people do not know how or why they might access this tremendous source of power and wisdom. The "how" part, or the magical techniques for contacting your animal spirits, can vary. This is because there are different categories of animal spirits. Before you venture into their world, knowing what these spirits are and how they influence you each day is wise.

Contrary to what you might first think, the term "animal spirit" does not refer to the spiritual body of a deceased animal. It isn't the ghost of your poodle, Chi-Chi, who died last week. An animal spirit is more of a symbolic manifestation. The animal spirit represents the contents of your physical, psychological, and emotional energies. In other words, it represents the contents of your unconscious, which is the wellspring from which your magical power pours forth. The unconscious is that part of your psyche that houses your urges, drives, and impulses. It is your wild, untamed self.

Familiar Self

Animal spirits have at least two main classifications. The first is what I call the familiar self. A familiar, as most readers know, is the animal power usually associated with Witches, and I use the term as a reference point to my own spiritual path. The familiar self is a representation of your own traits and abilities—both magical and mundane. For example, my familiar self is a fox because my unconscious self-expression makes me a bit of a "trickster." I didn't choose this animal spirit. In effect, it "chose" me because it represents the totality of my deeper self. It is through dreams, sacred visions, and deep trance work that you slowly uncover the powerful familiar self.

Familiar Teachers

Familiar teachers make up the second classification of animal spirits. A familiar teacher is an animal spirit that guides you through specific life problems and circumstances. You can have several teachers guiding you at once. You might have a bear teaching you about strength, while a ferret teaches you about playfulness. I offer the following technique to my students for contacting the familiar teacher:

1. To begin, think of a situation in your life that takes up emotional space. For your first attempt, I suggest that you use a situation that evokes a fairly strong emotional response, since that can provide a lucid psychic path for your first journey into the world of the animal spirits. Allow your thinking to drift into feeling. What emotion does this situation bring up for you?

2. Once you identify the feeling, then take note of where in your body you feel the emotional state first. It is crucial to this magical technique to know where you first feel the emotion, since animal spirits speak to you mainly through your body and your feeling states.

3. After you know where you feel the emotion connected to your situation, close your eyes and take several deep breaths. Slow your mind down. Slow your body down.

4. Imagine that you travel through your body to the spot where you feel the emotion connected to your situation. Give the spot a color and a shape. It can be any color, any shape. Then begin to exhale into the color and shape. With each outgoing breath, blow the color/shape up until it is larger than you are.

5. Once the color/shape looks larger then you, imagine that you step into it. What does it feel like to be inside this color and shape? Allow the color to dissolve into a landscape. Any type of landscape is likely to appear: a desert, meadow, or beach. In that landscape is a single animal. What is it? Ask the animal what it is there to teach you.

6. Once you have your answer you can open your eyes and begin journaling about the experience.

7. Action should follow. Don't allow the insight of the familiar teacher to become an interesting message *du jour*. Take action and create the transformation.

Languages of Healing
and Light

By Bernyce Barlow

When I agreed to do this article, I had a lot of apprehension. Spirit language is a topic that I take very seriously. It goes beyond ego, beyond conscious, and beyond subconscious. In recent years, I have become disappointed that the prayer languages have become a focus for ridicule, control, awe, and ego. The prayer language formally known as Glossolalia or "Speaking in Tongues" is not some mysterious freak of nature, nor is it the result of some kind of religious ecstacy trance. The language does not make one person better than another, nor does it mark the speaker or singer as especially spiritual or magical.

"Tongues" or the "Tongue of Angels" cannot be taught as a second language, it cannot be learned, and it is not a memorized chant. It is not the same prayer language that is practiced in high Masonic or Enochian magic. It cannot be claimed by one religion or group, because in truth it belongs to all of us. There is complete control over the gift. If someone has to fall into a trance to channel Tongues, that person is fooling you.

Tongues is, however, a beautiful expression of sound and resonance that represents creation, praise, healing, and light. Tongues has been claimed exclusively among the more recent religious coterie such as Christianity without much explanation as to its nature. On the other hand, within the same Christian fellowship, one segment uses it against another, destroying the purpose and beauty of this precious gift. Do not think I am picking on Christians, I am not. The gift of

Tongues has been defiled by other religious systems as well—systems that date back thousands of years. The gift has been claimed as a mystery, kept hidden, or used to exalt religious leaders' positions.

Tongues has been around as long as there has been spirit. It is not exclusive. Most cultures and spiritual societies have recognized its existence. It is a part of our creation, just like our arms and legs. It is seated somewhere in our brains, blanketed by the subconscious, and can be triggered through strong emotions of faith, unconditional love, and understanding. The emotions bypass the left brain by channeling through the limbotic system of the lower right brain, making the concept of a prayer language possible. You see, if the left brain got hold of this concept, it would reject it in a heartbeat before it reached the conscious. Tongues is a faith and physics thing.

The first language spoken on earth was not Tongues—rather it was the language of creation—but Tongues embodies that language in sound and resonance. If you listen to nature you will hear all of the consonants and vowel sounds in their long and short forms. Listen to a waterfall, the cracking of a tree branch, or the song of the owl. The first language imitated these sounds. A cracking sound may have represented the idea that someone or something was coming, and may have been imitated to convey that idea to others.

Language then evolved into a spiritual/symbolic tongue, assigning the original vowel groupings, meanings, and symbols. Eventually, specific concepts emerged from the subconscious, and the "knowing" of sound, song, and resonance was revealed to the conscious. Formalized speech was the last step in the communication link that evolved into the modern languages that are spoken today.

In concert with early language was the understanding of Earth resonance (knowing which musical note or sound vibrated to specific symbols, subjects, principles of physics, sacred sites, chakras, stars, and corresponding parts of the body). When a sacred tongue is combined with "understanding the harmony of Gaia's aria," light, healing, love, and knowledge often occur.

The structure of North American language includes Native American, English, and Mexican roots. All three languages use the same vowel sounds. There is a sequence of sounds that relate to specific concepts within the North American language. The sound of *ah,* for example, refers to the concept of purity, purists, and the type of ideas and folks who hold truth above all else. The sound of a long *a* represents placement, philosophy, and the physical side of placement. The *e* sounds resonate awareness and knowledge. The long *o* sound vibrates to the concept of innocence and the power of being teachable. The *oo* sound, like in the word *book,* represents all the concepts of the word carry, for example women carry children, banks carry loans, and animals carry loads.

These sounds, when released in spirit prayer or song, allow the above concepts to flow. Enlightenment comes when you don't get stuck in any one sound, but allow one to flow into another without attachment, in order to release a state of movement that progresses through the healing resonances. Also, in spirit song and prayer, tone and pitch are significant. Higher notes like high A resonate to the high chakras and their corresponding symbology, and lower notes such as low C resonate to lower chakra placements. When you join the power of the spoken word with love, resonance, and faith, it allows healing, protection, enlightenment, and light to dramatically intensify to raise spiritual consciousness.

This year while I was in Hawaii, I spent a great deal of time listening to first language. I listened intently to the sound of the waves at different sacred sites. One site was along a bay, another was in a lava sea cave, and then there was the sound of the waves upon a sandy beach, *ah wa ee*. In the Iao Valley, I heard the trees whisper their medicine names to the tradewinds that ascend the warrior canyons of the West Maui Mountains, and from the depths of the volcano Haleakala I heard the alto resonance of the Earth shift to a deep bass. Although first language and Tongues' physiology are different, prayers uttered in both heal.

There is also a spirit language with hidden and double meanings built into many modern languages. Since we have been speaking about Hawaii, I will use the Hawaiian language as an example. The word *kahuna* is a word most of us have heard before. A Hawaiian kahuna specializes in certain knowledge, perhaps herbal healing or navigation. We spell the word kahuna as it is seen and loosely translate the word to mean teacher or specialist, but the double meaning of the word is as follows (by the way, this is not a secret). Ka-huna means keeper of secrets, while Kahu-na means guardian of the secret Kahuna: Guardian of the secret, keeper of secrets.

As you can see, there is more than one meaning to Kahuna. The languages of the Pacific Islands, as well as Aboriginal Australia, include hidden or double meanings within the core structure of the speech. At times there are more than two expressive interpretations of a word. This hidden language is what is used in prayer and ceremony in many cultures. Kahunas are indeed keepers of the secrets of their specific trades, as seen in the word *ka huna*. If herbal healers were to tell all of their secrets they would be out of a job, but as the "guardian of the secret," the kahuna carries a special tabu, which enters into the secret shadow connected with the use of disassociated spirits and magic. This is the secret a true kahuna will take to his or her grave.

Prayer languages are powerful. Then again, any spoken word is powerful, whether it is uttered in a spirit language or not! Further, when it comes to prayer, the most important essence is not the word or hidden meaning, but the intent of the word. You see, our prayers are like arrows or spears. The aim of our prayers requires concentration, strength is found in our desire, the objective takes the arrow in the right direction, and the confidence that the arrow will meet its target has to do with faith. Desire is the most important emotional element involved in prayer, and can pierce through or make up for a lack of any of the above. The bottom line is that all the words on this planet cannot penetrate the covering of unconditional love.

Spirit languages have always been with us. Gaia speaks them, as do all her children. We reach out to the heavens with these languages, as well as into the depths of our inner selves. Spirit language is a gift each one of us has the potential to use, so next time you find yourself in a forest, on the prairie, along a river, or near the ocean, listen to the sounds. Take them into your ear and let them resonate, say the sounds out loud, become the wind, or the titter of the squirrel—recognize the symbology these sounds will bring up from your subconscious in thought and emotion. Then aim your arrow of light. Your prayer arrow will not miss if your heart's desire is pure and just, no matter what language it is uttered in.

THE POWER OF WORDS

BY JIM GARRISON

The spoken word is a great magical power. Words become living things. When created and given life by your will, and sent forth by being spoken into the ethers, words are vessels of intent, carriers of energy, and tools that shape perception and experience. Words are powerful, subtle, magical things.

Words can hurt or they can heal. Unaware of what they are doing, many people spew thoughtless, careless, hurtful words out into the midst of their lives, like verbal pollution. People respond. Do you really know what you've been saying? Take some time and think over the things you have said today, either out loud, or just to yourself. What you discover may prove enlightening.

Words are the way we communicate on a conscious level, but they can, and do, reach down to deeper levels. Salesmen and prophets, poets, and politicians all use words to get what they want by manipulating their words to create, shape, and guide their victims' responses. The trick is in knowing what sort of message to send with your words. Tell yourself that you can't do something, and you probably won't; tell yourself that you can, and you just might. It's not just a lot of hokey feel-good crap—it works. Find something to replace the negative messages you tell yourself over the course of your day. You just have to dare to make a conscious change in how you program yourself by your choice of words.

It is important to select the appropriate words for any given situation. Be aware of what you are saying whenever you call on a deity, or invite elementals to play in your kitchen. Know what your words mean, and the context from which they have been drawn if they are not your own words. Don't just piece together a ritual from cool-sounding bits you've lifted. Take that extra step and make the words work together in a coherent fashion. Better yet, rewrite them in your own words to suit your own will. You'll get better results, and learn a bit in the process as well.

THE POWER OF ALMONDS

BY JIM WEAVER

For centuries, people of the Near East have regarded the almond as a symbol of prosperity and fertility. To use almonds in rituals or recipes was thought to attract positive energy and good fortune.

Many years ago, for example, in certain rural areas of Greece, when a couple were to be married, family members would sometimes make a paste of ground almonds and honey. This paste would then be spread on the front door or step of the newlyweds' home. This was to ensure that fertility, prosperity, and the "sweetness of life" would be attracted to the new couple.

To this day, the first drink offered at many Greek and Arab weddings is an almond-flavored syrup diluted with cold water. It is the guests' way of showing that they wish only happiness for the bride and groom.

One of the best (and most delicious) ways to bring the positive power of almonds into your life is to bake up a batch of Greek almond butter cookies. Many people are familiar with them. They are the small, oval- or crescent-shaped cookies you'll see in Greek bakeries, and are dusted with confectioner's sugar.

These cookies have been prepared for centuries. Like magical rituals, old recipes take on a certain magical power of their own, especially those used in conjunction with any ceremony. That is the reason these cookies appear at many special occasions—weddings, baptisms, and any holiday celebration. They're believed to bring good luck.

The shape of these cookies is as important as the reason they are prepared. They are frequently shaped in the form of a crescent, which shows a Turkish influence, and perhaps an even older Pagan link. Some bakers shape them into "S" shapes. The "S" shape dates back to the Minoan civilization, which flourished on the island of Crete, and represents the snake. Snakes were respected by the Minoans for their healing powers.

If your fingers aren't too nimble, shaping the cookies in round or oval shapes is very acceptable. I hope they bring you happiness and prosperity!

GREEK ALMOND BUTTER COOKIES

2	sticks unsalted butter or margarine
¼	cup confectioner's sugar
1	egg yolk
½	teaspoon almond extract
¼	teaspoon orange blossom water (optional)*
½	cup (one small bag) very finely chopped, slivered, blanched almonds, lightly toasted
2¼	cups regular all-purpose flour; unsifted
	Confectioner's sugar, for coating

Preheat oven to 325° F. Toast chopped almonds on a small ungreased baking tray in the oven for about 5 minutes; stir once or twice with a spoon. Remove toasted almonds from oven and let cool to room temperature; set aside. In a large bowl beat the butter or margarine until creamy. Beat in the ¼ cup of confectioner's sugar, egg yolk, almond extract, orange blossom water, and chopped almonds. Mix in flour, adding a little extra if you have to, until the dough is soft, but not sticky. Pinch off small pieces of dough, about the size of a walnut, and shape as desired. Put on lightly greased cookie sheets and bake at 325° F for 30–35 minutes. Cookies are done when white on top and light golden brown on the bottom, or break one open; if there is no butter line, cookies are done. Let them cool completely, then place cookies on waxed paper. Sift confectioner's sugar over them, and roll cookies in sugar until completely covered. To serve, place each cookie in a paper baking cup and arrange on a platter. Enjoy! Makes about 2½ dozen.

*Author's Note: Orange blossom water is a fragrant water made by distilling water over orange blossoms. It can be purchased in Middle Eastern food stores or some health food stores.

Income Tax Magic

By Silver RavenWolf

Yes, it's that special time of year, the time for a fat income tax return check. No? Perhaps you view April 15 with fear and trepidation, sensing the vultures of the IRS circling overhead, biding their time to descend upon you with blood on their beaks and the Morrigan in their eyes. Yes, it's that mythical time when legends of poverty loom at our backs, and visions of bankruptcy dance in our heads. Is there anything an honest, magical person can do to make life with taxes any better? Of course! Here are some helpful tips to get you through the dreaded season of fear.

Before you begin the onerous task of collecting all your receipts, rummaging in the dresser drawer for that computer invoice dated January 2 of the previous year, or fretting over who should prepare your income tax return, take the time to do a reading with your favorite divination tool. For this article, I used *The Rune Oracle Cards*. I like the runes because they give you solutions as well as an outline of the situation. Check your divination tool to discover if there may be any glitches with the process of collecting, completing, or filing your return. For my reading I put down seven cards. Card one is for where I am right now; card two is for collecting data; card three represents the person who will calculate my return; card four is unforseen circumstances; card five is filing the return; card six is magic done for income tax purposes; and card seven is the outcome of the reading. You may wish to change the reading around to suit your preferences or the divination tool you chose.

If you see a problem, don't panic. If you are forewarned you can work around any possible difficulty. Check your divination tool throughout the filing process. Work magic accordingly.

After you have gathered all the necessary information, set your tax forms on your altar and banish any negative energies that may have attached themselves to them. Your cleansing procedures can include the use of the four elements, holy water, and magical sigils, such as the runes. (Hint: Use Algiz for protection against errors, Gyfu for finding a companionable and intelligent income tax preparer, Isa to freeze any misunderstandings that may result from your return information, Sol for easy navigation of your return through the system, and the Helm of Awe, which is not a rune, but a magical symbol, to ensure protection and right course of action).

Now that you've checked your divination tool, consider what type of ritual you would like to perform to aid you in your income tax venture. Protection from errors? Assistance in finding a good tax preparer? Help in filing on time? You know yourself and your history with taking care of your taxes; therefore, only you could design the proper ritual to fit your needs. Perhaps you don't want to perform a ritual at all. A set of simple spells might suffice as you work through the preparation procedure and eventual filing.

Who will guide you? Would you like to ask for assistance from your ancestors, your guardian angel, your spirit guide, or an archetype through the income tax season? Would you prefer to work with the Lord and Lady, or easier still, Spirit? You may choose an overall deity influence, then as you work specific rites or spells you may use several different archetypes, angels, or spirits. Check to make sure the energies of all deity and spirit influences blend well together.

When you've completed the tax preparation and the next step involves popping that envelope in the mail, take a ritual bath and then double check all of the information. Ask what you chose to guide you to give you wisdom to see any errors, or to remind you to include any important data you may have forgotten to add. Seal the documents in an envelope and put the envelope on your altar. Cleanse, consecrate, and bless the return, asking that the information arrive safely and on time.

Don't let the income tax monsters get you down! Take control of your finances through practical, magical applications.

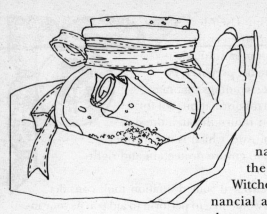

THE ANGEL BOTTLE

BY SILVER RAVENWOLF

Here's a sugary spell for financial success using the old technique of a Witches' bottle to attract financial abundance. You will need one green and one gold candle, a small jar of honey, three herbs you associate with money (mint, parsley, cinquefoil, High John the Conqueror root, cinnamon, sage, vervain, celandine, etc.), mortar and pestle, holy water or your favorite magical oil, one large, white feather, a dollar bill, a green cord or ribbon thirteen inches long, a green pen, and one small piece of parchment paper.

Moon phase choices for this spell would be Full, New, or crescent. Use the Sun (success) or Jupiter (monetary ventures) for your astrological associations, which would include either Sunday or Thursday, in the planetary hours of the Sun or Jupiter.

At the appropriate time, set the supplies on your altar, placing the herbs in the north, the feather in the east, the colored candles in the south, and the honey in the west. Place the dollar bill and the parchment paper (with writing instrument) in the center of the altar. Beginning in the north, working clockwise, cleanse, consecrate, and empower all supplies (ending with the money and parchment paper in the center).

On the parchment paper, write: "My life is filled with abundance and all my needs are met." Then sign your name underneath the affirmation. Dab oil or holy water on both sides of the dollar bill. Allow it to dry. Roll the dollar bill and affirmation paper together in a tight cylinder. Cast a magic circle with the white feather, then hold the feather out in front of you, and say:

> Guardian angel, I call you forth from the arms of Spirit
> To help me in my magic.
> Grace this working with your gifts of power, wisdom, and abundance.
> Hail and welcome, so mote it be.

Combine your magical herbs (in groups of three, seven, or nine) in the mortar with the pestle. As you grind the herbs in a clockwise motion, envision monetary abundance entering your life. Ask your guardian angel to help you make the magic of abundance.

Open the jar of honey. Drop in the money cylinder. Pour half of the powder into the honey. Hold your hands over the jar, and say:

> *As the energies of this potion blend together,*
> *I bring abundance into my life.*
> *Honey for sweet financial success.*
> *Herbs to blend and manifest.*
> *The symbol of money to connect with reward.*
> *I stir them together, then bind with a cord.*

Stir the mixture clockwise (deosil) three times, then close the jar. Bind your financial success to you by tying the green ribbon or cord around the jar. Light the gold and green candles, saying:

> *Gold for success, green for money*
> *I conjure harmony with herbs and honey.*

Sprinkle the remainder of your magical powder around the base of the candles. Hold the jar in your hands. Envision the mixture working to bring you financial success. Stare into the jar, seeing a kernel of your guardian angel's energy glowing at the center of the jar. If you've chosen a clear jar, hold the jar so that you can see the candle flames reflected in the honey.

Thank your guardian angel, and deactivate the magic circle. Allow the candles to burn out, or snuff them out and repeat lighting the candles and the visualization of the mixture working to bring you financial success every day until you have fully used the candles. Bury the candle ends in your back yard.

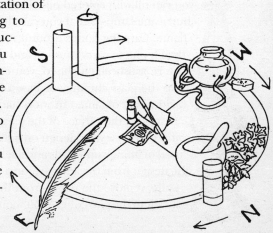

Each day pick up the jar and turn it clockwise nine times. As you turn the jar, continue the visualization of financial success.

Magical Tools

By Jim Garrison

When starting out on the magical path, you will probably hear a lot about all the tools everybody tells you to acquire. There are the various knives and wands, the chalice, pentacles, altar tables, candles, incense holders, and so on. True, you don't need fancy tools to do effective magic, but most folks eventually get involved in rituals and ceremonies that just seem to go better with a few tools. In the course of stocking your magical supply chest, there are a few tools to consider that you don't always hear about.

Staff

More theatrical than a wand, the staff is useful for drawing the attention of groups. You can use the staff to scribe a circle's boundaries. A staff can be used to denote a guardian of a particular quarter, each staff appropriately decorated for each of the sacred directions. With a bit of carving or painting, you can transform a staff into a powerful repository of runic or other energies. A staff can be a very handy tool if you like to work outdoors, and can serve as a very effective badge of office or distinguishing item to help you stand out from the crowd.

Lamps

A consecrated lamp filled with aromatic oil is a wonderful tool to include in your altar setup. In the quarters you can also use hurricane lamps or the more stylish oil lamps with floating wicks that you can fill with colored oils. The advantage of the old-style hurricane lamps is that you can dim them and adjust their flame. Carrying lamps around in ritual can be a bit safer than trying to carry candles, and they stay lit better, too. If you're artistically inclined, you can etch magical designs into the glass chimney or base of your lamp with a mild acid paste, obtained in most hardware stores. To do so, first clean the surface of the glass where you want to etch it. Then draw your design on a sheet of self-adhesive vinyl used in lining cupboards and shelves (contact paper). Cut the design from the adhesive vinyl with a craft or Exact-o™ knife, remove the paper from the back of the vinyl, and stick it to the glass where you want the design. Then apply the paste. After a few minutes, rinse off the paste and remove the vinyl. Wash the lamp one more time to remove any excess acid paste.

SCRYING BOWLS, SHEWSTONES, AND MAGIC MIRRORS

Any bowl can be painted black inside and used for scrying. You can fill the bowl with ink, water, or oil if you prefer.

Shewstones can be anything from an Austrian quartz crystal ball to a chunk of polished obsidian or a smoothly carved egg of tiger eye. You can pretty much use any sort of gemstone, mineral, or crystal you want. Some will work better than others, but the only way to determine that will be through experimentation. Generally, to work with a shewstone, you place it on a paten or pentacle. Some sources recommend using one made of beeswax, like Dr. John Dee used. If you can't acquire one made out of beeswax, you can hand-color a photocopy of Dr. Dee's design, or even draw your own. One word of warning: you may well want to do some sort of circle or create sacred space before working with a shewstone.

Mirrors are wonderful tools for doing Yesodic rites, working with moonlight, doing astral work, creating protective wards, doing revealing spells, clairvoyance work, or for returning unwanted or intrusive energies to their source.

If you are ambitious, you can remove the back of your mirror and scratch symbols into the the silver paint to create a magical circle, complete with sigils and arcane glyphs. Just be careful and remember that the image you are making is the reverse of what will be seen. Once you're finished scratching the symbols, either paint the back of the mirror with a coat of black paint, or cover the back with a sheet of black cardboard and then replace the backing.

CORDS

Made from silk, leather, cotton, or whatever material you prefer, cords are a great way to commemorate significant events such as rites of passage, or for signifying your dedication to a particular path, devotion, deity, or practice. Using different colors allows you to braid together a mixture of forces. For example, you might consecrate a strand of a particular color of cord to those planets that rule over those qualities that you want to bring into your life. Once each strand is properly consecrated, you can braid them together and seal the ends with thread, wax, jewelry findings, wire, or whatever your creativity inspires you to use. These cords then can be used to carry your athame in a sheath, or you might want to hang talismans or charms from them.

Another form of magical cord is the sort made for casting the circle. According to traditional sources, this cord is around nine feet in length for the individual, and from thirteen to twenty feet for a coven—depending on your tradition. These cords can be white, black, or red. You might consider braiding one with all three colors if that appeals to you.

SAND BOX

This is not the cat box, but rather a really fun tool for divination and spellwork. A simple box of sand can be used to ground energies. You can scribe symbols into the sand as part of a spell, or you might consider using a bed of sand laced with consecrated salt and herbs as a resting place for objects you wish to purify or cleanse. A sand box can also be used for classical geomancy. The box need not be extremely large—even something as small as four to five inches on a side is plenty useful. Fill the box with colored sand, aquarium gravel, or beach sand gathered under the Full Moon. You might consider using the sand box for doing sand-painting spells or rituals, which is ideal for small apartments. It's also easier to do sand-painting in the winter when you have a level surface to work on, instead of trying to fight with wind and snow. Another possibility is to create a miniature sand garden for meditative reflection, similar to rock gardens found in Zen centers.

RUGS, CUSHIONS, AND PILLOWS

Meditation is a staple of magical practice, and it's a good idea to have something to sit on. Cold floors can be distracting. Rugs can also be useful as roll-away magical circles. You can stuff dried herbs into your cushions and pillows, like you would a dream pillow.

POUCH

A fabric or leather bag in which you keep mementos and other items of significance is a very good thing to have. Don't worry about ripping off the idea of the medicine bundle or pouch of the indigenous peoples of North America—the Romans, Celts, Saxons, and Scandinavians all wore pouches and purses, too. When you are out walking in the woods it's handy to have something to hold all the rocks, acorns, leaves, twigs, herbs, feathers, or other gifts of nature that you come across and wish to hold on to for a bit.

A fabric pouch can be dyed, painted, stitched with designs, beaded, fringed, or otherwise decorated to suit your fancy. You may want to have more than one pouch to keep your special stones from getting mixed up with your matches, etc. This is especially useful at outdoor rituals, camping, or festivals.

Pens and Ink

If you ever decide to explore the process of making sigils, or you decide to make magical squares, kamea, or seals, you might find it enjoyable and rewarding to consecrate and dedicate a specific pen, or even set of pens, just for this sort of work. You can find designer fountain pens in a wide variety of materials and colors to lend the appropriate correspondences to your workings, or you might want to fashion your own pen from a stick of wood or a feather using an old-fashioned pen nib.

Once you have your pen, you can buy some colored inks to work with, selecting colors according to your favorite system of correspondences. Ambitious types might even want to try to craft their own ink.

Rattle

A rattle is a very effective tool for synchronizing people's heart rates and breathing in shamanistic sorts of workings. Quieter and easier to use than a drum, rattles are also much easier to take care of and to transport to rituals and gatherings.

Socks

In Minnesota where I live, it can get really cold, and running around on a chilly wood floor with bare feet is far from pleasant. A warm pair of wool ritual socks can be prepared by simply purifying them with incense and salt water, and maybe a touch of oil from the altar setup.

CORD MAGIC

By Estelle Daniels

O ne magical art that is not widely used is that of cord magic. Cords or ribbons of various colors are braided together while concentrating on a desired end. Then the cord is consecrated, blessed, and worn.

Many magical traditions use cords of various colors to designate attainment of degrees. This varies by tradition and region.

WAYS TO USE CORD MAGIC

Cord magic is widely adaptable. One very basic use is for protection. A cord can be made with the intent to protect the wearer from harm by psychic or magical energies. Then, when worn, the cord protects the wearer. Specialized cords can be made to protect from specific types of harm as the need arises. One caution: these protective cords should only be used when needed, not casually worn day in and day out. They work well when sleeping in an unfamiliar place, or visiting somewhere the wearer is uncertain about.

Another use for cords can be to help performance on the job. Weave them with the intent that you will do your job better, be more professional, make fewer mistakes, make a good impression on others, etc., then wear them under your clothes to work. You could wear them every day (taking them off after work), or maybe only on Monday, or the toughest day of your week. Eventually you will no longer need them, as you will have internalized the message.

Cord magic adapts well to helping others who may not use magic themselves. You weave the intent into the cords, and the person wears them knowing what spell you used and what the desired outcome is. You cannot give a person a cord and expect it to work without their knowledge and cooperation. The person wearing the cord must know what it is about and be a willing participant in the magical intent.

Some people use cords to invoke certain god or goddess energies. As deity has many aspects, you can use cords to symbolize a certain aspect of deity, and when woven with that in mind the cord acts as a link to that manifestation. These can also be used to invoke protection or aid from that particular god-form when worn.

A cord can also be used as a portable magical circle. Weave the cord inside a circle with the intent of reproducing that circle when worn. Then all you need to do is put the cords on, and you are in that circle. This works well when you are in a place where you cannot cast a full circle, or you need a circle but lack the time or equipment necessary. This type of cord needs to be recharged every so often to retain its potency and effectiveness.

BUYING AND PREPARING CORD MATERIALS

The materials used for a cord vary. I like the round silk cord (called rattail, mousetail, bugtail or other names), dyed various colors, and usually available by the yard or foot at craft, yarn, or fabric stores. It comes in varying widths and many colors. It braids easily, and looks nice when finished. Yarn can also be used. Thicker yarn is better as it stands up to wear, and wool is best. Natural fibers work best in cords. Colored ribbons can also be used, found in fabric stores for trim (not the ribbon used for decorating packages). Often they can be bought by the spool for a good price.

When planning for a specific cord, I go and buy the materials, usually all at once. It's easier to braid if you use the same material throughout, all silk or wool yarn, or ribbons. If the materials are bought in lengths, I measure to the length desired. The standard is three yards (nine feet) per strand. Longer lengths become difficult to work with, and shorter lengths make a less adaptable cord. When I get it all home, I coat the ends with melted wax (usually by running them into the melted wax at the base of a lighted candle) to seal the ends and prevent fraying. If you stick the cords in below the flame you can get the ends waxed and not burn the cord at all. After the wax hardens, I either start the braiding or I put the materials away until the time I have chosen to work on the cords.

BRAIDING THE CORD

When braiding, a tighter weave will make a shorter cord. A more elaborate weave will also probably end up shorter if you start with the same length of cord. The more strands used and the thicker strands used, generally the shorter the finished cord will be. You can secure the cord with a ring (it loops through to tie more easily with a ring), or you can just knot the ends together and braid if you don't want to use any metal.

When braiding, I plan enough time to finish the cord in one session. A simple three-strand braid can take twenty to forty minutes. With a seven or more strand braid it can take hours. As I braid, I recite the reasons for making this cord, perhaps making a rhyme or chant. I vary the words, using more than one rhyme or chant. I visualize the outcome desired; not how that outcome will happen, but just the end desired. If making the cord for another, I talk about the person and why this cord is being made and what I want it to do.

Once finished, I bless and consecrate the cord, then put it away until it is to be used. Cords make nice repositories for portable spells, and travel easily. You can wear them under your clothes or even as a belt, and they will do what you want, and be unobtrusive. You can carry them in a purse or pocket, ready to use when needed. Placed under a pillow, they offer protection at night while sleeping.

Cord magic is simple and effective, and adapts well to many purposes. Blessed Be.

MAGIC FINGERS

BY RACHEL RAYMOND

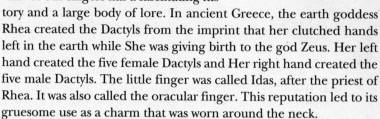

The symbolism and magical power of our fingers has a fascinating history and a large body of lore. In ancient Greece, the earth goddess Rhea created the Dactyls from the imprint that her clutched hands left in the earth while She was giving birth to the god Zeus. Her left hand created the five female Dactyls and Her right hand created the five male Dactyls. The little finger was called Idas, after the priest of Rhea. It was also called the oracular finger. This reputation led to its gruesome use as a charm that was worn around the neck.

The ring finger was said to be ruled by Venus, the goddess of love, and it was thought that a vein ran directly from that finger to the heart. This is why wedding rings are still placed on that finger today.

According to the ancient Romans, the middle finger belonged to the Father, or Jupiter, and was called the phallic finger—a symbolism that has lost nothing in the translation centuries later.

INDEX FINGER

The index finger, or command finger, belonged to the Mother, and was considered the most powerful. Just pointing it at someone could direct them, heal them, or curse them, which is why it is still considered rude to point, and why scolding or nagging women are shown wagging their index fingers. The index and middle finger crossed together was symbolic of sexual intercourse and was used as a protective charm.

THUMBS

The thumb symbolized the divine child. Newborns keep their thumbs close to their fist or enclosed within their fingers. As infants mature, they gradually raise their thumbs. After death, the thumb relaxes downward into the hand again. This may be why Romans giving a gladiator the death sentence gave the "thumbs down."

A thumb that turns back indicates someone who has trouble saving money, but wide thumbs mean that you will be good at making money. Long thumbs are supposed to indicate stubbornness. If, when clasping your hands, you fold your right thumb over your left you are said to be domineering and independent. If you cover your right thumb with your left, then you are said to be more comfortable following than leading. If you fold both thumbs under your clasped hands then you are said to have a guilty conscience.

HAND GESTURES

Different finger positions have different symbolic meanings. A finger raised to the lips indicates silence or secrecy. Two fingers raised means judgment or teaching, three fingers raised indicates the trinity. The Vulcan sign used by Spock to signify "Live long and prosper" is actually an ancient Jewish gesture of peace and good will.

Hindu deities are frequently shown with their hands in various symbolic positions, or *mudras*. Extending the index and little finger while holding down the thumb and two middle fingers was originally a mudra of the Hindu goddess Kali-Ma. It is also a sign of the crescent moon, and was used in Asia to signify the goddess Quan-Yin. Later it became a sign of the devil and was said to symbolize his horns. It was still used to avert evil. The gesture we use to signal "okay" was once the mudra used to indicate infinite perfection and spiritual bliss.

FINGERS IN THE MOUTH

A finger in the mouth has been used to indicate the ingestion of magical substances. The great Celtic bard Taliesen achieved his inspiration when he tasted the magical fluid from the goddess Cerridwen's cauldron. He inadvertently ingested a few drops when some of the scalding liquid splattered onto his finger, and he sucked on it. In other legends, a hero who defeats a dragon may inadvertently touch the sizzling dragon flesh and then put his finger in his mouth, thereby achieving the wisdom of the dragon. The Egyptian god Horus, in His infant form, is shown with His finger in his mouth. He is sucking on it because splattered on it is the magical milk of His mother, Isis.

FINGERNAILS

The strongest magical powers of fingers are reputed to be in the nails. Elaborate means for disposal of fingernail cuttings are traditional all over the world.

It is considered to be extremely bad luck to cut an infant's nails
before the child is a year old. It is
supposed to make the child "light-fingered"
(a thief).

It is said that walking on fingernail parings
will injure the person from whom they came. Having inadvertently
stepped on my own nail clippings from time to time with bare feet, I
can vouch for this idea, although I cannot say if I have been hurt
when someone else stepped on them.

Fingernails could heal as well as hurt. To heal epilepsy, all you
need to do is gather the sufferer's nail parings and hair cuttings and
bury them with a black cock at a crossroads at midnight. An ancient
remedy for ague specified putting nail clippings and hair trimmings
in the hollow of an elder or aspen tree.

Other entertaining fingernail beliefs include the following.
Those who bite their nails will not grow tall. It is bad luck to clean
your fingernails after dark. People with large half Moons at the base
of their fingertips are considered well bred and possessing of good
fortune. Prominent nail ridges indicate a nervous temperament.
Small, rounded nails indicate an honest person with a short fuse.
People with triangle-shaped nails have trouble keeping secrets. You
can count the white spots on your nails and make a wish. A white spot
on your pinkie indicates a journey is in store; on your ring finger it
bodes a letter or a new sweetheart; on your middle finger it augers for
a new enemy; and on your index finger a new friend. Finally, a white
spot on your thumbnail predicts a present is in your near future.

The most magical use of fingers is their ability to create and to
heal; to bring beautiful sounds from a waiting musical instrument; to
make a work of art from a collection of raw materials; to create a sa-
vory meal from a bag of groceries. Perhaps the greatest finger magic
of all is to bring comfort, joy, and pleasure to those we love through
the simple act of touch.

ELEMENTAL SPECIFICS

BY CERRIDWEN IRIS SHEA

When you are working in the sacred space of the cast circle, do you know what elemental energies you are working with and why? Are you just using elements and saying words because that's the way you've been taught?

EARTH

Take a look at your altar. What represents the element of earth? Clay? A dish of salt? Sand? Earth? A rock? Why is it there? The item I use will be the one with the closest meaning to the goal of my ritual.

AIR

The most common representation for air is incense. Is it stick or cone? What is the scent? Does the scent have meaning to the ritual? Have you decided to use a feather to represent air? If so, what kind of feather? From what bird? What meaning does that bird add to your ritual? Or are you using a pen or pencil, for inspiration? Incense can represent fire and air. A pencil, made of wood and graphite, can represent air (inspiration) and earth (wood/graphite).

FIRE

Are you using candles to represent fire? Are they anointed with oil? Does the oil compliment the incense you are using with the air element, or are they contradictory? Are you using a representation of a salamander? A disk with the Sun on it? Are you burning something in a cauldron (fire and water)? Each of these will bring something into the ritual.

WATER

Are you using a dish of water? Wine? A seashell (water and earth)? A representation of a water creature or a mermaid? Why are they there? What will they bring to the ritual?

Undines—Water Element

SPIRIT

Do you have something to represent spirit? Is spirit an unseen element in the ritual? Do you choose not to use spirit? Why or why not?

CASTING THE CIRCLE

Okay, you have chosen your elements and they are consecrated. You've cast your circle. How have you cast? Are you using words you read somewhere or that someone told you to say, or are you saying something that has personal mean-ing to you? My advice: if it has no personal meaning, change it.

Sylphs—Air Element

THE DIRECTIONS/WATCHTOWERS

It's time to call in the directions/watchtowers/whatever your tradi-tion calls them. Who are you calling in and why? Angels? Dragons? El-ementals? A combination? Are they there to guard, watch, or partic-ipate? If you are calling in more than one energy from a direction, does each one have a purpose in the circle? If so, specify the purpose. If not, don't call it in. Will everyone you've called in get along?

After you're finished, then what? I dislike the term "dismissing" the quarters. Who the heck am I to dismiss? To me, that is rather hi-erarchical and a bit insulting. Make sure you remember who you've in-vited in, so that you can thank each one specifically. I've been in cir-cles where the eagle was called in (and showed up), but it was the owl who was thanked and dismissed!

Okay, okay. It's far too much work and now you have a headache. But think about it. Take the time to know each element thorough-ly. What you put out there comes back. Treat elemental representations with respect. Make sure you know who you are calling in and why. It will boost the energy of the ritual, enhance your work, and build stronger working re-lationships, both on the physical and as-tral planes.

Gnomes—Earth Element

PLACES OF POWER

BY KEN JOHNSON

The earth is filled with geographic zones, both large and small, that possess powerful energy fields. Mystics and magicians call these energy zones "power spots" or "places of power." They can be found almost everywhere, even in the unlikeliest locations.

Different power spots resonate with different centers in our bodies. One may awaken the heart and help us experience bliss, while another may simply fill us with joy, and yet another may assist us in the process of spiritual healing. Then there is the opposite effect: some places can devastate our energy fields with such intensity that they may even cause disease to those who live near them.

Power spots may also be classified according to whether they are yin or yang, "masculine," or "feminine." A yang power spot fills us with a certain quality, while a yin spot dissolves or disperses things. This doesn't mean that yang spots are "positive" or that yin spots are "negative." A yin power spot can suck out disease and heal the human organism, while some yang spots merely fill us with egotism and bluster rather than with wisdom.

Ultimately, there are seven kinds of power spots: Those that are filled with beneficial energy and give this energy to us freely, as an act of love; those that awaken a particular chakra or inner center of power; those that actually help magicians and other spiritual seekers to shift their consciousness from one inner center to another; those that serve as "gateways between the worlds" and help us to enter different dimensions; those that bear the imprint of some very high or enlightened soul, such as the meditation places or graves of the masters; those that "suck out" or steal our life energies, causing illness of disease; and those that suck out the

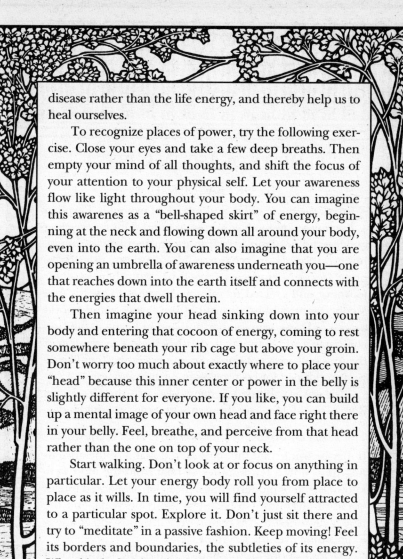

disease rather than the life energy, and thereby help us to heal ourselves.

To recognize places of power, try the following exercise. Close your eyes and take a few deep breaths. Then empty your mind of all thoughts, and shift the focus of your attention to your physical self. Let your awareness flow like light throughout your body. You can imagine this awarenes as a "bell-shaped skirt" of energy, beginning at the neck and flowing down all around your body, even into the earth. You can also imagine that you are opening an umbrella of awareness underneath you—one that reaches down into the earth itself and connects with the energies that dwell therein.

Then imagine your head sinking down into your body and entering that cocoon of energy, coming to rest somewhere beneath your rib cage but above your groin. Don't worry too much about exactly where to place your "head" because this inner center or power in the belly is slightly different for everyone. If you like, you can build up a mental image of your own head and face right there in your belly. Feel, breathe, and perceive from that head rather than the one on top of your neck.

Start walking. Don't look at or focus on anything in particular. Let your energy body roll you from place to place as it wills. In time, you will find yourself attracted to a particular spot. Explore it. Don't just sit there and try to "meditate" in a passive fashion. Keep moving! Feel its borders and boundaries, the subtleties of its energy. What kind of a place is it? Yin or yang? Does it resonate with a particular center inside your body? Which one? The type of power spot you choose will give you a clue as to the nature of your own magical gifts, because it will probably activate the center in which your own personal power is located.

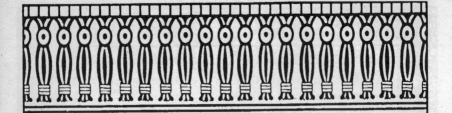

TEMPLES OF ISIS IN GREECE

BY deTRACI REGULA

Speak the name of Isis and images of pyramids, Egyptian temples, and the Nile spring to mind. This far-traveling goddess did not limit herself to the ancient land of Khem, however. Sailors, merchants, soldiers, priests, priestesses, princesses, and emperors carried her with them on their journeys, and erected temples and shrines to an Isis in a Mediterreanean guise. Instead of the shadowy underworld aspects of Osiris, who was her husband in Egypt, in the Greco-Roman world Isis was paired with Serapis, a descendent of the Apis bull aspect of Osiris. Serapis is a lively, Zeus-like divinity renowned for his prowess in healing and war.

Isis was worshipped at many places in the Greek and Roman world. Here are three sites that can be visited today.

DELOS: SACRED ISLAND OF THE AEGEAN

It may be ironic that the most sacred island of the ancient Aegean is only a few minutes by boat from the most well-known island of modern times, the celebrity-packed tourist island of Mykonos. Go back two thousand years, and the true "celebrities" of this region were the gods and goddesses presiding over the island of Delos.

Delos is a bright, windblown island, the birthplace of Apollo and Artemis. The island was ultimately considered so sacred that no mere mortal could be born or die on Delos. Pregnant women and those believed about to die were transported by boat to the neighboring islands. In 426 B.C.E. all the graves that existed on the island were exhumed and transported to the nearby island of Rheneia, where they

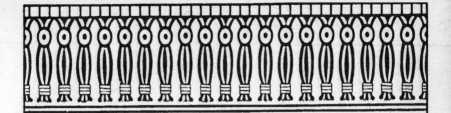

were reinterred. Among the remains found on the island of Rheneia was the burial of Philo, a priestess of Isis, who was laid to rest with a tiny inscribed gold ring bearing what is believed to be her name; earrings; and her sacred sistrum, a bronze rattle that she had used in her worship of Isis.

The temple at which Philo served still stands, clinging to the slopes of Mt. Cynthos, overlooking the sacred harbor where modern tour boats now dock. An unusual horned altar stands in front of the temple, evoking Babylonia rather than Egypt. Within the temple enclosure, a massive statue of Isis still stands, headless, but somehow no less powerful. The temple is roofless now, so the Sun pours in and the white marble of the statue glows in the light in a way it never did in ancient times. If the statue were complete, it would long ago have been removed to sterile safety in a museum. Instead, Isis is still on duty here, and at her feet dried flowers attest to the visits of modern worshippers. The statue's head may be missing, but the Goddess' heart is still present on Delos.

EPIDAUROS: HEALING CENTER OF ANCIENT GREECE

In the Greek world, as well as in her native Egypt, Isis was renowned as a goddess who heals. In the Greco-Egyptian city of Alexandria, she and Sarapis presided over the training of physicians at the most renowned medical university of the ancient world. With these credentials, it was not long before her worship was established at Epidauros, the sacred site of Asclepius, the Greek god of healing and medicine. Epidauros in those times was very similar to a modern healing spa. There was a large, 200-room "hotel" for patients and their families to stay at while receiving healings at the

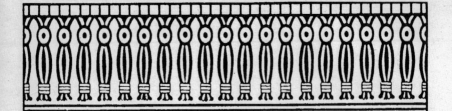

temples. Isis presided over her own Iseum, with a staff of medically trained clergy. To be a *pastophor,* a position held by both men and women, one needed to completely master the six sacred medical texts of the god Thoth, which Isis was said to have taught to her own son Horus. Pastophors understood anatomy, diagnosis, surgery, pharmacology, opthmalogy, and gynecology.

Isis also had an "annex," the smaller temple of the Egyptian deities, where she was worshipped along with Sarapis.

GORTYN: A ROMAN CITY OF CRETE

When Rome conquered a new nation, cities built on the Roman model were quickly erected as signs of Roman power and as administrative, religious, and commercial centers. Gortyn is a Roman city in the southwest of Crete, with extensive ruins that lie in the midst of olive groves. Wandering through the rocky remains, visitors have to avoid the nets spread beneath the olive trees during the harvest season. There is a more formal, more carefully kept site near the small museum and the well-preserved Christian basilica, but the dry weeds across the road beneath the olive trees conceal what remains of the temple of Isis and Sarapis. Here Isis was worshipped in an unusual guise, as Isis-Persephone, mated to Sarapis-Pluto. In the Heraklion Museum, the statues removed from the temple at Gortyn form an interesting family group. Isis-Persephone holds a sistrum next to her husband Sarapis-Pluto, and at his feet sits the family dog, three-headed Cerberus. Cerberus is more understandable when one realizes that at Gortyn, the triad of deities worshipped were Isis, Sarapis, and the jackal-headed god, Anubis.

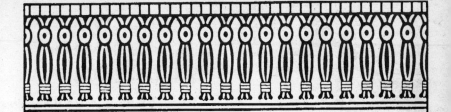

Gortyn is special because the temple's nilometer still exists. The nilometer was an artifact of the worship in Egypt, where they served the practical function of measuring the rise of the Nile during the flood. Temples of Isis often retained these nilometers far from the Nile, sometimes connected with a local river, but usually serving a purely symbolic function. At Gortyn, visitors can descend the steps of the nilometer and pause in front of three niches sacred to the deities of the temple. Standing in front of the niches, visitors are completely below the level of the ground. The sacred earth surrounds the visitor with silence. A few moments' meditation takes you back, beyond the time of the destruction of this temple, into the high holy days of the past, when this was an active and spiritually powerful place.

As Plutarch, a Greek priest and writer of the first century of this era, said, "Isis belongs to the Greeks," and her many temple sites attest to that fact. While her native Egypt was languishing under the conquest of the Greeks and, later, the Romans, Isis was busy with her own overseas conquest of the souls and hearts of countless inhabitants of the Aegean and beyond.

THE
LEGEND OF
LOST LEMURIA

BY KEN JOHNSON

Lemuria is not just a creation of the occultists. In fact, it enjoys great prominence in Pacific Island mythology, in marked contrast to the few references to Atlantis which may be found in Western myth. Among Pacific Islanders, there is a nearly universal belief in a sunken primordial continent. The Polynesians call it *Hawaiki* or *Havai'ki*.

This original homeland was an enormous land mass, covering most of the central Pacific. A lush, verdant land, it was here that the island people began. In those days, the land of Havai'ki was ruled by a semi-mystical race of aristocrats whom later legends call the People of the Mist. They are credited with giving the Polynesians all of their great cultural gifts and traditions. It is also said that the *menehunes,* the "little people" of Hawaiian folklore who are sometimes known as the *mu,* also came originally from Havai'ki.

At some point in prehistory, and because of some spiritual transgression that remains unclear, the vast continent of Havai'ki sank beneath the waves. The survivors became refugees, dispersed to all parts of the Pacific basin. After many millennia, the people, who still remembered their ancient homeland, began to voyage through the Pacific in their great canoes, and discovered the island remnants of their former home. So they returned, not, as the archaeologists would have it, to uninhabited coral atolls and volcanic islands, but to continental remnants that were, in many cases, still occupied by fugitive bands of Menehunes and the People of the Mist.

Havai'ki itself still survives, if only on the astral plane. According to Polynesian myth, it still exists as a mysterious island "in the west" or as a land beneath the sea where only heroes and shamans may travel, and where they may receive the wisdom of the ancestors.

FAIRIES

By Silver RavenWolf

Reality? Tradition? Lore? The kingdoms and populace of fairy-enchantment have long haunted imaginations of poets, dreamers, peasants, and scholars. Most fairy mythology indicates that fairies manifest as preternatural creatures living between the worlds. This gives them the ability to sneak through the human populace unseen when they choose, or blatantly appear in a variety of ways to serve their purposes if they so desire. Much like humans, members of the fairy realms have a checkered history when it comes to helping or harming those of us on the material plane.

The majority of fairy folk find their roots in European folklore, although legends and lore of similar entities circulate through most of human history, regardless of religious belief, cultural nuances, or socio-economic status. From Eskimos to the Japanese, the tales, antics, and dangers of the "little folk" persist. The belief in fairies appears linked to the same area of human consciousness that creates a connection between religious mythos and metaphysical practices.

Through the tumultuous history of humankind, the origin of fairies has been hotly debated. Are they spirits of the dead? Fallen angels? The essence of plant and tree energy? Do they resemble humans only because we want them to, or can they really manifest in pseudo-human form? Are they lore-remnants of a race of people who have long since merged with the dust of our ever-changing planet, or is our belief in them so strong that we have actually manifested them into the astral through our own process of thought creation? Is that crazy woman walking down the street and muttering to herself as she adjusts her red hat just an odd lady, or is she a Redcap? Sagas and legends evolve from traditional stories, that although containing fictional and imaginative elements, may have a historical basis. These sagas and legends could represent in the popular memory a real happening that was extraordinary enough to be remembered and embellished. Perhaps our fairies fit the profile of the saga or legend?

Fairy legend doesn't just revolve around cute little people with gossamer wings, or the helpful brownie. A compendium of fairy lore paints them, if not as downright malicious, with at least little regard for human morality. At best, quite a few legends portray the fairy population with prankster mentality. The most powerful and unpredictable personalities manifest as the *Sidhe*. Originally, the word sidhe meant mound or hill, or the dwelling place of the DeDanaan after their defeat by the Milesians. These ancient shining ones, thus exiled underground, became part of folk legend, metamorphosing into the fairies as Sidhe, the people of the hills. The traditional characteristics of fairies can be found in European literature as in Shakespeare's *A Midsummer Night's Dream* and *Romeo and Juliet* (in Mercutio's "Queen Mab" speech), and other great works. To escape the magics of the most dangerous of fairies, one would employ the use of iron, as this metal destroys all fairy magic. The majority of fairies appear to live in some sort of organized society, whether it be the ubiquitous fairyland or underground in the mythical terrain of the Sidhe. Whatever the fairy society, two factors appear to remain constant: The absence of sickness, and the absence of time.

If one wishes to contact the fairies, or receive their blessings, a customary offering of milk and honey should be left by the back door of your home on the first day of spring. Then, as the days warm and the world around you comes alive with the energy of manifestation, you should take walks around your home or spend time meditating outdoors, sending loving energy to the area. As your thoughts merge with the universal consciousness, you will be sending the signal that you come in peace, merging the spirit of yourself with the energy patterns of the land.

REFERENCES

Ellis, Peter Berresford. *A Dictionary of Irish Mythology.* Oxford Paperback Reference. Oxford University Press, 1987.

Evans-Wentz, W. Y. *The Fairy Faith in Celtic Countries.* Library of the Mystic Arts. Citadel Press, 1990 (1966 University Press).

Mercatante, Anthony. *The Facts on File Encyclopedia of World Mythology and Legend.* Facts on File, 1988.

THE FEY FOLK

BY LILITH SILVERHAIR

You can see them still across the Irish countryside—hundreds of burial mounds and barrow graves. What secrets do they hold? The Pagan folk knew. These were the sidh, the under hill homes of the fairies.

The Fair Folk have long been associated with the dead and ancestors. The Celtic peoples said that the fairies came out of their hills on Samhain, the night when the veil between the world of the living and the world of the dead was thinnest. *The Book of the Dun Cow* describes the realm of Fairy as a place where there is continual feasting, and no one ever dies or does anything bad. This was the Pagan afterlife, literally a land of milk and honey. Respect for the fairies and thus respect for the dead was never really stamped out by the Christian churches, who taught that the fairies were nothing more than devils and demons. While underground, Cornish miners would not make the sign of the cross, for they did not want to offend the fairies in their very homes by making gestures to invoke their enemy.

The fairies of old were not the diminutive winged beings one so often sees in storybooks. The Fair Folk of Ireland were gods, a race of giants—the Tuatha De Danann. The women of the fairy mounds—the *Bean Sidh*—later degenerated into banshees, the wailing demons whose voices foretold or brought about death. A "Who's Who" of the Fairy Realm could read something like this:

BROWNIES: These small men with wrinkled brown skin and a shaggy demeanor like to adopt homes. They will do various household chores in exchange for cream and honey cakes.

ELVES: This is the classic, pointed-eared fey. They are astonishingly beautiful, although very pale. The Old English and Norse words for *elf* (*aelf* and *alfr*) meant white. Very magical in nature, they were always thought to be powerful and somewhat frightening, depending on their disposition. They can be both beneficial and malevolent to humans, so it is best not to upset them in any way.

GNOMES: Here we have the earth elementals. It is said that each flower and plant has its own gnome attending it, so it is best to be very careful when dealing with the local flora of your area, lest you disturb a gnome. In ancient times this was said to bring about dire consequences.

GOBLINS: Having trouble finding things where you last put them? It could be that you have a goblin about engaging in its favorite pastime—snitching things. Goblins are olive-skinned, and their favorite time of year is Halloween. Goblins aren't necessarily evil. They are simply the pranksters of the Fairy Realm.

PIXIES: Found almost exclusively in Ireland, pixies are the most carefree of fey. They love to lead people astray simply to watch the consternation it causes. If you feel you have been duped by a pixie, your only recourse is to turn your clothing inside out to turn away the pixie magic.

To please the fair folk, you need do nothing more than accept them, not disturb their natural habitats, and perhaps leave pretty trinkets or a bit of bread and honey as an offering.

LORD OF THE WILD HUNT

BY D. J. CONWAY

The Lord of the Wild Hunt is the most misunderstood of all the Pagan God's aspects. He is the Celtic male counterpart of the Greek goddesses the Erinyes, deities who see that justice and what we call "fate" is carried out. Unfortunately, the early European Christians managed to convince people that the Lord of the Hunt was really their devil, who supposedly went out on dark, stormy nights and on Halloween to kidnap unsuspecting souls and carry them off to the Christian hell.

Actually, this Lord is very different from anything imagined by the Christians. The Lord of the Hunt carries out the will of the Goddess in Her role of recycling Mother and Fate. He makes certain that souls who are ready for the transition from life to physical death are in the right places at the right times to meet their destinies. It is also his duty to bring to justice those who have broken the laws of the Goddess.

The story of the Wild Hunt or the Ride of Death is known all over Europe. The Nordic and Germanic cultures say this Ride is led by Odhinn/Wodan, or the Erl King. Others also were said to lead a Wild Hunt: Dietrich of Berne (Teutonic); the French Grand Huntsman of Fontainebleau; the Celtic deity Arawn; the Norse Lusse (an evil spirit in the form of a great bird of prey); and King Arthur. Even the folk hero Robin Hood (whose story goes back much further than medieval times) was a type of Lord of the Hunt. He used his arrows to bring down and punish offenders.

Many Pagan male deities can be identified as the Lord of the Wild Hunt. Arawn of Wales was the god of Annwn, the Underground kingdom of the dead. Gwynn ap Nudd of Wales was the King of the Faeries and also ruler of a section of the Underworld. The Dagda of Ireland was known as the god of death and rebirth.

Odhinn had an aspect as Lord of Death. He was God of the Hanged, and collected his share of warrior-souls from the battlefields. His wolves, Geri and Freki, ran with Odhinn and the Valkyries when he

led the Hunt. A shape-shifter, he produced the battle panic called "battle-fetter," a psychological state that caused men to be unable to act.

The Danes knew Odhinn in his aspect as the Lord of the Hunt and called him the *Ellerkonge* (Erl King), or king of elves. The Erl King was associated with the elder tree and with Hel in her aspect as Old Lady of the Elder.

The Norse god Hod or Hodr, who slew Balder, was sometimes shown as a threatening god, wearing a death mask and a hood, very similar to the father of Robin Hood.

In his night ride through the sky, the Lord was accompanied by a pack of spectral hounds (a Goddess animal), and a great host of ethereal entities, who possibly represent the ancestors of the person he is seeking.

The Hounds of the Hunt are known by a variety of names. In England, they are called the Gabriel Hounds, Yeth Hounds, the Dartmoor Hounds, and the Wisht Hounds. The Irish called them the Hounds of Hell, while the Welsh knew them as the Cwn Annwn (Faery Hounds).

The God in his aspect as the Lord of the Hunt is not to be feared, for, contrary to many stories, he performs his task with compassion. Without his gentle guidance, our passage at death would be much harder. We shouldn't fear the Father whose firm but compassionate correction of our mistakes helps us live a better and more spiritual life.

The Erl King

A Ride with the Wild Hunt

By Ann Moura (Aoumiel)

The following dark aspect meditation, which may be recorded and then played back, is suggested for one to get a feeling for the unity of purpose between Dark Lord and Crone. This gives the participant the opportunity to approach the Dark Powers and feel how they work together. The word *raid* comes from the old Scottish word *rade*, which is "ride" as a noun. The Wild Hunt is an ancient image that depicts the Horned God as Death or the Hunter, racing across the night sky with his band of followers, gathering souls. It is also the image for chaos and violent storms. In this meditation, the visualization evokes the Hunter.

Sit in a darkened room. Breathe deeply and exhale. Now begin a simple breathing exercise of inhaling for two counts and holding for one, releasing for two counts and holding for one, etc. This will help you to relax and clear your mind. Once your mind is calm, the noise of stray thoughts is vanquished, and you are in your quiet inner space, listen and hear the distant thundering of horses' hooves. A horn sounds far away, and the noise of riders seems to become more distinct. Now you hear the pounding of horses' hooves coming closer; the rattle and squeak of harness and saddles; the heavy breath of the beasts; and again the blast of the horn. You know it is the Wild Hunt approaching.

You call out, "May I ride with the raid until break of day?" The Hunter calls back to you, "Catch hold my hand and dare not let go!" and as He passes, you grasp the hand held down to you. You are amazed at the fluid strength that quickly pulls you up to sit before the Hunter upon His mount. You hold fast to that hand and watch the raid from your privileged seat.

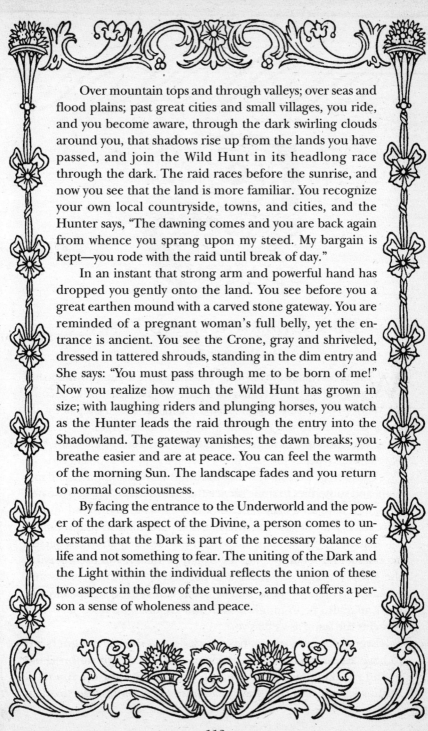

Over mountain tops and through valleys; over seas and flood plains; past great cities and small villages, you ride, and you become aware, through the dark swirling clouds around you, that shadows rise up from the lands you have passed, and join the Wild Hunt in its headlong race through the dark. The raid races before the sunrise, and now you see that the land is more familiar. You recognize your own local countryside, towns, and cities, and the Hunter says, "The dawning comes and you are back again from whence you sprang upon my steed. My bargain is kept—you rode with the raid until break of day."

In an instant that strong arm and powerful hand has dropped you gently onto the land. You see before you a great earthen mound with a carved stone gateway. You are reminded of a pregnant woman's full belly, yet the entrance is ancient. You see the Crone, gray and shriveled, dressed in tattered shrouds, standing in the dim entry and She says: "You must pass through me to be born of me!" Now you realize how much the Wild Hunt has grown in size; with laughing riders and plunging horses, you watch as the Hunter leads the raid through the entry into the Shadowland. The gateway vanishes; the dawn breaks; you breathe easier and are at peace. You can feel the warmth of the morning Sun. The landscape fades and you return to normal consciousness.

By facing the entrance to the Underworld and the power of the dark aspect of the Divine, a person comes to understand that the Dark is part of the necessary balance of life and not something to fear. The uniting of the Dark and the Light within the individual reflects the union of these two aspects in the flow of the universe, and that offers a person a sense of wholeness and peace.

BBS, Cyberspace, and Privacy

By Estelle Daniels

When the magicians of old talked about traveling to the astral planes, they never imagined that the internet would become the modern equivalent. Cyberspace is intangible, and it is a place without a place, not in the real-time world. You can travel far, yet never leave your home. There are also pitfalls, and issues that many who have enthusiastically jumped into cyberspace haven't considered.

The average person who uses the internet has a computer and modem, and subscribes to some service that allows them access to the net. They also have an e-mail address, which allows them to send and receive mail. They browse the internet, and participate in chat rooms.

The first illusion many internet users have is that what a person accesses and does on the net are totally private. If you use a service, the sysop (systems operator) also has access to your accounts and e-mail. This may only be so that he or she can retrieve lost passwords, but it may also be to monitor what you are doing, if necessary. This protects the sysop as well as you.

Every computer system has a back door, a way the designers left to have access in cases of emergency. Hackers delight in breaking in and checking out other computer systems just for the fun of it. Businesses and industry have elaborate encryption codes to help

maintain privacy, but the best encryption is only good until someone breaks it.

People have sent messages via e-mail and those messages have ended up in the hands of people they were never meant for. Even private and confidential e-mail messages can be opened and read by others if they know what to look for and how to get in. You should write each message with a thought about its impact if it were made public. Confidentiality and outing are big issues in magical groups. If you correspond and use a code name, avoid using any mundane name or home address. If you refer to others, use nicknames that would be meaningless to an outsider. Keep all descriptions general enough so as to not allow an outsider to identify people, places, or incidents.

Participating in a chat room is a great way to meet people and exchange information and find friends. Be aware that for every person who posts in a chat room, there are at least twenty "lurkers." These are people who log in, but do not actively post. Chat rooms are in effect gigantic party lines, and anyone can "listen in"—the kid next door, or the fundamentalists who think anything occult is satanic. Next time you post, think about that information getting into the hands of those people. Is there anything to identify you personally? People have been targeted with mailings, phone calls, and actual visits by fundamentalists eagerly wanting to reform them, and the information was obtained on the internet. Don't do that to yourself or a friend.

Some people are not "out" in their mundane lives. That is, they have chosen to keep private their religion, their magical affiliations, their sexual orientation, or their leisure activities. If they are on the internet, they have to be careful, because anyone can drop in to a chat room. If you are out, keep in mind the many who are not, and don't jeopardize their livelihoods or family relationships by casually dropping details of their lives such as where they work, their home addresses, their phone numbers, or their real names. Just because the Constitution guarantees religious freedom doesn't mean a vindictive boss can't fire you for other reasons, and sexual orientation is not protected under the Constitution.

Another thing you encounter in cyberspace is "flame wars." These are acrimonious exchanges between people who take disagreement to extremes. Chat rooms are semi-anonymous, and people have fewer inhibitions about getting down and dirty anonymously. Again, there is no guarantee of confidentiality. At the very least the sysop knows who you are, and people have been banned from chat rooms for going too far. Also, people who follow chat rooms for a while get to know regulars, and over time can gather information that just might allow them to identify participants. Then when things get really nasty, someone might say, "I know who you are, John Doe, you are really Joe Slob who lives at 666 Main Street." If you really are Joe Slob, your cover is blown, and people may respond more directly to your comments. If someone guessed wrong, and John Doe isn't really Joe Slob, you can bet Joe Slob will still be contacted about the matter in question, and then someone else's life has been made difficult by a thoughtless person. Even in private e-mail, don't do this kind of thing because that information (the kind that is potentially the most damaging) occasionally gets out. Murphy's Law. If you need to identify someone, use a handle, a magical or mundane nickname, or a description vague enough that an acquaintance in another arena of life would not identify the individual.

If you really need to talk in person, give out your phone number only. Those can be traced using a reverse directory, but that takes time and effort, and most BBSers would rather post and read than leave their computers. You can arrange to meet at a neutral place, wearing a carnation or a big hat. It's hokey but it still works.

In the same way, cellular and cordless phones are not really private either. Remember Princess Di and the Squidgie tapes? Neighbors can listen in on a cordless phone in a manner similar to the party lines of old. Cellular conversations can also be monitored with radio equipment.

The internet is a wonderland, and with a little care and forethought it can be safe as well. Eight words the Wiccan Rede fulfill, an ye harm none, do what ye will. Blessed Be.

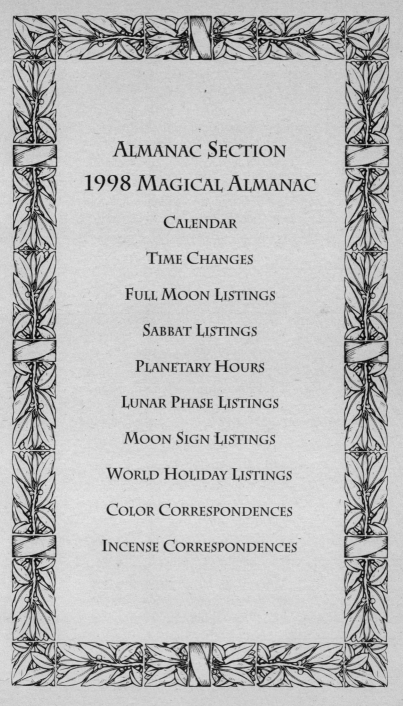

Almanac Section
1998 Magical Almanac

Calendar

Time Changes

Full Moon Listings

Sabbat Listings

Planetary Hours

Lunar Phase Listings

Moon Sign Listings

World Holiday Listings

Color Correspondences

Incense Correspondences

Almanac Listings

In these listings you will find the date, day, lunar phase, Moon sign, color and incense for the day, and festivals from around the world.

✤c The Date is used in numerological calculations that govern magical rites.

✤c Each day is ruled by a planet that possesses specific magical influences:

> Monday (Moon): Peace, sleep, compassion, healing, friends, psychic awareness, purification, fertility.
>
> Tuesday (Mars): Passion, sex, courage, aggression, protection.
>
> Wednesday (Mercury): The conscious mind, study, travel, divination, wisdom.
>
> Thursday (Jupiter): Expansion, money, prosperity, generosity.
>
> Friday (Venus): Love, friendship, reconciliation, beauty.
>
> Saturday (Saturn): Longevity, exorcism, endings, homes, and houses.
>
> Sunday (Sun): Protection, healing, spirituality, strength.

✤c The Lunar Phase is important in determining the best times for magic.

> The Waxing Moon (from the New Moon to the Full) is the ideal time for positive magic.

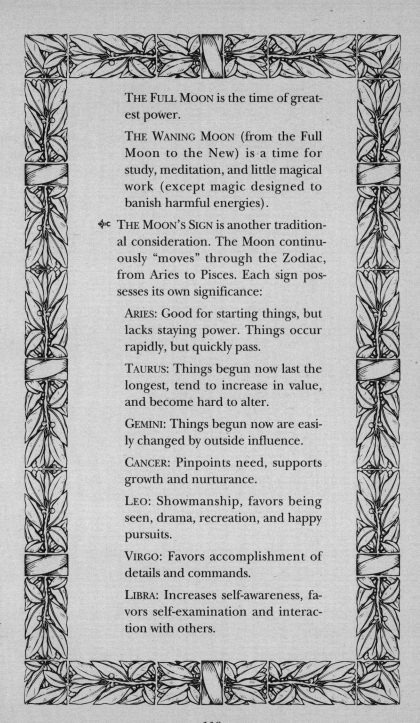

THE FULL MOON is the time of greatest power.

THE WANING MOON (from the Full Moon to the New) is a time for study, meditation, and little magical work (except magic designed to banish harmful energies).

❖c THE MOON'S SIGN is another traditional consideration. The Moon continuously "moves" through the Zodiac, from Aries to Pisces. Each sign possesses its own significance:

ARIES: Good for starting things, but lacks staying power. Things occur rapidly, but quickly pass.

TAURUS: Things begun now last the longest, tend to increase in value, and become hard to alter.

GEMINI: Things begun now are easily changed by outside influence.

CANCER: Pinpoints need, supports growth and nurturance.

LEO: Showmanship, favors being seen, drama, recreation, and happy pursuits.

VIRGO: Favors accomplishment of details and commands.

LIBRA: Increases self-awareness, favors self-examination and interaction with others.

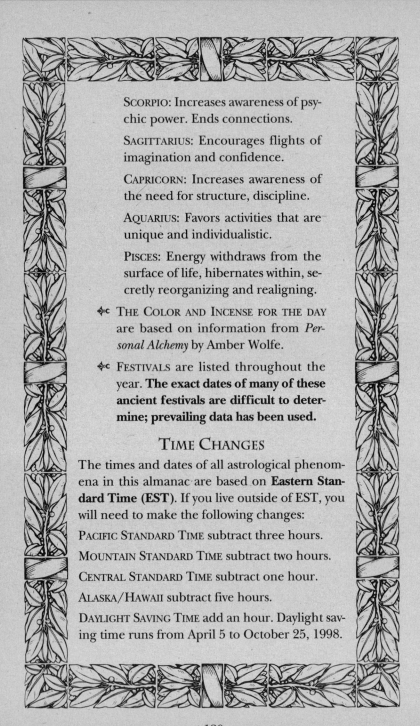

SCORPIO: Increases awareness of psychic power. Ends connections.

SAGITTARIUS: Encourages flights of imagination and confidence.

CAPRICORN: Increases awareness of the need for structure, discipline.

AQUARIUS: Favors activities that are unique and individualistic.

PISCES: Energy withdraws from the surface of life, hibernates within, secretly reorganizing and realigning.

❧ THE COLOR AND INCENSE FOR THE DAY are based on information from *Personal Alchemy* by Amber Wolfe.

❧ FESTIVALS are listed throughout the year. **The exact dates of many of these ancient festivals are difficult to determine; prevailing data has been used.**

TIME CHANGES

The times and dates of all astrological phenomena in this almanac are based on **Eastern Standard Time (EST)**. If you live outside of EST, you will need to make the following changes:

PACIFIC STANDARD TIME subtract three hours.

MOUNTAIN STANDARD TIME subtract two hours.

CENTRAL STANDARD TIME subtract one hour.

ALASKA/HAWAII subtract five hours.

DAYLIGHT SAVING TIME add an hour. Daylight saving time runs from April 5 to October 25, 1998.

1998 Sabbats and Full Moons

January 12	Full Moon 12:24 PM
February 2	Imbolc
February 11	Full Moon 5:23 AM
March 12	Full Moon 11:35 PM
March 20	Ostara (Spring Equinox)
April 11	Full Moon 5:24 PM
May 1	Beltane
May 11	Full Moon 9:30 AM
June 9	Full Moon 11:19 PM
June 21	Litha (Summer Solstice)
July 9	Full Moon 11:01 AM
August 1	Lammas
August 7	Full Moon 9:10 PM
September 6	Full Moon 6:22 AM
September 22	Mabon (Fall Equinox)
October 5	Full Moon 3:12 PM
October 31	Samhain
November 4	Full Moon 12:18 AM
December 3	Full Moon 10:20 AM
December 21	Yule (Winter Solstice)

THE PLANETARY HOURS

The selection of an auspicious time for starting any affair is an important matter. When a thing is once commenced, its existence tends to be of a nature corresponding to the conditions under which it was begun. Not only should you select the appropriate date, but when possible you should also start the affair under an appropriate planetary hour.

Each hour of the day is ruled by a planet, and so the nature of any time during the day corresponds to the nature of the planet ruling it. The nature of the planetary hours is the same as the description of each of the planets, except that you will not need to refer to the descriptions for Uranus, Neptune, and Pluto, as they are considered here as higher octaves of Mercury, Venus, and Mars, respectively. If something is ruled by Uranus, you can use the hour of Mercury.

The only other factor you need to know to use the Planetary Hours is the time of your local Sunrise and Sunset for any given day. This is given in the chart following.

EXAMPLE

Planetary hours for January 2, 1998, 10 degrees latitude.

1) Find sunrise (table, page 125) and sunset (table, page 126) for January 2, 1998, at 10 degrees latitude by following the 10º latitude column down to the January 2 row. In the case of our example this is the first entry in the upper left-hand corner of both the sunrise and sunset tables. You will see that sunrise for January 2, 1998, at 10 degrees latitude is at 6 hours and 16 minutes (or 6:16 AM) and sunset is at 17 hours and 49 minutes (or 5:49 PM).

2) Subtract sunrise time (6 hours 16 minutes) from sunset time (17 hours 49 minutes) to get the number of astrological daylight hours. It is easier to do this if you convert the hours into minutes. For example, 6 hours and 16 minutes = 376 minutes (6 hours x 60 minutes each = 360 minutes + 16 minutes = 376 minutes). 17 hours and 49 minutes = 1069

minutes (17 hours x 60 minutes = 1020 minutes + 49 minutes = 1069 minutes). Now subtract: 1069 minutes - 376 minutes = 693 minutes. If we then convert this back to hours by dividing by 60, we have 11 hours and 33 minutes of daylight planetary hours. However, it is easier to calculate the next step if you leave the number in minutes.

3) Next you should determine how many minutes are in a daylight planetary hour for that particular day (January 2, 1998, 10 degrees latitude). To do this divide 693 minutes by 12 (the number of hours of daylight at the equinoxes). The answer is 58, rounded off. Therefore, a daylight planetary hour for January 2, 1998, at 10 degrees latitude has 58 minutes. Remember that except on equinoxes, there is not an even amount of daylight and night time, so you will rarely have 60 minutes in a daylight hour.

4) Now you know that each daylight planetary hour is roughly 58 minutes. You also know, from step one, that sunrise is at 6:16 AM. To determine the starting times of each planetary hour, simply add 58 minutes to the sunrise time for the first planetary hour, 58 minutes to that number for the second planetary hour, etc. So the daylight planetary hours for our example are as follows: 1st hour 6:16 AM–7:14 AM; 2nd hour 7:15 AM–8:11 AM; 3rd hour 8:12 AM–9:08 AM; 4th hour 9:09 AM–10:05 AM; 5th hour 10:06 AM–11:02 AM; 6th hour 11:03 AM–11:59 AM; 7th hour 12:00 AM–12:56 PM; 8th hour 12:57 PM–1:53 PM; 9th hour 1:54 PM–2:50 PM; 10th hour 2:51 PM–3:47 PM; 11th hour 3:48 PM–4:44 PM; 12th hour 4:45 PM–5:51 PM. Note that because you rounded up, this isn't exact to the sunset table, which says that sunset is at 5:49 PM. This is a good reason to give yourself a little "fudge space" when using planetary hours. For most accurate sunrise or sunset times, consult your local newspaper.

5) Now, to determine which sign rules which daylight planetary hour, consult your calendar pages to determine which day of the week January 2 falls on. You'll find it's a Friday. Next, turn to page 127 to find the sunrise planetary hour chart. (It's the one on the top.) If you follow down the column for Thursday, you will see that the first planetary hour of the day is ruled by Venus, the second by Mercury, the third by the Moon, etc.

6) Now you've determined the daytime (sunrise) planetary hours. You can use the same formula to determine the night time (sunset) planetary hours. You know you have 11 hours and 33 minutes of sunrise planetary hours. Therefore subtract 11 hours and 33 minutes of sunrise hours from the 24 hours in a day to equal the number of sunset hours. 24 hours - 11 hours 13 minutes = 12 hours 47 minutes of sunset time. Now convert this to minutes $(12 \times 60) + 47 = (720) + 47 = 767$ minutes. (This equals 12.783 hours, but remember to leave it in minutes for now.)

7) Now go to step 3 and repeat the rest of the process for the sunset hours. When you get to step 5, remember to consult the sunset table on page 126 rather than the sunrise one. When you complete these steps you should get the following answers. There are (roughly) 63 minutes in a sunset planetary hour for this example. This means that the times for the sunset planetary hours are (starting from the 17:49 sunset time rather than the 6:16 sunrise time) first hour 5:49 PM; second 6:52 PM; third 7:55 PM; fourth 8:58 PM; fifth 10:01 PM; sixth 11:04 PM; seventh 12:07 AM; eighth 1:10 AM; ninth 2:13 AM; tenth 3:16 AM; eleventh 4:19 AM; twelfth 5:21 AM. You see which signs rule the hours by consulting the sunset hours chart on page 127.

SUNRISE

Latitude		+10°	+20°	+30°	+40°	+42°	+46°	+50°
		h:m	h:m	h:m	h:m	h:m	h:m	h:m
JAN	2	6:16	6:34	6:57	7:21	7:28	7:42	7:59
	14	6:21	6:34	6:55	7:20	7:26	7:39	7:53
	26	6:23	6:37	6:53	7:14	7:19	7:29	7:42
FEB	7	6:22	6:33	6:46	7:03	7:06	7:15	7:24
	19	6:18	6:27	6:36	6:48	6:50	6:56	7:03
	27	6:15	6:21	6:28	6:37	6:38	6:43	6:48
MAR	7	6:11	6:15	6:19	6:24	6:26	6:28	6:31
	19	6:05	6:05	6:05	6:05	6:05	6:05	6:05
	27	6:00	5:58	5:56	5:52	5:52	5:50	5:49
APR	12	5:51	5:44	5:37	5:27	5:25	5:19	5:14
	20	5:47	5:38	5:28	5:15	5:12	5:05	4:57
	28	5:44	5:33	5:20	5:04	5:00	4:52	4:42
MAY	6	5:41	5:28	5:13	4:54	4:50	4:40	4:28
	18	5:38	5:23	5:05	4:42	4:37	4:25	4:10
	26	5:38	5:21	5:01	4:36	4:30	4:17	4:01
JUN	3	5:38	5:20	4:59	4:32	4:26	4:12	3:54
	15	5:39	5:20	4:58	4:30	4:24	4:09	3:50
	23	5:41	5:22	5:00	4:32	4:25	4:10	3:51
JUL	1	5:43	5:24	5:02	4:35	4:28	4:13	3:55
	9	5:45	5:27	5:06	4:39	4:33	4:19	4:01
	17	5:47	5:30	5:10	4:45	4:39	4:26	4:10
	25	5:48	5:33	5:15	4:52	4:46	4:34	4:20
AUG	2	5:50	5:36	5:19	4:59	4:54	4:43	4:31
	10	5:51	5:38	5:24	5:07	5:02	4:53	4:42
	18	5:51	5:41	5:29	5:14	5:11	5:03	4:54
	26	5:51	5:43	5:34	5:22	5:19	5:13	5:06
SEP	3	5:51	5:45	5:38	5:29	5:27	5:23	5:18
	11	5:50	5:46	5:42	5:37	5:36	5:33	5:30
	19	5:49	5:48	5:47	5:45	5:44	5:43	5:42
	27	5:49	5:50	5:51	5:52	5:53	5:53	5:54
OCT	13	5:48	5:54	6:01	6:08	6:10	6:14	6:19
	21	5:49	5:57	6:06	6:17	6:19	6:25	6:31
	29	5:50	6:00	6:12	6:26	6:29	6:36	6:45
NOV	6	5:52	6:04	6:18	6:35	6:39	6:48	6:58
	14	5:54	6:08	6:24	6:44	6:49	6:59	7:11
	22	5:57	6:13	6:31	6:53	6:58	7:10	7:24
	30	6:01	6:18	6:37	7:02	7:07	7:20	7:35
DEC	8	6:05	6:23	6:44	7:09	7:15	7:29	7:45
	16	6:09	6:28	6:49	7:15	7:22	7:36	7:53
	24	6:13	6:32	6:53	7:20	7:26	7:40	7:57
	30	6:17	6:35	6:56	7:22	7:28	7:42	7:59

SUNSET

UNIVERSAL TIME FOR MERIDIAN OF GREENWICH

Latitude		+10°	+20°	+30°	+40°	+42°	+46°	+50°
		h:m	h:m	h:m	h:m	h:m	h:m	h:m
JAN	2	17:49	17:30	17:09	16:43	16:37	16:23	16:06
	14	17:57	17:41	17:22	16:58	16:52	16:40	16:25
	26	18:03	17:48	17:32	17:12	17:07	16:57	16:44
FEB	7	18:07	17:55	17:42	17:26	17:23	17:14	17:05
	19	18:09	18:01	17:52	17:40	17:38	17:32	17:25
	27	18:10	18:04	17:58	17:50	17:48	17:44	17:39
MAR	7	18:11	18:07	18:03	17:58	17:57	17:55	17:52
	19	18:11	18:11	18:11	18:11	18:11	18:11	18:11
	27	18:11	18:13	18:16	18:19	18:20	18:22	18:24
APR	12	18:10	18:17	18:25	18:35	18:38	18:43	18:49
	20	18:11	18:20	18:30	18:43	18:47	18:53	19:02
	28	18:11	18:22	18:35	18:52	18:55	19:04	19:14
MAY	6	18:12	18:25	18:41	19:00	19:04	19:14	19:26
	18	18:14	18:30	18:48	19:11	19:17	19:29	19:43
	26	18:16	18:33	18:53	19:18	19:24	19:38	19:54
JUN	3	18:18	18:37	18:57	19:24	19:30	19:45	20:02
	15	18:22	18:43	19:03	19:30	19:37	19:53	20:11
	23	18:23	18:42	19:05	19:33	19:39	19:55	20:13
JUL	1	18:25	18:43	19:05	19:33	19:39	19:54	20:12
	9	18:25	18:43	19:04	19:31	19:37	19:51	20:09
	17	18:25	18:42	19:02	19:27	19:33	19:46	20:02
	25	18:24	18:42	18:58	19:21	19:26	19:38	19:53
AUG	2	18:23	18:36	18:53	19:13	19:18	19:28	19:41
	10	18:20	18:32	18:46	19:03	19:07	19:17	19:28
	18	18:16	18:27	18:38	18:53	18:56	19:04	19:13
	26	18:12	18:20	18:30	18:41	18:44	18:50	18:57
SEP	3	18:08	18:14	18:20	18:28	18:30	18:35	18:40
	11	18:03	18:06	18:10	18:16	18:17	18:19	18:23
	19	17:58	17:59	18:00	18:02	18:03	18:04	18:05
	27	17:53	17:52	17:50	17:49	17:49	17:48	17:47
OCT	13	17:44	17:38	17:32	17:24	17:22	17:18	17:13
	21	17:40	17:32	17:23	17:12	17:09	17:04	16:57
	29	17:37	17:27	17:16	17:01	16:58	16:51	16:42
NOV	6	17:36	17:23	17:09	16:52	16:48	16:39	16:29
	14	17:35	17:21	17:04	16:45	16:40	16:30	16:17
	22	17:35	17:19	17:01	16:39	16:34	16:22	16:08
	30	17:36	17:19	17:00	16:36	16:30	16:17	16:02
DEC	8	17:39	17:21	17:00	16:35	16:28	16:15	15:58
	16	17:42	17:24	17:02	16:36	16:30	16:15	15:59
	24	17:46	17:27	17:06	16:40	16:33	16:19	16:02
	30	17:50	17:32	17:11	16:45	16:39	16:25	16:09

Sunrise and Sunset Hours

Sunrise

Hour	Sun	Mon	Tue	Wed	Thu	Fri	Sat
1	☉	☽	♂	☿	♃	♀	♄
2	♀	♄	☉	☽	♂	☿	♃
3	☿	♃	♀	♄	☉	☽	♂
4	☽	♂	☿	♃	♀	♄	☉
5	♄	☉	☽	♂	☿	♃	♀
6	♃	♀	♄	☉	☽	♂	☿
7	♂	☿	♃	♀	♄	☉	☽
8	☉	☽	♂	☿	♃	♀	♄
9	♀	♄	☉	☽	♂	☿	♃
10	☿	♃	♀	♄	☉	☽	♂
11	☽	♂	☿	♃	♀	♄	☉
12	♄	☉	☽	♂	☿	♃	♀

Sunset

Hour	Sun	Mon	Tue	Wed	Thu	Fri	Sat
1	♃	♀	♄	☉	☽	♂	☿
2	♂	☿	♃	♀	♄	☉	☽
3	☉	☽	♂	☿	♃	♀	♄
4	♀	♄	☉	☽	♂	☿	♃
5	☿	♃	♀	♄	☉	☽	♂
6	☽	♂	☿	♃	♀	♄	☉
7	♄	☉	☽	♂	☿	♃	♀
8	♃	♀	♄	☉	☽	♂	☿
9	♂	☿	♃	♀	♄	☉	☽
10	☉	☽	♂	☿	♃	♀	♄
11	♀	♄	☉	☽	♂	☿	♃
12	☿	♃	♀	♄	☉	☽	♂

☉ Sun; ☿ Mercury; ♄ Saturn; ♂ Mars; ♀ Venus; ☽ Moon; ♃ Jupiter

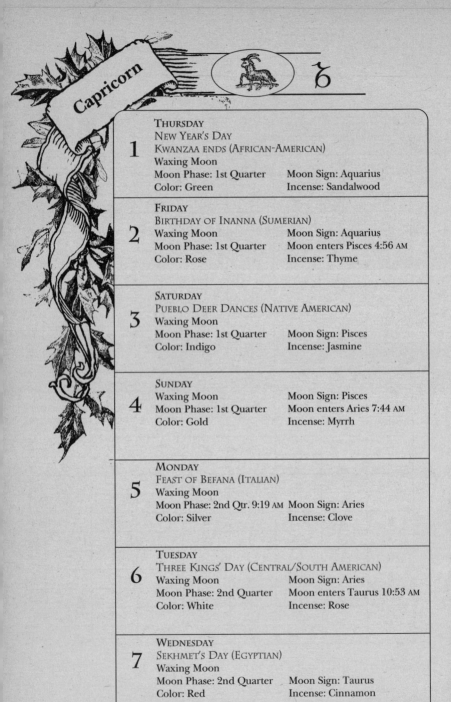

Capricorn ♑

THURSDAY
NEW YEAR'S DAY
1 KWANZAA ENDS (AFRICAN-AMERICAN)
Waxing Moon
Moon Phase: 1st Quarter   Moon Sign: Aquarius
Color: Green   Incense: Sandalwood

FRIDAY
BIRTHDAY OF INANNA (SUMERIAN)
2 Waxing Moon   Moon Sign: Aquarius
Moon Phase: 1st Quarter   Moon enters Pisces 4:56 AM
Color: Rose   Incense: Thyme

SATURDAY
PUEBLO DEER DANCES (NATIVE AMERICAN)
3 Waxing Moon
Moon Phase: 1st Quarter   Moon Sign: Pisces
Color: Indigo   Incense: Jasmine

SUNDAY
Waxing Moon   Moon Sign: Pisces
4 Moon Phase: 1st Quarter   Moon enters Aries 7:44 AM
Color: Gold   Incense: Myrrh

MONDAY
FEAST OF BEFANA (ITALIAN)
5 Waxing Moon
Moon Phase: 2nd Qtr. 9:19 AM Moon Sign: Aries
Color: Silver   Incense: Clove

TUESDAY
THREE KINGS' DAY (CENTRAL/SOUTH AMERICAN)
6 Waxing Moon   Moon Sign: Aries
Moon Phase: 2nd Quarter   Moon enters Taurus 10:53 AM
Color: White   Incense: Rose

WEDNESDAY
SEKHMET'S DAY (EGYPTIAN)
7 Waxing Moon
Moon Phase: 2nd Quarter   Moon Sign: Taurus
Color: Red   Incense: Cinnamon

8 THURSDAY
Waxing Moon
Moon Phase: 2nd Quarter
Color: Turquoise

Moon Sign: Taurus
Moon enters Gemini 2:42 PM
Incense: Frankincense

9 FRIDAY
FESTIVAL OF JANUS
Waxing Moon
Moon Phase: 2nd Quarter
Color: Pink

Moon Sign: Gemini
Incense: Bay Laurel

10 SATURDAY
GERAINT'S DAY (WELSH)
Waxing Moon
Moon Phase: 2nd Quarter
Color: Blue

Moon Sign: Gemini
Moon enters Cancer 7:43 PM
Incense: Delphinium

11 SUNDAY
FESTIVAL OF CARMENTALIA (ROMAN)
Waxing Moon
Moon Phase: 2nd Quarter
Color: Orange

Moon Sign: Cancer
Incense: Thyme

12 MONDAY
NEZ PERCE WAR DANCES (NATIVE AMERICAN)
Waxing Moon
Moon Phase: Full 12:24 PM
Color: White

Moon Sign: Cancer
Incense: Ginger

13 TUESDAY
MIDVINTERSBLOT (NORSE)
Waning Moon
Moon Phase: 3rd Quarter
Color: White

Moon Sign: Cancer
Moon enters Leo 2:45 AM
Incense: Lavender

14 WEDNESDAY
MAKAR SANKRATI (HINDU)
Waning Moon
Moon Phase: 3rd Quarter
Color: Peach

Moon Sign: Leo
Incense: Sandalwood

Capricorn ♑

THURSDAY
15 BLACK CHRIST FESTIVAL (GUATEMALAN)
Waning Moon — Moon Sign: Leo
Moon Phase: 3rd Quarter — Moon enters Virgo 12:31 PM
Color: White — Incense: Almond

FRIDAY
16 FESTIVAL OF GANESHA (HINDU)
Waning Moon
Moon Phase: 3rd Quarter — Moon Sign: Virgo
Color: White — Incense: Lilac

SATURDAY
17 ST. ANTHONY'S DAY (MEXICAN)
Waning Moon
Moon Phase: 3rd Quarter — Moon Sign: Virgo
Color: Gray — Incense: Clove

SUNDAY
18 SURYA (HINDU)
Waning Moon — Moon Sign: Virgo
Moon Phase: 3rd Quarter — Moon enters Libra 12:45 AM
Color: Yellow — Incense: Cedar

MONDAY
19 MARTIN LUTHER KING, JR. DAY
Waning Moon
Moon Phase: 3rd Quarter — Moon Sign: Libra
Color: Lavender — Incense: Lily

TUESDAY
20 FESTIVAL OF THORABLOTTAR (ICELANDIC)
Waning Moon — Moon Sign: Libra
Moon Phase: 4th Qtr. 2:41 PM — Sun enters Aquarius 1:46 AM
Color: Gray — Moon enters Scorpio 1:35 PM
— Incense: Sage

WEDNESDAY
21 SANTA INES' DAY (MEXICAN)
Waning Moon
Moon Phase: 4th Quarter — Moon Sign: Scorpio
Color: White — Incense: Rose

THURSDAY
22 ST. VINCENT'S DAY
Waning Moon
Moon Phase: 4th Quarter   Moon Sign: Scorpio
Color: Violet   Incense: Hyacinth

FRIDAY
23 Waning Moon   Moon Sign: Scorpio
Moon Phase: 4th Quarter   Moon enters Sagittarius 12:26 AM
Color: Peach   Incense: Maple

SATURDAY
24 BLESSING OF THE HAPPY WOMAN'S CANDLE (HUNGARIAN)
Waning Moon
Moon Phase: 4th Quarter   Moon Sign: Sagittarius
Color: Brown   Incense: Sandalwood

SUNDAY
25 BURNS' NIGHT (SCOTTISH)
Waning Moon   Moon Sign: Sagittarius
Moon Phase: 4th Quarter   Moon enters Capricorn 7:40 AM
Color: Peach   Incense: Cedar

MONDAY
26 FESTIVAL OF EKEKO (BOLIVIAN)
Waning Moon
Moon Phase: 4th Quarter   Moon Sign: Capricorn
Color: Gray   Incense: Peony

TUESDAY
27 SEMENTIVAE FERIA (ROMAN)
Waning Moon   Moon Sign: Capricorn
Moon Phase: 4th Quarter   Moon enters Aquarius 11:27 AM
Color: Red   Incense: Mint

WEDNESDAY
28 UPELLY-AA (SCOTTISH)
Waning Moon
Moon Phase: New 1:01 AM   Moon Sign: Aquarius
Color: Brown   Incense: Pine

Aquarius

THURSDAY
MARTYR'S DAY (NEPALESE)

29
Waxing Moon
Moon Phase: 1st Quarter
Color: Green

Moon Sign: Aquarius
Moon enters Pisces 1:09 PM
Incense: Rosemary

FRIDAY
HOLY DAY OF THE THREE HIERARCHS (EAST. ORTHODOX)

30
Waxing Moon
Moon Phase: 1st Quarter
Color: Rose

Moon Sign: Pisces
Incense: Ginger

SATURDAY
HECATE'S FEAST (GREEK)

31
Waxing Moon
Moon Phase: 1st Quarter
Color: Indigo

Moon Sign: Pisces
Moon enters Aries 2:21 PM
Incense: Lavender

JANUARY BIRTHSTONES
Ancient: Garnet
Modern: Garnet

JANUARY FLOWERS
Carnations
Snowdrops

FEBRUARY BIRTHSTONES
Ancient: Amethyst
Modern: Amethyst

FEBRUARY FLOWERS
Violets
Primroses

SUNDAY

1

ST. BRIGHID'S FEAST DAY
Waxing Moon
Moon Phase: 1st Quarter   Moon Sign: Aries
Color: Gold   Incense: Vanilla

MONDAY

2

IMBOLC
Waxing Moon   Moon Sign: Aries
Moon Phase: 1st Quarter   Moon enters Taurus 4:25 PM
Color: Silver   Incense: Lilac

TUESDAY

3

POWAMU FESTIVAL (HOPI)
Waxing Moon
Moon Phase: 2nd Qtr. 5:53 PM   Moon Sign: Taurus
Color: Red   Incense: Patchouli

WEDNESDAY

4

KING FROST DAY (ENGLISH)
Waxing Moon   Moon Sign: Taurus
Moon Phase: 2nd Quarter   Moon enters Gemini 8:09 PM
Color: Yellow   Incense: Cedar

THURSDAY

5

FEAST OF ST. AGATHA (SICILIAN)
Waxing Moon
Moon Phase: 2nd Quarter   Moon Sign: Gemini
Color: Green   Incense: Pine

FRIDAY

6

FESTIVAL OF APHRODITE (GREEK)
Waxing Moon
Moon Phase: 2nd Quarter   Moon Sign: Gemini
Color: Rose   Incense: Bayberry

SATURDAY

7

SELENE'S DAY (GREEK)
Waxing Moon   Moon Sign: Gemini
Moon Phase: 2nd Quarter   Moon enters Cancer 1:58 AM
Color: Indigo   Incense: Jasmine

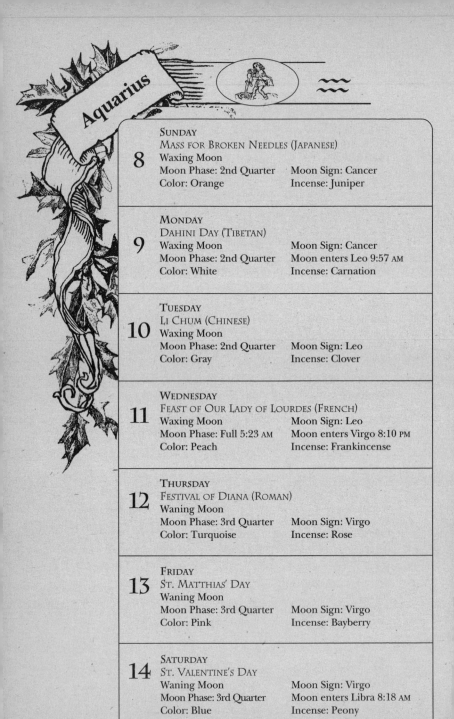

Aquarius

SUNDAY
8 MASS FOR BROKEN NEEDLES (JAPANESE)
Waxing Moon
Moon Phase: 2nd Quarter   Moon Sign: Cancer
Color: Orange   Incense: Juniper

MONDAY
9 DAHINI DAY (TIBETAN)
Waxing Moon   Moon Sign: Cancer
Moon Phase: 2nd Quarter   Moon enters Leo 9:57 AM
Color: White   Incense: Carnation

TUESDAY
10 LI CHUM (CHINESE)
Waxing Moon
Moon Phase: 2nd Quarter   Moon Sign: Leo
Color: Gray   Incense: Clover

WEDNESDAY
11 FEAST OF OUR LADY OF LOURDES (FRENCH)
Waxing Moon   Moon Sign: Leo
Moon Phase: Full 5:23 AM   Moon enters Virgo 8:10 PM
Color: Peach   Incense: Frankincense

THURSDAY
12 FESTIVAL OF DIANA (ROMAN)
Waning Moon
Moon Phase: 3rd Quarter   Moon Sign: Virgo
Color: Turquoise   Incense: Rose

FRIDAY
13 ST. MATTHIAS' DAY
Waning Moon
Moon Phase: 3rd Quarter   Moon Sign: Virgo
Color: Pink   Incense: Bayberry

SATURDAY
14 ST. VALENTINE'S DAY
Waning Moon   Moon Sign: Virgo
Moon Phase: 3rd Quarter   Moon enters Libra 8:18 AM
Color: Blue   Incense: Peony

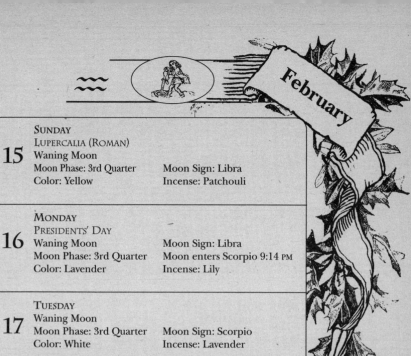

15 SUNDAY
LUPERCALIA (ROMAN)
Waning Moon
Moon Phase: 3rd Quarter   Moon Sign: Libra
Color: Yellow   Incense: Patchouli

16 MONDAY
PRESIDENTS' DAY
Waning Moon   Moon Sign: Libra
Moon Phase: 3rd Quarter   Moon enters Scorpio 9:14 PM
Color: Lavender   Incense: Lily

17 TUESDAY
Waning Moon
Moon Phase: 3rd Quarter   Moon Sign: Scorpio
Color: White   Incense: Lavender

18 WEDNESDAY
SPENTA ARMAITI (ZOROASTRIAN)
Waning Moon   Moon Sign: Scorpio
Moon Phase: 3rd Quarter   Sun enters Pisces 3:55 PM
Color: Brown   Incense: Sage

19 THURSDAY
MAHASHIVATRI (INDIAN)
Waning Moon   Moon Sign: Scorpio
Moon Phase: 4th Qtr. 10:27 AM Moon enters Sagittarius 8:56 AM
Color: White   Incense: Hyacinth

20 FRIDAY
DAY OF TACITA (ROMAN)
Waning Moon
Moon Phase: 4th Quarter   Moon Sign: Sagittarius
Color: Peach   Incense: Almond

21 SATURDAY
Waning Moon
Moon Phase: 4th Quarter   Moon Sign: Sagittarius
Color: Gray   Moon enters Capricorn 5:30 PM
                               Incense: Mint

Pisces

22 SUNDAY
WASHINGTON'S BIRTHDAY
Waning Moon
Moon Phase: 4th Quarter   Moon Sign: Capricorn
Color: Peach   Incense: Cedar

23 MONDAY
TERMINALIA (ROMAN)
Waning Moon   Moon Sign: Capricorn
Moon Phase: 4th Quarter   Moon enters Aquarius 10:10 PM
Color: Gray   Incense: Mint

24 TUESDAY
Waning Moon
Moon Phase: 4th Quarter   Moon Sign: Aquarius
Color: Black   Incense: Lily

25 WEDNESDAY
ASH WEDNESDAY
Waning Moon   Moon Sign: Aquarius
Moon Phase: 4th Quarter   Moon enters Pisces 11:42 PM
Color: White   Incense: Frankincense

26 THURSDAY
HYGEIA'S DAY (NORTH AFRICAN)
Waning Moon
Moon Phase: New 12:26 PM   Moon Sign: Pisces
Color: Violet   Incense: Lilac

27 FRIDAY
FEAST OF ESTHER (HEBREW)
Waxing Moon   Moon Sign: Pisces
Moon Phase: 1st Quarter   Moon enters Aries 11:42 PM
Color: White   Incense: Floral

28 SATURDAY
BUDDHA'S CONCEPTION (TIBETAN)
Waxing Moon
Moon Phase: 1st Quarter   Moon Sign: Aries
Color: Brown   Incense: Thyme

March

1 SUNDAY
MATRONALIA (ROMAN)
Waxing Moon
Moon Phase: 1st Quarter   Moon Sign: Aries
Color: Gold   Incense: Sandalwood

2 MONDAY
MOTHER'S MARCH (BULGARIAN)
Waxing Moon   Moon Sign: Aries
Moon Phase: 1st Quarter   Moon enters Taurus 12:01 AM
Color: Silver   Incense: Almond

3 TUESDAY
DOLL FESTIVAL (JAPANESE)
Waxing Moon
Moon Phase: 1st Quarter   Moon Sign: Taurus
Color: Red   Incense: Rosemary

4 WEDNESDAY
FEAST OF RHIANNON (WELSH)
Waxing Moon   Moon Sign: Taurus
Moon Phase: 1st Quarter   Moon enters Gemini 2:15 AM
Color: Yellow   Incense: Pine

5 THURSDAY
CELEBRATION OF ISIS (NORTH AFRICAN)
Waxing Moon
Moon Phase: 2nd Qtr. 3:41 AM   Moon Sign: Gemini
Color: Green   Incense: Musk

6 FRIDAY
MARS' DAY (ROMAN)
Waxing Moon   Moon Sign: Gemini
Moon Phase: 2nd Quarter   Moon enters Cancer 7:27 AM
Color: Rose   Incense: Ginger

7 SATURDAY
JUNONALIA (ROMAN)
Waxing Moon
Moon Phase: 2nd Quarter   Moon Sign: Cancer
Color: Indigo   Incense: Honeysuckle

Pisces ♓

SUNDAY
8
BIRTHDAY OF MOTHER EARTH (CHINESE)
Waxing Moon   Moon Sign: Cancer
Moon Phase: 2nd Quarter   Moon enters Leo 3:46 PM
Color: Orange   Incense: Sandalwood

MONDAY
9
FEAST OF THE FORTY MARTYRS (GREEK)
Waxing Moon
Moon Phase: 2nd Quarter   Moon Sign: Leo
Color: Lavender   Incense: Honeysuckle

TUESDAY
10
HOLI (INDIAN)
Waxing Moon
Moon Phase: 2nd Quarter   Moon Sign: Leo
Color: White   Incense: Lilac

WEDNESDAY
11
HERCULES' DAY (GREEK)
Waxing Moon   Moon Sign: Leo
Moon Phase: 2nd Quarter   Moon enters Virgo 2:36 AM
Color: Peach   Incense: Myrrh

THURSDAY
12
FEAST OF MARDUK (MESOPOTAMIAN)
Waxing Moon
Moon Phase: Full 11:35 PM Moon Sign: Virgo
Color: Turquoise   Incense: Sandalwood

FRIDAY
13
PURIFICATION FEAST (BALINESE)
Waning Moon   Moon Sign: Virgo
Moon Phase: 3rd Quarter   Moon enters Libra 2:59 PM
Color: Pink   Incense: Patchouli

SATURDAY
14
VETURIUS MAMURIUS (ROMAN)
Waning Moon
Moon Phase: 3rd Quarter   Moon Sign: Libra
Color: Blue   Incense: Delphinium

15 SUNDAY
IDES OF MARCH (ROMAN)
Waning Moon
Moon Phase: 3rd Quarter   Moon Sign: Libra
Color: Yellow   Incense: Maple

16 MONDAY
FESTIVAL OF DIONYSUS (GREEK)
Waning Moon   Moon Sign: Libra
Moon Phase: 3rd Quarter   Moon enters Scorpio 3:51 AM
Color: White   Incense: Sandalwood

17 TUESDAY
ST. PATRICK'S DAY (IRISH)
Waning Moon
Moon Phase: 3rd Quarter   Moon Sign: Scorpio
Color: Gray   Incense: Myrrh

18 WEDNESDAY
SHEELAH'S DAY (ICELANDIC)
Waning Moon   Moon Sign: Scorpio
Moon Phase: 3rd Quarter   Moon enters Sagittarius 3:56 PM
Color: Brown   Incense: Pine

19 THURSDAY
DAY OF AGANYU (SANTERÍA)
Waning Moon
Moon Phase: 3rd Quarter   Moon Sign: Sagittarius
Color: White   Incense: Almond

20 FRIDAY
OSTARA (SPRING EQUINOX)
Waning Moon   Moon Sign: Sagittarius
Moon Phase: 3rd Quarter   Sun enters Aries 2:54 PM
Color: Peach   Incense: Bay Laurel

21 SATURDAY
TEA AND TEPHI DAY (IRISH)
Waning Moon   Moon Sign: Sagittarius
Moon Phase: 4th Qtr. 2:38 AM   Moon enters Capricorn 1:43 AM
Color: Gray   Incense: Rosemary

Aries ♈

SUNDAY
22
PURIM BEGINS (JEWISH)
Waning Moon
Moon Phase: 4th Quarter
Color: Peach

Moon Sign: Capricorn
Incense: Cedar

MONDAY
23
PURIM ENDS (JEWISH)
Waning Moon
Moon Phase: 4th Quarter
Color: Gray

Moon Sign: Capricorn
Moon enters Aquarius 8:02 AM
Incense: Ginger

TUESDAY
24
Waning Moon
Moon Phase: 4th Quarter
Color: Black

Moon Sign: Aquarius
Incense: Vanilla

WEDNESDAY
25
ANUNCIACIÓN (MEXICAN)
Waning Moon
Moon Phase: 4th Quarter
Color: Brown

Moon Sign: Aquarius
Moon enters Pisces 10:43 AM
Incense: Patchouli

THURSDAY
26
PLOWING DAY (SLAVIC)
Waning Moon
Moon Phase: 4th Quarter
Color: Violet

Moon Sign: Pisces
Incense: Peony

FRIDAY
27
SMELL THE BREEZE DAY (EGYPTIAN)
Waning Moon
Moon Phase: New 10:14 PM
Color: White

Moon Sign: Pisces
Moon enters Aries 10:49 AM
Incense: Lilac

SATURDAY
28
BIRTHDAY OF KWAN YIN (CHINESE)
Waxing Moon
Moon Phase: 1st Quarter
Color: Brown

Moon Sign: Aries
Incense: Juniper

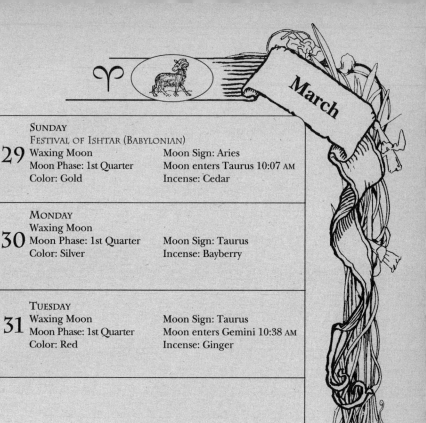

SUNDAY
29
FESTIVAL OF ISHTAR (BABYLONIAN)
Waxing Moon   Moon Sign: Aries
Moon Phase: 1st Quarter   Moon enters Taurus 10:07 AM
Color: Gold   Incense: Cedar

MONDAY
30
Waxing Moon
Moon Phase: 1st Quarter   Moon Sign: Taurus
Color: Silver   Incense: Bayberry

TUESDAY
31
Waxing Moon   Moon Sign: Taurus
Moon Phase: 1st Quarter   Moon enters Gemini 10:38 AM
Color: Red   Incense: Ginger

MARCH BIRTHSTONES
Ancient: Jasper
Modern: Bloodstone

MARCH FLOWERS
Daffodils
Jonquils

Aries

1	**WEDNESDAY** APRIL FOOL'S DAY Waxing Moon Moon Phase: 1st Quarter — Moon Sign: Gemini Color: Yellow — Incense: Sandalwood

1

WEDNESDAY
APRIL FOOL'S DAY
Waxing Moon
Moon Phase: 1st Quarter   Moon Sign: Gemini
Color: Yellow   Incense: Sandalwood

2

THURSDAY
ST. URBAN'S DAY
Waxing Moon   Moon Sign: Gemini
Moon Phase: 1st Quarter   Moon enters Cancer 2:10 PM
Color: Green   Incense: Cedar

3

FRIDAY
BIRTHDAY OF BUDDHA
Waxing Moon
Moon Phase: 2nd Qtr. 3:19 PM   Moon Sign: Cancer
Color: Rose   Incense: Rose

4

SATURDAY
MEGALESIA BEGINS (ROMAN)
Waxing Moon   Moon Sign: Cancer
Moon Phase: 2nd Quarter   Moon enters Leo 9:36 PM
Color: Indigo   Incense: Bayberry

5

SUNDAY
PALM SUNDAY (CHRISTIAN))
DAYLIGHT-SAVING TIME BEGINS AT 2 AM
Waxing Moon
Moon Phase: 2nd Quarter   Moon Sign: Leo
Color: Gold   Incense: Clove

6

MONDAY
CHING MING (CHINESE)
Waxing Moon
Moon Phase: 2nd Quarter   Moon Sign: Leo
Color: Silver   Incense: Lavender

7

TUESDAY
FEAST OF BLAGINI (ROMANIAN)
Waxing Moon   Moon Sign: Leo
Moon Phase: 2nd Quarter   Moon enters Virgo 8:26 AM
Color: Red   Incense: Wintergreen

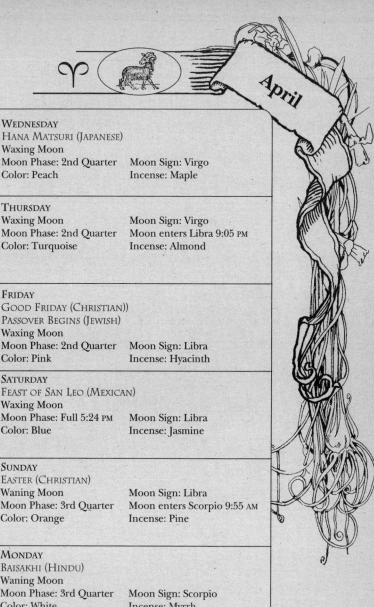

April

8 WEDNESDAY
HANA MATSURI (JAPANESE)
Waxing Moon
Moon Phase: 2nd Quarter · Moon Sign: Virgo
Color: Peach · Incense: Maple

9 THURSDAY
Waxing Moon
Moon Phase: 2nd Quarter · Moon Sign: Virgo
Color: Turquoise · Moon enters Libra 9:05 PM
· Incense: Almond

10 FRIDAY
GOOD FRIDAY (CHRISTIAN))
PASSOVER BEGINS (JEWISH)
Waxing Moon
Moon Phase: 2nd Quarter · Moon Sign: Libra
Color: Pink · Incense: Hyacinth

11 SATURDAY
FEAST OF SAN LEO (MEXICAN)
Waxing Moon
Moon Phase: Full 5:24 PM · Moon Sign: Libra
Color: Blue · Incense: Jasmine

12 SUNDAY
EASTER (CHRISTIAN)
Waning Moon · Moon Sign: Libra
Moon Phase: 3rd Quarter · Moon enters Scorpio 9:55 AM
Color: Orange · Incense: Pine

13 MONDAY
BAISAKHI (HINDU)
Waning Moon
Moon Phase: 3rd Quarter · Moon Sign: Scorpio
Color: White · Incense: Myrrh

14 TUESDAY
SOMMARSBLÖT (NORSE)
Waning Moon · Moon Sign: Scorpio
Moon Phase: 3rd Quarter · Moon enters Sagittarius 9:52 PM
Color: Gray · Incense: Patchouli

Aries ♈

WEDNESDAY
15
FEAST OF TELLUS MATER (ROMAN)
Waning Moon
Moon Phase: 3rd Quarter   Moon Sign: Sagittarius
Color: White   Incense: Honeysuckle

THURSDAY
16
ST. PADARM'S DAY (CELTIC)
Waning Moon
Moon Phase: 3rd Quarter   Moon Sign: Sagittarius
Color: Violet   Incense: Rose

FRIDAY
17
Waning Moon   Moon Sign: Sagittarius
Moon Phase: 3rd Quarter   Moon enters Capricorn 8:05 AM
Color: Peach   Incense: Mango

SATURDAY
18
PASSOVER ENDS (JEWISH))
Waning Moon
Moon Phase: 3rd Quarter   Moon Sign: Capricorn
Color: Peach   Incense: Blackberry

SUNDAY
19
ORTHODOX EASTER (CHRISTIAN)
Waning Moon   Moon Sign: Capricorn
Moon Phase: 4th Qtr. 2:53 PM Moon enters Aquarius 3:42 PM
Color: Yellow   Incense: Sage

MONDAY
20
YAQUI PAGEANT (NATIVE AMERICAN)
Waning Moon   Moon Sign: Aquarius
Moon Phase: 4th Quarter   Sun enters Taurus 1:56 AM
Color: Yellow   Incense: Sandalwood

TUESDAY
21
Waning Moon   Moon Sign: Aquarius
Moon Phase: 4th Quarter   Moon enters Pisces 8:07 PM
Color: Black   Incense: Myrrh

WEDNESDAY
22
EARTH DAY
Waning Moon
Moon Phase: 4th Quarter   Moon Sign: Pisces
Color: Brown   Incense: Patchouli

THURSDAY
23
ST. GEORGE'S DAY (BRITISH)
Waning Moon   Moon Sign: Pisces
Moon Phase: 4th Quarter   Moon enters Aries 9:31 PM
Color: White   Incense: Almond

FRIDAY
24
CHILDREN'S DAY (ICELANDIC)
Waning Moon
Moon Phase: 4th Quarter   Moon Sign: Aries
Color: Peach   Incense: Bay Laurel

SATURDAY
25
FEAST OF SAN JORGE (MEXICAN)
Waning Moon   Moon Sign: Aries
Moon Phase: 4th Quarter   Moon enters Taurus 9:09 PM
Color: Gray   Incense: Cinnamon

SUNDAY
26
FLOWER PARADES (DUTCH)
Waning Moon
Moon Phase: New 6:42 AM   Moon Sign: Taurus
Color: Peach   Incense: Coconut

MONDAY
27
Waxing Moon   Moon Sign: Taurus
Moon Phase: 1st Quarter   Moon enters Gemini 8:56 PM
Color: Lavender   Incense: Vanilla

TUESDAY
28
FLORALIA BEGINS (ROMAN)
Waxing Moon
Moon Phase: 1st Quarter   Moon Sign: Gemini
Color: Gray   Incense: Thyme

Taurus

	WEDNESDAY	
29	Waxing Moon	Moon Sign: Gemini
	Moon Phase: 1st Quarter	Moon enters Cancer 10:57 AM
	Color: Yellow	Incense: Sandalwood

	THURSDAY	
30	WALPURGISNACHT (GERMAN)	
	Waxing Moon	
	Moon Phase: 1st Quarter	Moon Sign: Cancer
	Color: Green	Incense: Juniper

APRIL BIRTHSTONES
Ancient: Sapphire
Modern: Diamond

APRIL FLOWERS
Daisies
Sweet Peas

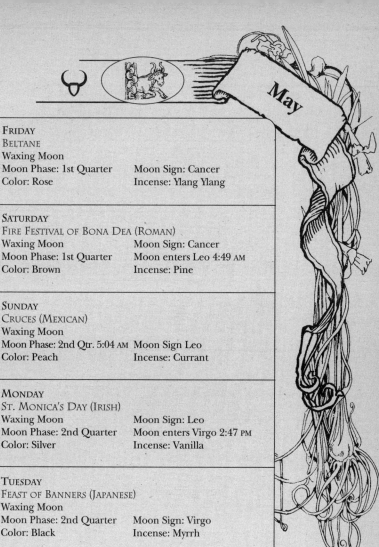

May

FRIDAY
BELTANE
Waxing Moon
Moon Phase: 1st Quarter   Moon Sign: Cancer
Color: Rose   Incense: Ylang Ylang

1

SATURDAY
FIRE FESTIVAL OF BONA DEA (ROMAN)
Waxing Moon   Moon Sign: Cancer
Moon Phase: 1st Quarter   Moon enters Leo 4:49 AM
Color: Brown   Incense: Pine

2

SUNDAY
CRUCES (MEXICAN)
Waxing Moon
Moon Phase: 2nd Qtr. 5:04 AM Moon Sign Leo
Color: Peach   Incense: Currant

3

MONDAY
ST. MONICA'S DAY (IRISH)
Waxing Moon   Moon Sign: Leo
Moon Phase: 2nd Quarter   Moon enters Virgo 2:47 PM
Color: Silver   Incense: Vanilla

4

TUESDAY
FEAST OF BANNERS (JAPANESE)
Waxing Moon
Moon Phase: 2nd Quarter   Moon Sign: Virgo
Color: Black   Incense: Myrrh

5

WEDNESDAY
EYVIND KELVE (NORSE)
Waxing Moon
Moon Phase: 2nd Quarter   Moon Sign: Virgo
Color: Brown   Incense: Cedar

6

THURSDAY
Waxing Moon   Moon Sign: Virgo
Moon Phase: 2nd Quarter   Moon enters Libra 3:19 AM
Color: White   Incense: Jasmine

7

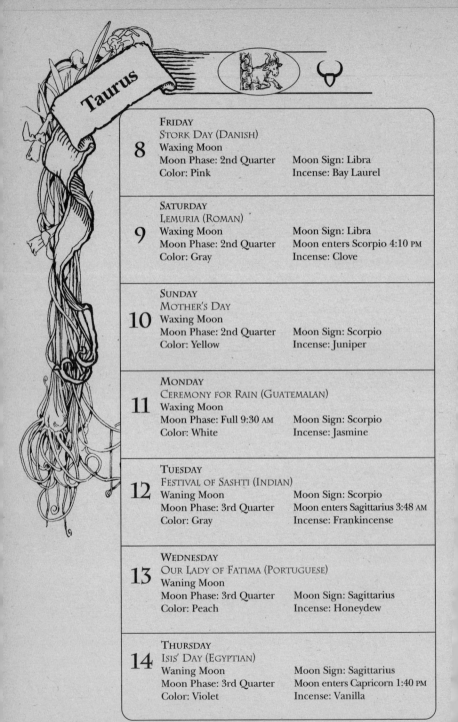

Taurus

FRIDAY
STORK DAY (DANISH)

8
Waxing Moon
Moon Phase: 2nd Quarter   Moon Sign: Libra
Color: Pink   Incense: Bay Laurel

SATURDAY
LEMURIA (ROMAN)

9
Waxing Moon   Moon Sign: Libra
Moon Phase: 2nd Quarter   Moon enters Scorpio 4:10 PM
Color: Gray   Incense: Clove

SUNDAY
MOTHER'S DAY

10
Waxing Moon
Moon Phase: 2nd Quarter   Moon Sign: Scorpio
Color: Yellow   Incense: Juniper

MONDAY
CEREMONY FOR RAIN (GUATEMALAN)

11
Waxing Moon
Moon Phase: Full 9:30 AM   Moon Sign: Scorpio
Color: White   Incense: Jasmine

TUESDAY
FESTIVAL OF SASHTI (INDIAN)

12
Waning Moon   Moon Sign: Scorpio
Moon Phase: 3rd Quarter   Moon enters Sagittarius 3:48 AM
Color: Gray   Incense: Frankincense

WEDNESDAY
OUR LADY OF FATIMA (PORTUGUESE)

13
Waning Moon
Moon Phase: 3rd Quarter   Moon Sign: Sagittarius
Color: Peach   Incense: Honeydew

THURSDAY
ISIS' DAY (EGYPTIAN)

14
Waning Moon   Moon Sign: Sagittarius
Moon Phase: 3rd Quarter   Moon enters Capricorn 1:40 PM
Color: Violet   Incense: Vanilla

May

FRIDAY
15 FEAST OF ISIDRO (FILIPINO)
Waning Moon
Moon Phase: 3rd Quarter   Moon Sign: Capricorn
Color: White   Incense: Bayberry

SATURDAY
16 SAVITU-VRATA (INDIAN)
Waning Moon
Moon Phase: 3rd Quarter   Moon Sign: Capricorn
Color: Blue   Moon enters Aquarius 9:31 PM
Incense: Lilac

SUNDAY
17 MUT-L-ARD (MOROCCAN)
Waning Moon
Moon Phase: 3rd Quarter   Moon Sign: Aquarius
Color: Orange   Incense: Cedar

MONDAY
18 Waning Moon
Moon Phase: 4th Qtr. 11:36 PM   Moon Sign: Aquarius
Color: Lavender   Incense: Peony

TUESDAY
19 FEAST OF PUDENCIANA (MEXICAN)
Waning Moon   Moon Sign: Aquarius
Moon Phase: 4th Quarter   Moon enters Pisces 3:04 AM
Color: Red   Incense: Thyme

WEDNESDAY
20 MJOLLNIR (GERMAN)
Waning Moon
Moon Phase: 4th Quarter   Moon Sign: Pisces
Color: Yellow   Incense: Pine

THURSDAY
21 DAY OF TEFNUT (EGYPTIAN)
Waning Moon   Moon Sign: Pisces
Moon Phase: 4th Quarter   Sun enters Gemini 1:05 AM
Color: Green   Moon enters Aries 6:06 AM
Incense: Wintergreen

Gemini ♊

22	**FRIDAY** RAGNAR LODBROK'S DAY (ODINIST) Waning Moon Moon Phase: 4th Quarter Moon Sign: Aries Color: Peach Incense: Myrrh

22 FRIDAY
RAGNAR LODBROK'S DAY (ODINIST)
Waning Moon
Moon Phase: 4th Quarter   Moon Sign: Aries
Color: Peach   Incense: Myrrh

23 SATURDAY
SEMIK (RUSSIAN)
Waning Moon   Moon Sign: Aries
Moon Phase: 4th Quarter   Moon enters Taurus 7:06 AM
Color: Indigo   Incense: Hyacinth

24 SUNDAY
THE THREE MARIES (FRENCH)
Waning Moon
Moon Phase: 4th Quarter   Moon Sign: Taurus
Color: Gold   Incense: Vanilla

25 MONDAY
MEMORIAL DAY (OBSERVED)
Waning Moon   Moon Sign: Taurus
Moon Phase: New 2:32 PM   Moon enters Gemini 7:25 AM
Color: Gray   Incense: Ginger

26 TUESDAY
Waxing Moon
Moon Phase: 1st Quarter   Moon Sign: Gemini
Color: White   Incense: Lavender

27 WEDNESDAY
Waxing Moon   Moon Sign: Gemini
Moon Phase: 1st Quarter   Moon enters Cancer 8:58 AM
Color: Brown   Incense: Juniper

28 THURSDAY
Waxing Moon
Moon Phase: 1st Quarter   Moon Sign: Cancer
Color: Turquoise   Incense: Rose

29 FRIDAY
OAK APPLE DAY (ENGLISH)
Waxing Moon
Moon Phase: 1st Quarter
Color: Rose

Moon Sign: Cancer
Moon enters Leo 1:38 PM
Incense: Rosemary

30 SATURDAY
MEMORIAL DAY
Waxing Moon
Moon Phase: 1st Quarter
Color: Brown

Moon Sign: Leo
Incense: Maple

31 SUNDAY
DAY OF OGGUM (CUBAN)
Waxing Moon
Moon Phase: 1st Quarter
Color: Peach

Moon Sign: Leo
Moon enters Virgo 10:21 PM
Incense: Sandalwood

MAY BIRTHSTONES
Ancient: Agate
Modern: Emerald

MAY FLOWERS
Lilies of the Valley
Hawthorn

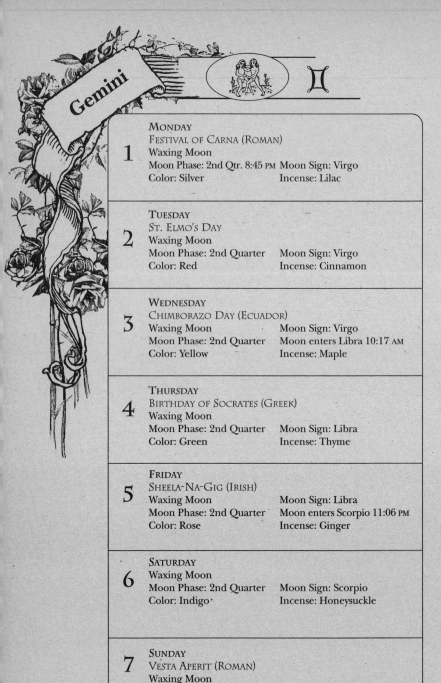

Gemini

MONDAY
1
FESTIVAL OF CARNA (ROMAN)
Waxing Moon
Moon Phase: 2nd Qtr. 8:45 PM   Moon Sign: Virgo
Color: Silver   Incense: Lilac

TUESDAY
2
ST. ELMO'S DAY
Waxing Moon
Moon Phase: 2nd Quarter   Moon Sign: Virgo
Color: Red   Incense: Cinnamon

WEDNESDAY
3
CHIMBORAZO DAY (ECUADOR)
Waxing Moon   Moon Sign: Virgo
Moon Phase: 2nd Quarter   Moon enters Libra 10:17 AM
Color: Yellow   Incense: Maple

THURSDAY
4
BIRTHDAY OF SOCRATES (GREEK)
Waxing Moon
Moon Phase: 2nd Quarter   Moon Sign: Libra
Color: Green   Incense: Thyme

FRIDAY
5
SHEELA-NA-GIG (IRISH)
Waxing Moon   Moon Sign: Libra
Moon Phase: 2nd Quarter   Moon enters Scorpio 11:06 PM
Color: Rose   Incense: Ginger

SATURDAY
6
Waxing Moon
Moon Phase: 2nd Quarter   Moon Sign: Scorpio
Color: Indigo·   Incense: Honeysuckle

SUNDAY
7
VESTA APERIT (ROMAN)
Waxing Moon
Moon Phase: 2nd Quarter   Moon Sign: Scorpio
Color: White   Incense: Frankincense

June

MONDAY

8

LINDISFARNE DAY (ODINIST)
Waxing Moon   Moon Sign: Scorpio
Moon Phase: 2nd Quarter   Moon enters Sagittarius 10:35 AM
Color: Lavender   Incense: Thyme

TUESDAY

9

VESTALIA (ROMAN)
Waxing Moon
Moon Phase: Full 11:19 PM   Moon Sign: Sagittarius
Color: White   Incense: Vanilla

WEDNESDAY

10

DAY OF ANAHITA (PERSIAN)
Waning Moon   Moon Sign: Sagittarius
Moon Phase: 3rd Quarter   Moon enters Capricorn 7:51 PM
Color: Brown   Incense: Patchouli

THURSDAY

11

KING KAMEHAMEHA I DAY (HAWAIIAN)
Waning Moon
Moon Phase: 3rd Quarter   Moon Sign: Capricorn
Color: Turquoise   Incense: Myrrh

FRIDAY

12

Waning Moon
Moon Phase: 3rd Quarter   Moon Sign: Capricorn
Color: Pink   Incense: Clove

SATURDAY

13

TIBETAN ALL SOULS' DAY
Waning Moon   Moon Sign: Capricorn
Moon Phase: 3rd Quarter   Moon enters Aquarius 3:03 AM
Color: Blue   Incense: Hyacinth

SUNDAY

14

VIDAR'S DAY (ODINIST)
Waning Moon
Moon Phase: 3rd Quarter   Moon Sign: Aquarius
Color: Yellow   Incense: Sandalwood

Gemini

15 MONDAY
ST. VITUS' DAY
Waning Moon — Moon Sign: Aquarius
Moon Phase: 3rd Quarter — Moon enters Pisces 8:32 AM
Color: White — Incense: Vanilla

16 TUESDAY
NIGHT OF THE DROP (EGYPTIAN)
Waning Moon
Moon Phase: 3rd Quarter — Moon Sign: Pisces
Color: Gray — Incense: Clove

17 WEDNESDAY
LUDI PISCATARI (ROMAN)
Waning Moon — Moon Sign: Pisces
Moon Phase: 4th Qtr. 5:38 AM — Moon enters Aries 12:23 PM
Color: Peach — Incense: Pine

18 THURSDAY
Waning Moon
Moon Phase: 4th Quarter — Moon Sign: Aries
Color: White — Incense: Rose

19 FRIDAY
WAA-LAA BEGINS (NATIVE AMERICAN)
Waning Moon — Moon Sign: Aries
Moon Phase: 4th Quarter — Moon enters Taurus 2:47 PM
Color: Peach — Incense: Bay Laurel

20 SATURDAY
DAY OF IX CHEL (MAYAN)
Waning Moon
Moon Phase: 4th Quarter — Moon Sign: Taurus
Color: Gray — Incense: Rosemary

21 SUNDAY
LITHA (SUMMER SOLSTICE)
Waning Moon — Moon Sign: Taurus
Moon Phase: 4th Quarter — Sun enters Cancer 9:02 AM
Color: Orange — Moon enters Gemini 4:26 PM
Incense: Blackberry

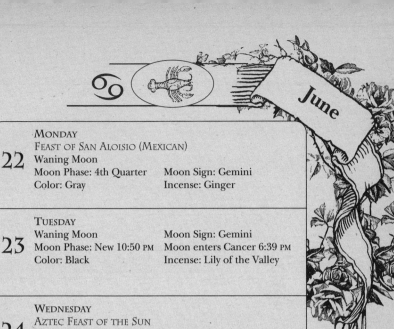

June

MONDAY
22 FEAST OF SAN ALOISIO (MEXICAN)
Waning Moon
Moon Phase: 4th Quarter   Moon Sign: Gemini
Color: Gray   Incense: Ginger

TUESDAY
23 Waning Moon   Moon Sign: Gemini
Moon Phase: New 10:50 PM   Moon enters Cancer 6:39 PM
Color: Black   Incense: Lily of the Valley

WEDNESDAY
24 AZTEC FEAST OF THE SUN
Waxing Moon
Moon Phase: 1st Quarter   Moon Sign: Cancer
Color: White   Incense: Myrrh

THURSDAY
25 WELL-DRESSING FESTIVAL (BRITISH)
Waxing Moon   Moon Sign: Cancer
Moon Phase: 1st Quarter   Moon enters Leo 11:04 PM
Color: Violet   Incense: Carnation

FRIDAY
26 IROQUOIS GREEN CORN FESTIVAL (NATIVE AMERICAN)
Waxing Moon
Moon Phase: 1st Quarter   Moon Sign: Leo
Color: White   Incense: Lavender

SATURDAY
27 Waxing Moon
Moon Phase: 1st Quarter   Moon Sign: Leo
Color: Brown   Incense: Sandalwood

SUNDAY
28 FESTIVAL OF THE TARASQUE (FRENCH)
Waxing Moon   Moon Sign: Leo
Moon Phase: 1st Quarter   Moon enters Virgo 6:55 AM
Color: Peach   Incense: Juniper

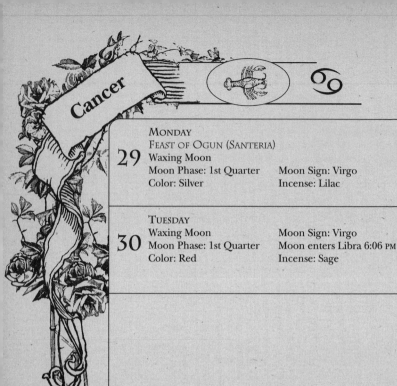

Cancer

MONDAY
FEAST OF OGUN (SANTERIA)
29 Waxing Moon
Moon Phase: 1st Quarter   Moon Sign: Virgo
Color: Silver   Incense: Lilac

TUESDAY
30 Waxing Moon   Moon Sign: Virgo
Moon Phase: 1st Quarter   Moon enters Libra 6:06 PM
Color: Red   Incense: Sage

JUNE BIRTHSTONES
Ancient: Emerald
Modern: Agate

JUNE FLOWERS
Roses
Honeysuckle

♋ July

WEDNESDAY
1
CANADA DAY
Waxing Moon
Moon Phase: 2nd Qtr. 1:44 PM   Moon Sign: Libra
Color: Yellow   Incense: Patchouli

THURSDAY
2
FEAST OF EXPECTANT MOTHERS (EUROPEAN)
Waxing Moon
Moon Phase: 2nd Quarter   Moon Sign: Libra
Color: Green   Incense: Clove

FRIDAY
3
INDEPENDENCE DAY (OBSERVED)
SOTHIS (EGYPTIAN)
Waxing Moon   Moon Sign: Libra
Moon Phase: 2nd Quarter   Moon enters Scorpio 6:46 AM
Color: White   Incense: Almond

SATURDAY
4
INDEPENDENCE DAY
Waxing Moon
Moon Phase: 2nd Quarter   Moon Sign: Scorpio
Color: Indigo   Incense: Lavender

SUNDAY
5
OLD MIDSUMMER'S DAY
Waxing Moon   Moon Sign: Scorpio
Moon Phase: 2nd Quarter   Moon enters Sagittarius 6:24 PM
Color: Gold   Incense: Cedar

MONDAY
6
Waxing Moon
Moon Phase: 2nd Quarter   Moon Sign: Sagittarius
Color: Silver   Incense: Vanilla

TUESDAY
7
TANABATA (JAPANESE)
Waxing Moon
Moon Phase: 2nd Quarter   Moon Sign: Sagittarius
Color: Red   Incense: Clover

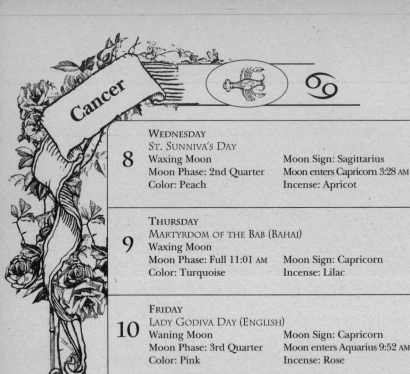

Cancer

8	**WEDNESDAY** **ST. SUNNIVA'S DAY** Waxing Moon Moon Phase: 2nd Quarter Color: Peach	Moon Sign: Sagittarius Moon enters Capricorn 3:28 AM Incense: Apricot

9	**THURSDAY** **MARTYRDOM OF THE BAB (BAHAI)** Waxing Moon Moon Phase: Full 11:01 AM Color: Turquoise	Moon Sign: Capricorn Incense: Lilac

10	**FRIDAY** **LADY GODIVA DAY (ENGLISH)** Waning Moon Moon Phase: 3rd Quarter Color: Pink	Moon Sign: Capricorn Moon enters Aquarius 9:52 AM Incense: Rose

11	**SATURDAY** **NAADAM FESTIVAL (MONGOLIAN)** Waning Moon Moon Phase: 3rd Quarter Color: Blue	Moon Sign: Aquarius Incense: Thyme

12	**SUNDAY** Waning Moon Moon Phase: 3rd Quarter Color: Orange	Moon Sign: Aquarius Moon enters Pisces 2:22 PM Incense: Clove

13	**MONDAY** **REED DANCE DAY (AFRICAN)** Waning Moon Moon Phase: 3rd Quarter Color: White	Moon Sign: Pisces Incense: Bay Laurel

14	**TUESDAY** **BASTILLE DAY (FRENCH)** Waning Moon Moon Phase: 3rd Quarter Color: Black	Moon Sign: Pisces Moon enters Aries 5:45 PM Incense: Lilac

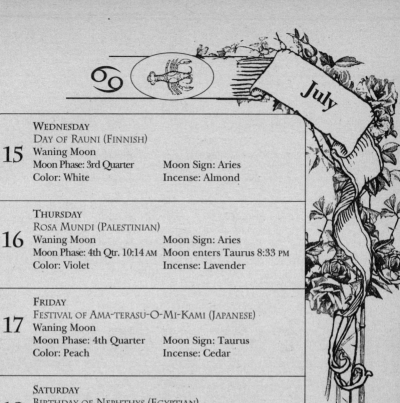

July

WEDNESDAY
15 DAY OF RAUNI (FINNISH)
Waning Moon
Moon Phase: 3rd Quarter   Moon Sign: Aries
Color: White   Incense: Almond

THURSDAY
16 ROSA MUNDI (PALESTINIAN)
Waning Moon   Moon Sign: Aries
Moon Phase: 4th Qtr. 10:14 AM   Moon enters Taurus 8:33 PM
Color: Violet   Incense: Lavender

FRIDAY
17 FESTIVAL OF AMA-TERASU-O-MI-KAMI (JAPANESE)
Waning Moon
Moon Phase: 4th Quarter   Moon Sign: Taurus
Color: Peach   Incense: Cedar

SATURDAY
18 BIRTHDAY OF NEPHTHYS (EGYPTIAN)
Waning Moon   Moon Sign: Taurus
Moon Phase: 4th Quarter   Moon enters Gemini 11:18 PM
Color: Gray   Incense: Thyme

SUNDAY
19 WEDDING OF ADONIS AND APHRODITE (GREEK)
Waning Moon
Moon Phase: 4th Quarter   Moon Sign: Gemini
Color: Yellow   Incense: Sandalwood

MONDAY
20 BINDING OF THE WREATHS (LITHUANIAN)
Waning Moon
Moon Phase: 4th Quarter   Moon Sign: Gemini
Color: Violet   Incense: Lavender

TUESDAY
21 DAMO'S DAY (GREEK)
Waning Moon   Moon Sign: Gemini
Moon Phase: 4th Quarter   Moon enters Cancer 2:43 AM
Color: Gray   Incense: Myrrh

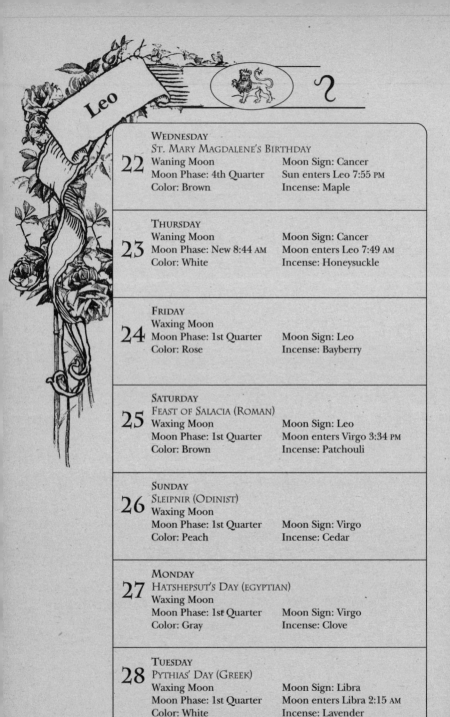

Leo

WEDNESDAY
22 ST. MARY MAGDALENE'S BIRTHDAY
Waning Moon   Moon Sign: Cancer
Moon Phase: 4th Quarter   Sun enters Leo 7:55 PM
Color: Brown   Incense: Maple

THURSDAY
23 Waning Moon   Moon Sign: Cancer
Moon Phase: New 8:44 AM   Moon enters Leo 7:49 AM
Color: White   Incense: Honeysuckle

FRIDAY
24 Waxing Moon
Moon Phase: 1st Quarter   Moon Sign: Leo
Color: Rose   Incense: Bayberry

SATURDAY
25 FEAST OF SALACIA (ROMAN)
Waxing Moon   Moon Sign: Leo
Moon Phase: 1st Quarter   Moon enters Virgo 3:34 PM
Color: Brown   Incense: Patchouli

SUNDAY
26 SLEIPNIR (ODINIST)
Waxing Moon
Moon Phase: 1st Quarter   Moon Sign: Virgo
Color: Peach   Incense: Cedar

MONDAY
27 HATSHEPSUT'S DAY (EGYPTIAN)
Waxing Moon
Moon Phase: 1st Quarter   Moon Sign: Virgo
Color: Gray   Incense: Clove

TUESDAY
28 PYTHIAS' DAY (GREEK)
Waxing Moon   Moon Sign: Libra
Moon Phase: 1st Quarter   Moon enters Libra 2:15 AM
Color: White   Incense: Lavender

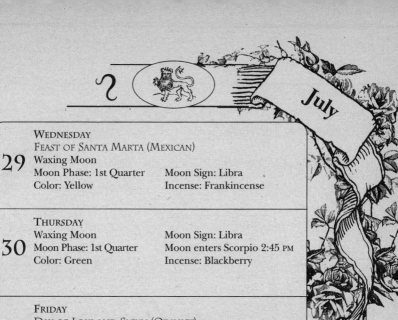

WEDNESDAY
FEAST OF SANTA MARTA (MEXICAN)

29 Waxing Moon
Moon Phase: 1st Quarter   Moon Sign: Libra
Color: Yellow   Incense: Frankincense

THURSDAY
Waxing Moon   Moon Sign: Libra
30 Moon Phase: 1st Quarter   Moon enters Scorpio 2:45 PM
Color: Green   Incense: Blackberry

FRIDAY
DAY OF LOKI AND SIGYN (ODINIST)
31 Waxing Moon
Moon Phase: 2nd Qtr. 7:05 AM   Moon Sign: Scorpio
Color: White   Incense: Lilac

JULY BIRTHSTONES
Ancient: Onyx
Modern: Ruby

JULY FLOWERS
Water Lilies
Larkspur

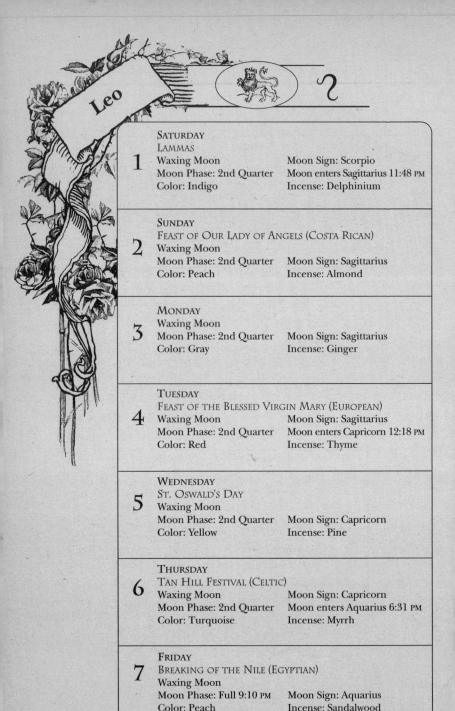

Leo

♌

1
SATURDAY
LAMMAS
Waxing Moon   Moon Sign: Scorpio
Moon Phase: 2nd Quarter   Moon enters Sagittarius 11:48 PM
Color: Indigo   Incense: Delphinium

2
SUNDAY
FEAST OF OUR LADY OF ANGELS (COSTA RICAN)
Waxing Moon
Moon Phase: 2nd Quarter   Moon Sign: Sagittarius
Color: Peach   Incense: Almond

3
MONDAY
Waxing Moon
Moon Phase: 2nd Quarter   Moon Sign: Sagittarius
Color: Gray   Incense: Ginger

4
TUESDAY
FEAST OF THE BLESSED VIRGIN MARY (EUROPEAN)
Waxing Moon   Moon Sign: Sagittarius
Moon Phase: 2nd Quarter   Moon enters Capricorn 12:18 PM
Color: Red   Incense: Thyme

5
WEDNESDAY
ST. OSWALD'S DAY
Waxing Moon
Moon Phase: 2nd Quarter   Moon Sign: Capricorn
Color: Yellow   Incense: Pine

6
THURSDAY
TAN HILL FESTIVAL (CELTIC)
Waxing Moon   Moon Sign: Capricorn
Moon Phase: 2nd Quarter   Moon enters Aquarius 6:31 PM
Color: Turquoise   Incense: Myrrh

7
FRIDAY
BREAKING OF THE NILE (EGYPTIAN)
Waxing Moon
Moon Phase: Full 9:10 PM   Moon Sign: Aquarius
Color: Peach   Incense: Sandalwood

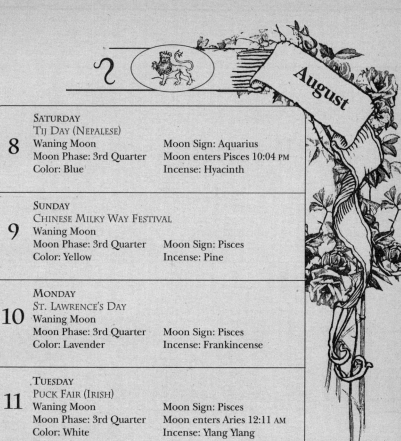

August

SATURDAY
TIJ DAY (NEPALESE)

8

Waning Moon
Moon Phase: 3rd Quarter
Color: Blue

Moon Sign: Aquarius
Moon enters Pisces 10:04 PM
Incense: Hyacinth

SUNDAY
CHINESE MILKY WAY FESTIVAL

9

Waning Moon
Moon Phase: 3rd Quarter
Color: Yellow

Moon Sign: Pisces
Incense: Pine

MONDAY
ST. LAWRENCE'S DAY

10

Waning Moon
Moon Phase: 3rd Quarter
Color: Lavender

Moon Sign: Pisces
Incense: Frankincense

TUESDAY
PUCK FAIR (IRISH)

11

Waning Moon
Moon Phase: 3rd Quarter
Color: White

Moon Sign: Pisces
Moon enters Aries 12:11 AM
Incense: Ylang Ylang

WEDNESDAY
LIGHTS OF ISIS (EGYPTIAN)

12

Waning Moon
Moon Phase: 3rd Quarter
Color: Peach

Moon Sign: Aries
Incense: Patchouli

THURSDAY
HECATE'S DAY (GREEK)

13

Waning Moon
Moon Phase: 3rd Quarter
Color: White

Moon Sign: Aries
Moon enters Taurus 2:05 AM
Incense: Rose

FRIDAY
FIESCHI'S CAKE DAY (ITALIAN)

14

Waning Moon
Moon Phase: 4th Qtr. 2:49 PM
Color: Rose

Moon Sign: Taurus
Incense: Lily of the Valley

Leo ♌

SATURDAY
MOON FESTIVAL FOR CHANG-O (CHINESE)
15
Waning Moon
Moon Phase: 4th Quarter
Color: Gray
Moon Sign: Taurus
Moon enters Gemini 4:46 AM
Incense: Wintergreen

SUNDAY
FESTIVAL OF MINSTRELS (EUROPEAN)
16
Waning Moon
Moon Phase: 4th Quarter
Color: Orange
Moon Sign: Gemini
Incense: Patchouli

MONDAY
AMENARTUS (EGYPTIAN)
17
Waning Moon
Moon Phase: 4th Quarter
Color: White
Moon Sign: Gemini
Moon enters Cancer 8:56 AM
Incense: Peony

TUESDAY
BLESSING OF THE GRAPES (ARMENIAN)
18
Waning Moon
Moon Phase: 4th Quarter
Color: Gray
Moon Sign: Cancer
Incense: Rosemary

WEDNESDAY
RUSTIC VINALIA (ROMAN)
19
Waning Moon
Moon Phase: 4th Quarter
Color: White
Moon Sign: Cancer
Moon entes Leo 3:01 PM
Incense: Bayberry

THURSDAY
DAY OF INANNA (MESOPOTAMIAN)
20
Waning Moon
Moon Phase: 4th Quarter
Color: Violet
Moon Sign: Leo
Incense: Rose

FRIDAY
21
Waning Moon
Moon Phase: New 9:03 PM
Color: Pink
Moon Sign: Leo
Moon enters Virgo 11:22 PM
Incense: Ginger

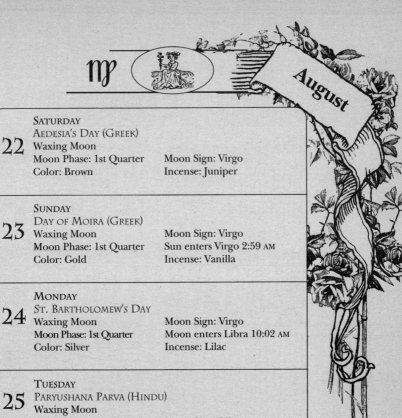

SATURDAY
AEDESIA'S DAY (GREEK)
22 Waxing Moon
Moon Phase: 1st Quarter   Moon Sign: Virgo
Color: Brown   Incense: Juniper

SUNDAY
DAY OF MOIRA (GREEK)
23 Waxing Moon
Moon Phase: 1st Quarter   Moon Sign: Virgo
    Sun enters Virgo 2:59 AM
Color: Gold   Incense: Vanilla

MONDAY
ST. BARTHOLOMEW'S DAY
24 Waxing Moon
Moon Phase: 1st Quarter   Moon Sign: Virgo
    Moon enters Libra 10:02 AM
Color: Silver   Incense: Lilac

TUESDAY
PARYUSHANA PARVA (HINDU)
25 Waxing Moon
Moon Phase: 1st Quarter   Moon Sign: Libra
Color: Black   Incense: Almond

WEDNESDAY
FEAST DAY OF ILMATAR (FINNISH)
26 Waxing Moon   Moon Sign: Libra
Moon Phase: 1st Quarter   Moon enters Scorpio 10:25 PM
Color: Brown   Incense: Sage

THURSDAY
WORSHIP OF MOTHER GODDESS DEVAKI (EAST INDIAN)
27 Waxing Moon
Moon Phase: 1st Quarter   Moon Sign: Scorpio
Color: Green   Incense: Bay Laurel

FRIDAY
28 Waxing Moon
Moon Phase: 1st Quarter   Moon Sign: Scorpio
Color: White   Incense: Hyacinth

SATURDAY
29 HATHOR'S DAY (EGYPTIAN)
Waxing Moon   Moon Sign: Scorpio
Moon Phase: 1st Quarter   Moon enters Sagittarius 10:55 AM
Color: Indigo   Incense: Hyacinth

SUNDAY
30 ST. ROSE OF LIMA DAY (PERUVIAN)
Waxing Moon
Moon Phase: 2nd Qtr. 12:07 AM   Moon Sign: Sagittarius
Color: Peach   Incense: Mango

MONDAY
31 Waxing Moon   Moon Sign: Sagittarius
Moon Phase: 2nd Quarter   Moon enters Capricorn 9:23 PM
Color: Lavender   Incense: Rose

AUGUST BIRTHSTONES
Ancient: Carnelian
Modern: Topaz

AUGUST FLOWERS
Gladiolus
Poppies

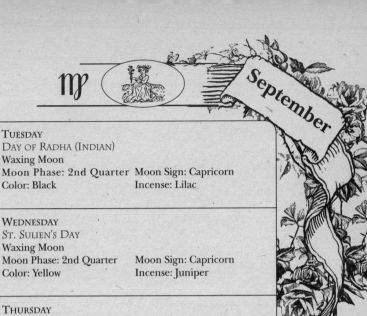

TUESDAY
DAY OF RADHA (INDIAN)
1
Waxing Moon
Moon Phase: 2nd Quarter   Moon Sign: Capricorn
Color: Black   Incense: Lilac

WEDNESDAY
ST. SULIEN'S DAY
2
Waxing Moon
Moon Phase: 2nd Quarter   Moon Sign: Capricorn
Color: Yellow   Incense: Juniper

THURSDAY
LA KON (NATIVE AMERICAN)
3
Waxing Moon   Moon Sign: Capricorn
Moon Phase: 2nd Quarter   Moon enters Aquarius 4:21 AM
Color: Violet   Incense: Honeysuckle

FRIDAY
4
Waxing Moon
Moon Phase: 2nd Quarter   Moon Sign: Aquarius
Color: Rose   Incense: Bayberry

SATURDAY
DAY OF NANDA DEVI (EAST INDIAN)
5
Waxing Moon   Moon Sign: Aquarius
Moon Phase: 2nd Quarter   Moon enters Pisces 7:48 AM
Color: Brown   Incense: Sandalwood

SUNDAY
6
Waxing Moon
Moon Phase: Full 6:22 AM   Moon Sign: Pisces
Color: Gold   Incense: Cedar

MONDAY
LABOR DAY
7
FESTIVAL OF DURGA (BENGALESE)
Waning Moon   Moon Sign: Pisces
Moon Phase: 3rd Quarter   Moon enters Aries 8:53 AM
Color: Lavender   Incense: Lavender

Virgo ♍

TUESDAY

8

PINNHUT FESTIVAL (NATIVE AMERICAN)
Waning Moon
Moon Phase: 3rd Quarter   Moon Sign: Aries
Color: White   Incense: Hyacinth

WEDNESDAY

9

HORNED DANCE AT ABBOTS BROMLEY (ENGLISH)
Waning Moon   Moon Sign: Aries
Moon Phase: 3rd Quarter   Moon enters Taurus 9:17 AM
Color: Peach   Incense: Honeydew

THURSDAY

10

Waning Moon
Moon Phase: 3rd Quarter   Moon Sign: Taurus
Color: White   Incense: Carnation

FRIDAY

11

EGYPTIAN DAY OF QUEENS
Waning Moon   Moon Sign: Taurus
Moon Phase: 3rd Quarter   Moon enters Gemini 10:41 AM
Color: Pink   Incense: Bay Laurel

SATURDAY

12

ASTRAEA'S DAY (GREEK)
Waning Moon
Moon Phase: 4th Qtr. 8:58 PM Moon Sign: Gemini
Color: Blue   Incense: Lilac

SUNDAY

13

LECTISTERNIA (ROMAN)
Waning Moon   Moon Sign: Gemini
Moon Phase: 4th Quarter   Moon enters Cancer 2:20 PM
Color: Orange   Incense: Thyme

MONDAY

14

FEAST OF LIGHTS (EGYPTIAN)
Waning Moon
Moon Phase: 4th Quarter   Moon Sign: Cancer
Color: Gray   Incense: Rosemary

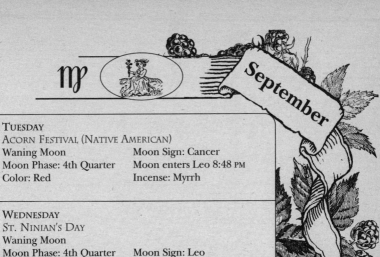

15 TUESDAY
ACORN FESTIVAL (NATIVE AMERICAN)
Waning Moon
Moon Phase: 4th Quarter
Color: Red

Moon Sign: Cancer
Moon enters Leo 8:48 PM
Incense: Myrrh

16 WEDNESDAY
ST. NINIAN'S DAY
Waning Moon
Moon Phase: 4th Quarter
Color: White

Moon Sign: Leo
Incense: Hyacinth

17 THURSDAY
HILDEGARD OF BINGEN'S DAY (GERMAN)
Waning Moon
Moon Phase: 4th Quarter
Color: Green

Moon Sign: Leo
Incense: Blackberry

18 FRIDAY
Waning Moon
Moon Phase: 4th Quarter
Color: White

Moon Sign: Leo
Moon enters Virgo 5:51 AM
Incense: Vanilla

19 SATURDAY
FAST OF THOTH (EGYPTIAN)
Waning Moon
Moon Phase: 4th Quarter
Color: Gray

Moon Sign: Virgo
Incense: Clove

20 SUNDAY
ROSH HASHANAH BEGINS (JEWISH)
Waning Moon
Moon Phase: New 12:01 PM
Color: Yellow

Moon Sign: Virgo
Moon enters Libra 4:57 PM
Incense: Eucalyptus

21 MONDAY
RAUD THE STRONG'S MARTYRDOM (NORWEGIAN)
Waxing Moon
Moon Phase: 1st Quarter
Color: White

Moon Sign: Libra
Incense: Lavender

Libra

TUESDAY
22
ROSH HASHANAH ENDS (JEWISH)
Waxing Moon
Moon Phase: 1st Quarter | Moon Sign: Libra
Color: Gray | Incense: Clove

WEDNESDAY
23
MABON (FALL EQUINOX)
Waxing Moon | Moon Sign: Libra
Moon Phase: 1st Quarter | Moon enters Scorpio 5:22 AM
Color: Brown | Sun enters Libra 12:37 AM
| Incense: Sandalwood

THURSDAY
24
FEAST OF OBATALA (SANTERIA)
Waxing Moon
Moon Phase: 1st Quarter | Moon Sign: Scorpio
Color: Turquoise | Incense: Myrrh

FRIDAY
25
Waxing Moon | Moon Sign: Scorpio
Moon Phase: 1st Quarter | Moon enters Sagittarius 6:05 PM
Color: Peach | Incense: Coconut

SATURDAY
26
FEAST OF SANTA JUSTINA (MEXICAN)
Waxing Moon
Moon Phase: 1st Quarter | Moon Sign: Sagittarius
Color: Indigo | Incense: Lavender

SUNDAY
27
DAY OF WILLOWS (MESOPOTAMIAN)
Waxing Moon
Moon Phase: 1st Quarter | Moon Sign: Sagittarius
Color: Peach | Incense: Cedar

MONDAY
28
CONFUCIUS' BIRTHDAY
Waxing Moon | Moon Sign: Sagittarius
Moon Phase: 2nd Qtr. 4:12 PM | Moon enters Capricorn 5:31 AM
Color: Silver | Incense: Clove

September

TUESDAY
29 YOM KIPPUR BEGINS (JEWISH)
Waxing Moon
Moon Phase: 2nd Quarter   Moon Sign: Capricorn
Color: Black   Incense: Vanilla

WEDNESDAY
30 YOM KIPPUR ENDS (JEWISH)
Waxing Moon   Moon Sign: Capricorn
Moon Phase: 2nd Quarter   Moon enters Aquarius 1:54 PM
Color: Yellow   Incense: Patchouli

SEPTEMBER BIRTHSTONES
Ancient: Chrysolite
Modern: Beryl

SEPTEMBER FLOWERS
Morning Glories
Asters

Libra

THURSDAY
1
Waxing Moon
Moon Phase: 2nd Quarter   Moon Sign: Aquarius
Color: Green   Incense: Plum

FRIDAY
2
OLD MAN'S DAY (ENGLISH)
Waxing Moon   Moon Sign: Aquarius
Moon Phase: 2nd Quarter   Moon enters Pisces 6:24 PM
Color: Peach   Incense: Vanilla

SATURDAY
3
FESTIVAL OF DIONYSUS (GREEK)
Waxing Moon
Moon Phase: 2nd Quarter   Moon Sign: Pisces
Color: Brown   Incense: Pine

SUNDAY
4
SUKKOT BEGINS (JEWISH)
Waxing Moon   Moon Sign: Pisces
Moon Phase: 2nd Quarter   Moon enters Aries 7:32 PM
Color: Peach   Incense: Almond

MONDAY
5
ROMANIAN WINE FESTIVAL
Waxing Moon
Moon Phase: Full 3:12 PM   Moon Sign: Aries
Color: Gray   Incense: Ginger

TUESDAY
6
SUKKOT ENDS (JEWISH)
Waning Moon   Moon Sign: Aries
Moon Phase: 3rd Quarter   Moon enters Taurus 6:58 PM
Color: Red   Incense: Sandalwood

WEDNESDAY
7
PALLAS ATHENA'S DAY (ROMAN)
Waning Moon
Moon Phase: 3rd Quarter   Moon Sign: Taurus
Color: Yellow   Incense: Juniper

THURSDAY

8 Waning Moon
Moon Phase: 3rd Quarter
Color: Turquoise

Moon Sign: Taurus
Moon enters Gemini 6:44 PM
Incense: Frankincense

FRIDAY
ST. DENIS' DAY

9 Waning Moon
Moon Phase: 3rd Quarter
Color: White

Moon Sign: Gemini
Incense: Lilac

SATURDAY

10 Waning Moon
Moon Phase: 3rd Quarter
Color: Gray

Moon Sign: Gemini
Moon enters Cancer 8:48 PM
Incense: Thyme

SUNDAY
VINALIA (ROMAN)

11 Waning Moon
Moon Phase: 3rd Quarter
Color: Yellow

Moon Sign: Cancer
Incense: Frankincense

MONDAY
COLUMBUS' DAY

12 Waning Moon
Moon Phase: 4th Qtr. 6:11 AM
Color: Lavender

Moon Sign: Cancer
Incense: Honeysuckle

TUESDAY
OUR LADY OF FATIMA (PORTUGUESE)

13 Waning Moon
Moon Phase: 4th Quarter
Color: White

Moon Sign: Cancer
Moon enters Leo 2:25 AM
Incense: Violet

WEDNESDAY
VINTERSBLÓT (NORTHERN EUROPEAN))

14 Waning Moon
Moon Phase: 4th Quarter
Color: Peach

Moon Sign: Leo
Incense: Bayberry

Libra

15 THURSDAY
IDES OF OCTOBER (ROMAN)
Waning Moon   Moon Sign: Leo
Moon Phase: 4th Quarter   Moon enters Virgo 11:32 AM
Color: White   Incense: Delphinium

16 FRIDAY
FESTIVAL OF PANDROSUS (GREEK)
Waning Moon
Moon Phase: 4th Quarter   Moon Sign: Virgo
Color: Pink   Incense: Ginger

17 SATURDAY
FESTIVAL OF HENGEST (ANGLO-SAXON)
Waning Moon   Moon Sign: Virgo
Moon Phase: 4th Quarter   Moon enters Libra 11:02 PM
Color: Blue   Incense: Rosemary

18 SUNDAY
FESTIVAL OF HERNE (CELTIC)
Waning Moon
Moon Phase: 4th Quarter   Moon Sign: Libra
Color: Orange   Incense: Thyme

19 MONDAY
Waning Moon
Moon Phase: 4th Quarter   Moon Sign: Libra
Color: White   Incense: Lilac

20 TUESDAY
FESTIVAL OF ANCESTORS (CHINESE)
Waning Moon   Moon Sign: Libra
Moon Phase: New 5:10 AM   Moon enters Scorpio 11:37 AM
Color: Gray   Incense: Cinnamon

21 WEDNESDAY
FESTIVAL OF ISHHARA (MESOPOTAMIAN)
Waxing Moon
Moon Phase: 1st Quarter   Moon Sign: Scorpio
Color: Brown   Incense: Sandalwood

THURSDAY
22
Waxing Moon
Moon Phase: 1st Quarter   Moon Sign: Scorpio
Color: Violet   Incense: Violet

FRIDAY
23
SWALLOWS OF SAN JUAN CAPISTRANO DAY (MEXICAN)
Waxing Moon   Moon Sign: Scorpio
Moon Phase: 1st Quarter   Moon enters Sagittarius 12:17 AM
Color: Rose   Sun enters Scorpio 9:59 AM
    Incense: Myrrh

SATURDAY
24
UNITED NATIONS DAY
Waxing Moon
Moon Phase: 1st Quarter   Moon Sign: Sagittarius
Color: Indigo   Incense: Jasmine

SUNDAY
25
ST. CRISPIN'S DAY
DAYLIGHT-SAVING TIME ENDS AT 2 AM
Waxing Moon   Moon Sign: Sagittarius
Moon Phase: 1st Quarter   Moon enters Capricorn 12:05 PM
Color: Gold   Incense: Sandalwood

MONDAY
26
ABAN JASHAN (JAPANESE)
Waxing Moon
Moon Phase: 1st Quarter   Moon Sign: Capricorn
Color: Silver   Incense: Frankincense

TUESDAY
27
OWAGIT (NATIVE AMERICAN)
Waxing Moon   Moon Sign: Capricorn
Moon Phase: 1st Quarter   Moon enters Aquarius 9:45 PM
Color: Black   Incense: Lilac

WEDNESDAY
28
FYRIBOD (CELTIC)
Waxing Moon
Moon Phase: 2nd Qtr. 6:46 AM   Moon Sign: Aquarius
Color: White   Incense: Myrrh

Scorpio ♏

29	**THURSDAY** IROQUOIS FEAST OF THE DEAD (NATIVE AMERICAN) Waxing Moon Moon Phase: 2nd Quarter Color: Turquoise	Moon Sign: Aquarius Incense: Frankincense
30	**FRIDAY** LOS ANGELITOS (MEXICAN) Waxing Moon Moon Phase: 2nd Quarter Color: Peach	Moon Sign: Aquarius Moon enters Pisces 3:58 AM Incense: Kiwi
31	**SATURDAY** SAMHAIN HALLOWEEN Waxing Moon Moon Phase: 2nd Quarter Color: Brown	Moon Sign: Pisces Incense: Patchouli

OCTOBER BIRTHSTONES
Ancient: Aquamarine
Modern: Pearl

OCTOBER FLOWERS
Calendula
Cosmos

SUNDAY

1 ALL SAINTS' DAY
Waxing Moon
Moon Phase: 2nd Quarter
Color: Yellow

Moon Sign: Pisces
Moon enters Aries 6:27 AM
Incense: Thyme

MONDAY

2 ANIMAS (MEXICAN)
Waxing Moon
Moon Phase: 2nd Quarter
Color: Gray

Moon Sign: Aries
Incense: Ginger

TUESDAY

3 FESTIVAL FOR THE NEW YEAR (GAELIC)
Waxing Moon
Moon Phase: 2nd Quarter
Color: White

Moon Sign: Aries
Moon enters Taurus 6:12 AM
Incense: Musk

WEDNESDAY

4 Waxing Moon
Moon Phase: Full 12:18 AM
Color: Brown

Moon Sign: Taurus
Incense: Patchouli

THURSDAY

5 GUY FAWKES' NIGHT (BRITISH)
Waning Moon
Moon Phase: 3rd Quarter
Color: Turquoise

Moon Sign: Taurus
Moon enters Gemini 5:11 AM
Incense: Hyacinth

FRIDAY

6 BIRTHDAY OF TIAMAT (BABYLONIAN)
Waning Moon
Moon Phase: 3rd Quarter
Color: Peach

Moon Sign: Gemini
Incense: Vanilla

SATURDAY

7 MAKAHIKI FESTIVAL (HAWAIIAN)
Waning Moon
Moon Phase: 3rd Quarter
Color: Brown

Moon Sign: Gemini
Moon enters Cancer 5:39 AM
Incense: Pine

Scorpio ♏

8	**SUNDAY** FESTIVAL OF KAMI OF THE HEARTH (JAPANESE) Waning Moon Moon Phase: 3rd Quarter — Moon Sign: Cancer Color: Peach — Incense: Blackberry

SUNDAY
8
FESTIVAL OF KAMI OF THE HEARTH (JAPANESE)
Waning Moon
Moon Phase: 3rd Quarter   Moon Sign: Cancer
Color: Peach   Incense: Blackberry

MONDAY
9
Waning Moon   Moon Sign: Cancer
Moon Phase: 3rd Quarter   Moon enters Leo 9:33 AM
Color: Lavender   Incense: Rose

TUESDAY
10
FESTIVAL OF THE GODDESS OF REASON (FRENCH)
Waning Moon
Moon Phase: 4th Qtr. 7:29 PM Moon Sign: Leo
Color: Red   Incense: Sage

WEDNESDAY
11
GURU NANAK'S BIRTHDAY (SIKH)
Waning Moon   Moon Sign: Leo
Moon Phase: 4th Quarter   Moon enters Virgo 5:38 PM
Color: White   Incense: Violet

THURSDAY
12
BIRTHDAY OF BAHA'U'LLAH (BAHA'I)
Waning Moon
Moon Phase: 4th Quarter   Moon Sign: Virgo
Color: Violet   Incense: Lilac

FRIDAY
13
FESTIVAL OF JUPITER (ROMAN)
Waning Moon
Moon Phase: 4th Quarter   Moon Sign: Virgo
Color: White   Incense: Myrrh

SATURDAY
14
MOCCAS' DAY (CELTIC)
Waning Moon   Moon Sign: Virgo
Moon Phase: 4th Quarter   Moon enters Libra 4:58 AM
Color: Blue   Incense: Thyme

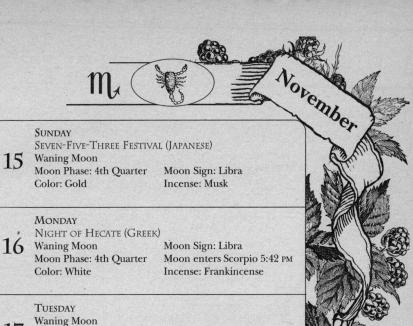

15 SUNDAY
SEVEN-FIVE-THREE FESTIVAL (JAPANESE)
Waning Moon
Moon Phase: 4th Quarter   Moon Sign: Libra
Color: Gold   Incense: Musk

16 MONDAY
NIGHT OF HECATE (GREEK)
Waning Moon   Moon Sign: Libra
Moon Phase: 4th Quarter Moon enters Scorpio 5:42 PM
Color: White   Incense: Frankincense

17 TUESDAY
Waning Moon
Moon Phase: 4th Quarter   Moon Sign: Scorpio
Color: Black   Incense: Lily of the Valley

18 WEDNESDAY
DAY OF ARDVI SURA (PERSIAN)
Waning Moon
Moon Phase: New 11:27 PM   Moon Sign: Scorpio
Color: Peach   Incense: Musk

19 THURSDAY
FEAST OF SANTA ISABEL (MEXICAN)
Waning Moon   Moon Sign: Scorpio
Moon Phase: 1st Quarter Moon enters Sagittarius 6:13 AM
Color: Green   Incense: Vanilla

20 FRIDAY
ST. EDMUND'S DAY
Waning Moon
Moon Phase: 1st Quarter   Moon Sign: Sagittarius
Color: Pink   Incense: Patchouli

21 SATURDAY
DAY OF CAILLEACH (CELTIC)
Waning Moon   Moon Sign: Sagittarius
Moon Phase: 1st Quarter Moon enters Capricorn 5:46 PM
Color: Pink   Incense: Floral

Sagittarius

22 SUNDAY
YDALIR (NORSE)
Waxing Moon
Moon Phase: 1st Quarter
Color: Orange

Moon Sign: Capricorn
Sun enters Sagittarius 7:34 AM
Incense: Patchouli

23 MONDAY
SHINJOSAI (JAPANESE)
Waxing Moon
Moon Phase: 1st Quarter
Color: Silver

Moon Sign: Capricorn
Incense: Myrrh

24 TUESDAY
STIR-UP SUNDAY (BRITISH)
Waxing Moon
Moon Phase: 1st Quarter
Color: Gray

Moon Sign: Capricorn
Moon enters Aquarius 3:43 AM
Incense: Frankincense

25 WEDNESDAY
FEAST OF SANTA CATALINA DE ALEJANDRÍA (MEXICAN)
Waxing Moon
Moon Phase: 1st Quarter
Color: Yellow

Moon Sign: Aquarius
Incense: Patchouli

26 THURSDAY
THANKSGIVING DAY
Waxing Moon
Moon Phase: 2nd Qtr. 7:22 PM
Color: White

Moon Sign: Aquarius
Moon enters Pisces 11:14 AM
Incense: Hyacinth

27 FRIDAY
Waxing Moon
Moon Phase: 2nd Quarter
Color: Rose

Moon Sign: Pisces
Incense: Lavender

28 SATURDAY
DAY OF SOPHIA (GREEK)
Waxing Moon
Moon Phase: 2nd Quarter
Color: Indigo

Moon Sign: Pisces
Moon enters Aries 3:34 PM
Incense: Musk

Look for our complete line of almanacs, date books and calendars.

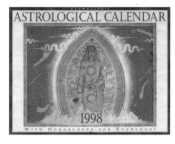

To order your copy today, call
1-800-THE MOON.

Llewellyn Worldwide
P.O. Box 64383, Dept. SK-935
St. Paul, MN 55164-0383

GET 15% OFF YOUR NEXT PURCHASE!

WE WANT TO KNOW ABOUT YOU! Knowing about our audience helps Llewellyn to keep developing quality products with YOU in mind. Please fill out this survey and send it in to receive a catalog and coupon for 15% off your next purchase of Llewellyn products.

Name: _____

Address: _____

City: _____State: _____ Zip: _____

Please check the boxes that apply:

Gender: ☐ Male ☐ Female

Age: ☐ Under 18 yrs old ☐ 18-26 ☐ 27-36
☐ 37-54 ☐ 55-65 ☐ 65+

Marital Status: ☐ Single ☐ Married
☐ Divorced ☐ Other

Do you have children? ☐ Yes ☐ No

Income: ☐ less than $15,000 ☐ $15,000-20,000
☐ $20,000-30,000 ☐ $30,000-40,000
☐ $40,000-50,000 ☐ $50,000+

Where did you purchase this product? ☐ Independent bookstore
☐ Chain bookstore ☐ Newsstand
☐ Mail order ☐ Other_____

What attracted you to this product? (choose all that apply):
☐ Interested in subject/content ☐ Artwork
☐ Friend's recommendation ☐ Gift for someone
☐ Received as a gift ☐ Buy it every year
☐ First time purchased ☐ Book review

How many books do you purchase a year? _____

What subject matter would you like to see more of?_____

We welcome your suggestions and content ideas. Write to: Attn: Annuals Editor, Llewellyn Worldwide, P.O. Box 64383, St Paul, MN 55164-0383

29 SUNDAY
SONS OF SATURN FESTIVAL (ROMAN)
Waxing Moon
Moon Phase: 2nd Quarter   Moon Sign: Aries
Color: Yellow   Incense: Maple

30 MONDAY
Waxing Moon
Moon Phase: 2nd Quarter   Moon Sign: Aries
Color: Lavender   Moon enters Taurus 4:52 PM
                               Incense: Lilac

NOVEMBER BIRTHSTONES
Ancient: Topaz
Modern: Topaz

NOVEMBER FLOWERS
Chrysanthemums
Dahlias

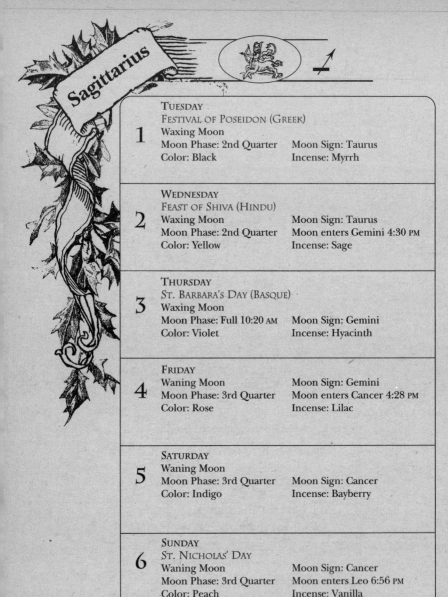

Sagittarius

TUESDAY
FESTIVAL OF POSEIDON (GREEK)
1 Waxing Moon
Moon Phase: 2nd Quarter   Moon Sign: Taurus
Color: Black   Incense: Myrrh

WEDNESDAY
FEAST OF SHIVA (HINDU)
2 Waxing Moon   Moon Sign: Taurus
Moon Phase: 2nd Quarter   Moon enters Gemini 4:30 PM
Color: Yellow   Incense: Sage

THURSDAY
ST. BARBARA'S DAY (BASQUE)
3 Waxing Moon
Moon Phase: Full 10:20 AM   Moon Sign: Gemini
Color: Violet   Incense: Hyacinth

FRIDAY
4 Waning Moon   Moon Sign: Gemini
Moon Phase: 3rd Quarter   Moon enters Cancer 4:28 PM
Color: Rose   Incense: Lilac

SATURDAY
5 Waning Moon
Moon Phase: 3rd Quarter   Moon Sign: Cancer
Color: Indigo   Incense: Bayberry

SUNDAY
ST. NICHOLAS' DAY
6 Waning Moon   Moon Sign: Cancer
Moon Phase: 3rd Quarter   Moon enters Leo 6:56 PM
Color: Peach   Incense: Vanilla

MONDAY
BURNING THE DEVIL (GUATEMALAN)
7 Waning Moon
Moon Phase: 3rd Quarter   Moon Sign: Leo
Color: Silver   Incense: Musk

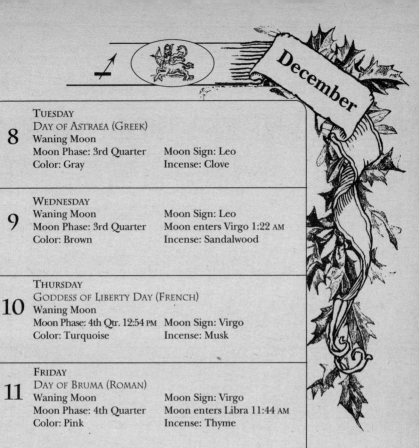

TUESDAY

8

DAY OF ASTRAEA (GREEK)
Waning Moon
Moon Phase: 3rd Quarter   Moon Sign: Leo
Color: Gray   Incense: Clove

WEDNESDAY

9

Waning Moon   Moon Sign: Leo
Moon Phase: 3rd Quarter   Moon enters Virgo 1:22 AM
Color: Brown   Incense: Sandalwood

THURSDAY

10

GODDESS OF LIBERTY DAY (FRENCH)
Waning Moon
Moon Phase: 4th Qtr. 12:54 PM   Moon Sign: Virgo
Color: Turquoise   Incense: Musk

FRIDAY

11

DAY OF BRUMA (ROMAN)
Waning Moon   Moon Sign: Virgo
Moon Phase: 4th Quarter   Moon enters Libra 11:44 AM
Color: Pink   Incense: Thyme

SATURDAY

12

SADA (ZOROASTRIAN)
Waning Moon
Moon Phase: 4th Quarter   Moon Sign: Libra
Color: Blue   Incense: Honeysuckle

SUNDAY

13

ST. LUCY'S DAY (SWEDISH)
Waning Moon
Moon Phase: 4th Quarter   Moon Sign: Libra
Color: Yellow   Incense: Cedar

MONDAY

14

CHANUKKAH BEGINS (JEWISH)
FESTIVAL OF NOSTRADAMUS (FRENCH)
Waning Moon   Moon Sign: Libra
Moon Phase: 4th Quarter   Moon enters Scorpio 12:17 AM
Color: White   Incense: Frankincense

Sagittarius

15 TUESDAY
FESTIVAL OF ALCYONE (GREEK)
Waning Moon
Moon Phase: 4th Quarter   Moon Sign: Scorpio
Color: Red   Incense: Ginger

16 WEDNESDAY
Waning Moon   Moon Sign: Scorpio
Moon Phase: 4th Quarter   Moon enters Sagittarius 12:47 PM
Color: White   Incense: Myrrh

17 THURSDAY
FEAST OF BABAL-UAIYE (SANTERIA)
Waning Moon
Moon Phase: 4th Quarter   Moon Sign: Sagittarius
Color: Green   Incense: Thyme

18 FRIDAY
SATURNALIA BEGINS (ROMAN)
Waning Moon   Moon Sign: Sagittarius
Moon Phase: New 5:42 PM   Moon enters Capricorn 11:55 PM
Color: Peach   Incense: Plum

19 SATURDAY
Waxing Moon
Moon Phase: 1st Quarter   Moon Sign: Capricorn
Color: Gray   Incense: Bayberry

20 SUNDAY
MOTHER NIGHT (ODINIST)
Waxing Moon
Moon Phase: 1st Quarter   Moon Sign: Capricorn
Color: Orange   Incense: Vanilla

21 MONDAY
YULE (WINTER SOLSTICE)/CHANUKKAH ENDS (JEWISH))
Waxing Moon   Moon Sign: Capricorn
Moon Phase: 1st Quarter   Sun enters Capricorn 8:56 PM
Color: Lavender   Moon enters Aquarius 9:17 AM
Incense: Lilac

22 TUESDAY
PRYDERI'S BIRTHDAY (CELTIC)
Waxing Moon
Moon Phase: 1st Quarter   Moon Sign: Aquarius
Color: Black   Incense: Almond

23 WEDNESDAY
ACCA LARENTIS (ROMAN)
Waxing Moon
Moon Phase: 1st Quarter   Moon Sign: Aquarius
Color: Peach   Moon enters Pisces 4:45 PM
   Incense: Patchouli

24 THURSDAY
CHRISTMAS EVE
Waxing Moon
Moon Phase: 1st Quarter   Moon Sign: Pisces
Color: Violet   Incense: Lavender

25 FRIDAY
CHRISTMAS DAY
Waxing Moon   Moon Sign: Pisces
Moon Phase: 1st Quarter   Moon enters Aries 10:04 PM
Color: Rose   Incense: Vanilla

26 SATURDAY
KWANZAA BEGINS (AFRICAN-AMERICAN)
Waxing Moon
Moon Phase: 2nd Qtr. 5:46 AM   Moon Sign: Aries
Color: Brown   Incense: Pine

27 SUNDAY
FEAST OF ST. JOHN THE EVANGELIST
Waxing Moon
Moon Phase: 2nd Quarter   Moon Sign: Aries
Color: Gold   Incense: Frankincense

28 MONDAY
BAIRNS' DAY (SCOTTISH)
Waxing Moon   Moon Sign: Aries
Moon Phase: 2nd Quarter   Moon enters Taurus 1:05 AM
Color: Gray   Incense: Bayberry

TUESDAY
BIRTHDAY OF RA (EGYPTIAN)

29 Waxing Moon
Moon Phase: 2nd Quarter   Moon Sign: Taurus
Color: Red   Incense: Sage

WEDNESDAY
ISIS' BIRTHDAY (EGYPTIAN)

30 Waxing Moon   Moon Sign: Taurus
Moon Phase: 2nd Quarter   Moon enters Gemini 2:22 AM
Color: Yellow   Incense: Patchouli

THURSDAY
NEW YEAR'S EVE

31 Waxing Moon
Moon Phase: 2nd Quarter   Moon Sign: Gemini
Color: Green   Incense: Cedar

DECEMBER BIRTHSTONES
Ancient: Ruby
Modern: Bloodstone

DECEMBER FLOWERS
Narcissus
Holly

THE SUMMER SOLSTICE: A GARDEN OF DELIGHTS

BY SIRONA KNIGHT

Last fall, as I sat with my knees in the dirt, digging, my five-year-old son came up and asked, "Mommy, why are you pulling up the flowers you planted?" I could see by the look in his eyes he could not fathom why I would dig up something that I had spent so much time last spring planting. While sitting in the stone circle that was now covered by the spent stalks and wicker baskets filled with corms and seeds where last summer at the solstice a rainbow of gladioluses and a golden ray of sunflowers flourished in splendor, I had to stop and think about what I was doing. My son's question sparked something inside of me, and I started thinking of how each thing we do is part of a pattern, which in turn is part of an ever-larger pattern. I reflected on the natural cycles and patterns of the seasons, and how my intention through my actions influenced these patterns, and at the same time set up new ones. By collecting and storing the corms and seeds in the fall, I set up a pattern where these seeds can be planted in the spring so as to reach their time of brilliance during Midsummer, precisely at the time of the summer solstice.

In Celtic mythology, the god of the rising Sun, Belenus, rules from Yule at the winter solstice to Letha's Day at the summer solstice, when the days grow longer and the Sun stronger. Lugh, the god of the setting Sun, rules from the summer solstice to the winter solstice, when the days grow shorter and darkness of night and

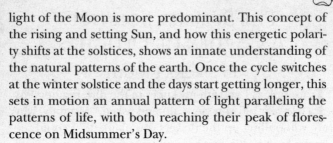

light of the Moon is more predominant. This concept of the rising and setting Sun, and how this energetic polarity shifts at the solstices, shows an innate understanding of the natural patterns of the earth. Once the cycle switches at the winter solstice and the days start getting longer, this sets in motion an annual pattern of light paralleling the patterns of life, with both reaching their peak of florescence on Midsummer's Day.

The summer solstice is the realization of the patterns we have planted and nourished during the year. In this sense the summer solstice is all of our intentions and desires manifested. This is why so many traditions stress being clear with your intention as a key for getting what you expect and desire in life. A practical example of this is seen in the Celtic Druid Tradition in the making of the pentacle.

After being initiated into the Gwyddonic Druid Tradition, you become a First Degree student, working your way through five magical works. These works are intended to teach the initiates various skills on their way to becoming Third Degree Craftmasters. The second magical work initiates perform is called "making a pentacle," where they learn to set up a pattern, and practice the steps for making the pattern come to fruition.

The first step in making a pentacle is to be clear in your intention or expectation as to the purpose and eventual manifested form of the pattern. In terms of a garden, you might ask yourself what you expect from your garden. Whether food, cut flowers, or a secret place to hide away, your expectation plays heavily into what you should plant in your garden. Once you are clear about your intention, you can then begin outlining the five steps involved in making the pentacle or pattern. With the garden the steps are: 1) collecting and storing the seeds, 2) tilling the soil, 3) planting the seeds, 4) watering and caring for the plants, and 5) harvesting the garden when it comes to fruition.

When doing a pentacle, you assign personal symbols for each of the steps, and then use the symbols to further infuse the steps into your awareness, enhancing the chances for a successful pattern. Once you have outlined the five steps of the pentacle, you merge with oneness to bring your pattern into manifested reality. By being one with each seed you plant, and aiding the natural cycles, your garden on the summer solstice can match the intentions and desires you had when you first planted it.

The final step in making a pentacle, creating a pattern, or planting a garden is to actively do each of the steps necessary to make it happen. Our patterns in life, from work habits to relationships, are just like gardens in that they reflect our intentions toward life and our participation. Without planning and effort, we become, at best, victims of our own randomness. You need to be specific, focusing your intention on the successful completion of the chosen pattern at hand.

This past spring, my young son helped me plant the bulbs and seeds we gathered in the fall. As the weeks passed and the little sprouts grew larger, I could see his understanding of the cycles and patterns of life were increasing, as was my own perception. By the summer solstice, everything seemed to erupt with life, and everywhere I looked, I saw the fruition of the patterns we had planted. Standing in the middle of this garden of delights, I reveled in my connection to these patterns and to the Great Goddess, the Mother of all things.

Planting an Enchanting Sunflower Circle

By Silver RavenWolf

Here's how to create a perfect place for fairies to romp and play. You will need sunflower seeds, tall wooden or bamboo stakes (sunflowers can grow six feet high), and a very sunny spot. Sunflowers do not grow well in shady areas.

If you like, you can begin growing your sunflowers indoors, beginning a month before planting time for your area. Purchase potting soil and a little fertilizer and plant in small pots. However, if you are not the indoor gardener type, don't despair. On a nice sunny day, after the frost is a memory, take your seeds, your athame, a cord (long cord for a big circle, small cord for a little circle) small stakes to mark, a watering can, fertilizer, and a digging stick (with a point on it), and march out to your back yard.

Mark the Circle

Determine where the center of your circle will be. Put a loop in the cord at one end. Put the loop around your athame and stick the athame in the ground at the center of your circle. Pull the cord taut and decide how wide you want your circle to be. Using the taut cord, mark out your circle with the small stakes. (Tent states will do as this is only temporary.)

Plant the Seeds

At inteverals of your choice (about eight inches is good) dig a small hole two inches deep and scatter two seeds in the hole. Cover with dirt. Water with a mixture of fertilizer and water. (Follow the directions on the back of the fertilizer product.) Complete your circle by repeating the process at eight-inch intervals. Note that sunflowers are annual plants. They will grow all season long and then die. They will not come up the next year. Cuttings of human hair can be scattered around the base of the plants to keep small animals from eating them.

Caring for the Plants

As your plants grow, you will need to thin them out. Do it slowly, a few at a time, until you have a strong, perfect circle.

Next comes the task of staking them to keep them from bending too far or breaking in a bad storm. Try not to hit the root system as you put the stakes in. You can tie the plant to the stakes using products from a nursery or gardening supply stores. If you can't afford that, don't worry, use strips of colored cloth. As your plants grow, continue to tie them loosely to the stakes (not so loose they flop around but not so tight that the cloth cuts into them). *Editor's note: You may also put the stakes in at the time of planting so that the roots will grow around them and you won't need to worry about disturbing them later.*

Magic

Write a ritual for both planting and harvesting. Remember to ask the plant's permission before cutting and leave a gift at your final harvest. Cut the stalk at one to two inches from the head. Tie a string around the stalk and hang the head in a dry place. Sunflower heads are best harvested when they are half open for magical and decorative use. Leave the heads on the plants until all the petals fall off to harvest seeds for the following year.

Decorations

Get creative. Line the outside of the circle with colorful rocks and make your own rock garden, perhaps with a tier of marigolds outside of the sunflowers. Plants that climb, like morning glories or Moon flowers, can be planted on the outside of your circle and trained to grow up the sunflower stalks for a magical hideaway.

THE BUFFALO DANCE

BY MARGUERITE ELSBETH

The People sit in lawn chairs, wearing brightly colored blankets or flowery woolen shawls to keep out the winter cold. They speak softly in the ancient language of this Pueblo Indian tribe, or wait silently for the Buffalo Dance to begin.

Shivering and expectant, I sit among them. A desert wind kicks up air spirits and clay dust. Singers and drummers move slowly from within the kiva, the tribal place of emergence, on to the plaza. They leave room for the dancers, who follow through the narrow dirt pathway lined with adobe houses.

The dancers trace the footsteps of their ancestors, remembering. A shaman-dancer leads the way in an antlered headdress, his loincloth etched with symbols. Red fox and coyote tails adorn his waist, and evergreen boughs circle his wrists and ankles. He shakes a turtle-shell rattle to alert the frozen sky and sleeping earth to the presence of the dancers. A young Indian woman, her long dark hair flowing over a simple black dress embroidered with clouds, lightning bolts, rain, and corn symbols, dances at his side. She is the Animal Mother. A line of hunter-dancers guided by men in buffalo headdresses follows the shaman and Animal Mother into the clearing, cedar bows poised, eyes searching for signs of the life-giving spirit animals.

The Animal Mother passes through the line of hunters, her downcast eyes supplicating the earth. The evergreen boughs she holds in each hand invite the earth, and all creatures and things, to rise up and meet the sky. She stands facing the shaman, who shakes his rattle, mirroring her movements. Earth and sky meet in the middle, and the animal-dancers—elk, deer, ram—enter the plaza hunched on walking sticks, their antlered heads bobbing and feathered hindquarters swaying to the steady beat of the drum.

The hunters train their bows on their prey, but the animal-dancers bolt with a jingling of bells, taking shelter in the crowd. Led by the Animal Mother and shaman-dancer, the hunters circle the plaza in an undulating spiral dance.

The Buffalo Dance is a purposeful waking dream: dance the hunt so that the animals will come and the people will eat. The power of sensation, sound, and movement is strong, intricate, simple, and archetypal—I might be watching any tribe of any culture dancing for nourishment and sustenance on any continent anywhere on the planet. Still, the dance is fundamentally the same. Indeed, tribal people the world over dance for any number of reasons—initiation and puberty, courtship, mating and fertility, or dancing for animal guardians, healers, and helpers.

Tribal dance causes me to see life as a continuum, an unbroken circle, a spiral spinning around the spirit world and this one. The dancer calls to the spirits to gather insight, obtain knowledge, to communicate and receive vital information, honor the ancestors, and to retrieve, cure, and guide the magical journey of the soul.

Let us return to our tribal roots. Dance for the Great Spirit and Mother Earth, the animals, trees, stones and primal forces, our desires, our memories, our friends, and our foes. Perhaps the spirits will come out to dance with us also.

ROCKHOUNDING

BY MARGUERITE ELSBETH

Crystals, gems, and minerals grow wild, in caves, quarries, old mining sites, and river beds. A journey to find the perfect stone can lift us out of ordinary reality into nature's realm. Rockhounding is harmless, provided it's done with respect for Mother Earth. Little is required for a solitary mining adventure; only a few tools for gathering, labeling, and identifying specimens are necessary, along with careful attention to weather, drinking water, snakes, and biting insects, of course!

SEEKING THE STONE SPIRITS

Choose a stone that attracts your attention in a natural way. Gather information about the stone spirit you seek, as some stones need special handling when found.

Discover where the stone you have chosen to mine is located. Make arrangements to visit the area for a day or overnight trip, and find out whether or not a permit is required.

Gather up the things you will need. Essential items are a hammer or geologist's pick, a small chisel, a prybar or crowbar, a pocket knife, a stiff brush, work gloves, an old newspaper, and a carrying bag. Crystal mining requires protective glasses. It shatters like glass and cuts like a razor. Also include tobacco and coins, as the Earth spirits enjoy a good smoke, and coins are associated with earth in many magical systems.

Once you arrive at the site, sit on the ground and meditate on what you are about to do. Speak with the spirits of the place, letting them know why you have come. Thank them for sharing their space with you. Smoke or leave a tobacco offering on the ground where you sit.

Now, ask Mother Earth's permission to take one of her stone people home with you. Look at the clouds, listen to the wind, the birds, and critters, and track your bodily sensations for the answer. If the omens are gentle, it is okay to harvest the stone. If the

Sun moves behind a cloud, the wind gusts up, or your body hurts after you ask the question, wait a while, then ask again. Mother Earth may need time to become accustomed to the idea.

Leave coins in the mine or cave entrance, toss coins into the river bed, or wherever your stone is to be found, as soon as you receive Mother Earth's permission.

Set to harvesting. Talk to the stone while you work, letting it know that you have come as a friend and protector. Place tobacco in the hole once the stone has been removed from its nest.

Leave the digging site immediately, and examine the stone carefully, noting its color, temperature, shape, and the sensation it produces as you turn it over in your hand, just like a psychometrist does to evaluate unseen radiations and impressions.

Ask the stone to tell you its message and to grant permission to use it in the future. The answers will arise through your body, the environment, or the stone itself, if you listen.

Thank the rock spirit and Mother Earth before making your way back to ordinary reality.

CRYSTAL ENCHANTMENT

By D. J. Conway

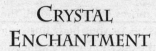

Crystals have fascinated humans for many thousands of years. These stones were so strange, unique, and powerful that early humans called them "frozen or petrified ice" or "earth stars." It took only a short time for certain skilled members of a culture to learn that crystals could be very helpful in day-to-day living.

The early healers used crystals to amplify their personal power to correct illnesses. By rubbing crystals on the diseased area or setting several stones in certain patterns on the body of the sick person, they could reverse, halt, or heal a great many illnesses.

Spiritual leaders discovered that the crystal could enable them to see into the past, present, and future. Seeing into the past, for example, helped them to pass judgment on disputed events, recall forgotten information, and correctly add to their people's history. By being aware of what occurred in the present and future, they could help avoid possible troubles and natural disasters, and foresee dangers. Both of these methods of using crystal are still in practice today.

It has become commonplace for people to own crystals, even if they haven't the faintest desire or idea how to use them. Other people won't have a crystal around, as they think their use is evil. Crystals aren't good or evil, in the terms we think of such abstract concepts, but are merely a superb source of power in its purest form.

Although the most commonly imagined shape for crystal is the crystal ball, the shape and size of a crystal is no indication of its possible use. Many people, however, shy away from using crystals for divination because they think only a crystal ball will work for this. Contrary to some writings, a tiny piece of inexpensive crystal will work just as well as a crystal ball, especially if it has at least one smooth edge. The crystal not only acts as a mirror into the future, but it also amplifies personal psychic abilities.

The trick in learning to use a crystal for divination is to discover where your abilities lie. Don't assume that you must see something in the crystal with your physical eyes for it to be working. A crystal may intensify your intuitive hunches, give you inner visions when you close your eyes, bring on prophetic dreams, or drop information directly into your conscious mind.

Another misconception is that the most powerful crystals are double-terminated, or have two pointed ends. These are usually very expensive, more so than the single-terminated ones. Each crystal has its own individual power, which has nothing to do with pointed ends.

There is also a great debate over natural versus manmade crystals. This is actually a matter of choice and checkbook. Personally, I've found little difference. All crystals, regardless of being manmade or natural, have to be cleansed after you purchase them to get rid of the vibrations of everyone who has handled them. You should also hold each crystal before buying to determine if the vibration feels right for you.

Crystals have a much wider use than many people have imagined. They can act as filters for negativity simply by hanging in an environment. A note of caution, though: It isn't wise to have a crystal hanging where sunlight can pass through it. Crystals can act as magnifiers and start fires in cars and homes this way. Also, sunlight is detrimental to a crystal's power, where moonlight enhances it.

If you are new to the use of crystals or are looking for new ways to use them, here are a few suggestions. Try setting five crystals (of whatever shape) in a semicircle when you use tarot cards, runes, etc. By placing them above your reading area in this manner, you are affecting both the turn of the cards and your own intuition. The same method will work when you are doing a meditation.

If you are having difficulty with a house plant, put a crystal in the pot temporarily. It charges the soil with healing energy, which naturally affects the plant. I'm not a believer in permanently burying crystals or other stones.

Such stones have a finite replacement supply, and we shouldn't be wasting them.

To amplify any magical working, place crystals around your altar and/or around your ritual area. I've found that five crystals placed on an altar in a rough pentagram shape can increase the raised power by as much as 75 percent. For around the edges of a circle, thirteen crystals set equal distance apart provide an impregnable wall against negatives, especially when working protection rituals.

Even broken pieces of crystal are usable. This breakage sometimes happens when they are accidentally dropped, or the rough edges break from use. Use these pieces in rattles or make a stress-bowl.

A stress-bowl is simply a small bowl filled with tiny pieces of crystal or other helpful stones. When you need to relax, run your fingers through these stones and feel the tensions fade away. It is a good idea to have a cover for this bowl, or children and pets may have them spread all over your floor in a short time.

Crystals will also amplify the power of other stones. To be certain what powers you are enhancing, read up on the other stones before deliberately using them with a crystal.

If you have a list of goals you want to achieve, put this list under a pyramid along with a crystal. This pyramid can be made out of wood or, if you are as unskilled as I am with a saw, cut one out of cardboard and tape the sides together. Align one flat side of the pyramid to the north, and put your list underneath it, with a crystal on top of the list. To enhance the process, you can put a picture of yourself and/or your family on top of the list. Be sure this is set in a place where it won't be moved, bumped, or tampered with. I've used the same cardboard pyramid-crystal technique for several years and had excellent results. Every three or four months, I cross off goals that have been reached or make a new list.

Crystals can be used in endless ways. Let your imagination soar, and see what personal methods you can discover.

GREEK ORACLE SITES

BY deTRACI REGULA

The clear light of the Sun and the fresh, flowing air of Greece make it easy to believe in divine presences, and perhaps this is why Greece was and is home to so many oracle sites of various gods and goddesses. The veil between the material and the spiritual is thin throughout the land, but certain sites have been revered for thousands of years as places where communion with the divine—whether with the bright king of the sky, Apollo, or the dark lord of the underworld, Pluto—is easier to achieve.

THE NEKROMANTICON OF PERGA

There are several sites in Greece where Pluto is believed to have abducted Persephone, and these sites are considered to be openings to the underworld where consultations with the divinities of the dead, or the deceased souls themselves, can be obtained. In Northwest Greece, the Nekromanticon, or oracle of the dead, served as the local site of the abduction of Persephone, where the ground opened up to allow Pluto to ride out and snatch her up, plunging the earth into an unending winter as Demeter, the mother of Persephone, searched for her daughter.

The Nekromanticon is located inland from the coast, at what used to be the far end of a marshy swamp fed by the River Styx. The souls of the dead were believed to be ferried from the coast to the Nekromanticon. A ferryman was necessary since the marshy lands were filled with clogged water passages and an unguided soul might never reach the dubious pleasures of Pluto's kingdom.

Today, the Nekromanticon looks like a small castle of the dead, and would easily serve as a horror or vampire movie location. From a short distance, the huge, carefully fitted stones, covered with moss and lichens, give off a suitably forbidding aura. Entering the site, the visitor follows the same labyrinthine pathway that once was used to

confuse supplicants and those undergoing initiation into the mysteries of Persephone and Pluto. An open, grass-choked courtyard room contains a rickety metal stairway, seemingly leading straight down into the ground. Some of the metal steps are rusted through, as if even metal here falls under the domain of the lord of death and the underworld. Reaching the bottom step, visitors find themselves in a vaulted cavern. Above, there are stone archways holding up the ceiling, but the floor beneath is moist, wet earth, fed by a stream of the River Styx itself. A few lightbulbs, a concession to modern visitors, only serve to throw shadows and make the cavern's darkness less penetrable by keeping the eyes from adjusting to the dim light dribbling in from the stairwell. Here the initiates were brought, after being kept for many days in complete darkness, to participate in a ritual or to make their request for a consultation with the dead. At a key moment, a stone would be removed from the ceiling by a priest outside the chamber, and a laser-like beam of sunlight would fall on the initiates, filling them with ecstasy or blinding them with terror.

The cavern, which once stretched much farther, now ends in a wall. When the site was reconsecrated to the Christian faith, a little chapel was placed directly above the most powerful portion of the Nekromanticon, and the wall was built to contain the forces neatly under the chapel precinct. Blocked and denied, the mysteries still continue. There are no images of Pluto or Persephone remaining, but a huge toad lives, neck pulsing, in the far corner of the cavern. Unafraid of visitors, kept company itself by a large spider higher on the wall, this representative of the chthonic forces seems to announce that nothing is ever destroyed, only rechanneled.

Outside and above, the little chapel built to tame these unruly underworld deities sits, slowly decaying. Even here, darkness touches the walls. At the far end of the chapel, the visitor's eye is drawn to a large niche containing a brightly painted, round portrait of Jesus. Surrounding and containing this image, invisible except at certain angles, is the Black Madonna, stretching out her hands, gathering all

to her dark breast. These unusual images of (supposedly) Mary are often found in chapels and churches built over old temple sites, particularly those of Persephone, Isis, and other ancient goddesses with underworld aspects or portrayed with dark images. Visitors report that while looking at the wall paintings, the numbers of the candles burning in the brass quiver by the door will change, added or subtracted by invisible hands, and offerings of coins will rearrange themselves. The chapel is only reached by a narrow creaky catwalk in full view of the rest of the Nekromanticon, so it's unlikely another visitor could come and go so swiftly, completely unobserved. The unseen remain active, no matter what names they are called.

Dodona: Oracle of Zeus and Dione

Dodona is a high mountain valley surrounded by still higher peaks, reached by curving, steep roads. Across from the entrance to the site, tall trees seem to generate their own wind to speak by and in ancient times, the wind through the trees was used as a method of divination. The priestesses and priests would add to the music of the wind by hanging copper vessels in the trees, presumably to give more detail to their divinations. Dodona is believed to be the most ancient site of habitation in this region of northwestern mainland Greece, and a few minutes spent in the remains of this ancient oracle city gives the first oracular answer. You *know* why this site was considered sacred. Its fertility and beauty washes over the visitor. Even in late autumn, Dodona speaks of springtime. Flowers of all kinds press up through the green grass, kept moist by the mountain dew and unseen springs.

Dodona was sacred to Dione, a goddess of the earth, the sky, and of springs. Her name means "goddess of the bright sky," but the joy of this mountain retreat is perhaps due to the influence of Aphrodite, of whom Dione was considered to be a form, or, in one version, the mother of the goddess of love herself. She was joined in this site by Zeus, apparently first in his aspect as a god of springs and water. The knowledge of oracles was supposed to have been brought to Dodona

by a dove from Egypt, leading some to suspect that an Egyptian priestess may have once traveled to Dodona. Though the dove is associated with Dodona, one of the most beautiful artifacts found here is a verdigris bronze eagle, a symbol of Zeus that is curiously gentle for an eagle. Perhaps it is a memory of its predecessor, the ancient dove.

Supplicants at the oracle inscribed small lead strips with their questions, poignant in their simplicity and timelessness. One man asks if a child is his; a young woman asks which of two suitors she should marry. Another question is more curious to our modern ears. The querent asks the oracle to please tell him which god in the pantheon he should worship.

By the two ancient temple sites of Dione, the oracle of Zeus surrounds an oak tree planted by archeologists in memory of the ancient oracle oak long ago cut down. Nearby, the remains of a shrine to Heracles competes with a church built, as usual, to claim new converts by creating a house of worship at an ancient accustomed site.

DELPHI

The modern town of Delphi lies only a couple of hours away from Athens by bus or car, so the days when a trip to the oracle took extensive planning and weeks or months of travel are long in the past. After a drive through agricultural country, past Gypsy camps and cotton fields, the road begins to climb. Suddenly, in a high pass, Delphi emerges, only a few feet from the narrow modern road.

In modern terms, Delphi is an energy vortex spot, and the power is tangible. In ancient times, the elaborately carved *omphalos,* or navel stone, marked the spot of the twirling earth chakra. Now the original has been removed to the museum, and only a blank, roughly formed, egg-shaped stone marks the spot. No matter. To the sensitive, the energy is still spinning and can be felt as a pulsing, rotating wheel emanating from the site of the substitute omphalos stone.

Apollo is said to have slain the dragon or snake occupying this site, and the remains of the large temple dedicated to him overlook

the Rock of the Pythoness, where the oracles were delivered. While Apollo's conquest of the snake here has been offered as evidence of the triumph of a male patriarchal god over an earlier female earth goddess, the story may instead be a metaphor for the conquest and control of the powerful energies of the vortex and energy lines emanating from it. Ley lines, the "power lines" of the earth energies, are often represented as masculine dragons or snakes. The female powers are also enshrined at Delphi. The name itself means womb, recognizing the vortex of power at this site and its equivalent in women. It is said that the pythoness, or oracle-priestess, inhaled mysterious vapors from the earth to induce her trance state, though no evidence of this has been discovered, and even ancient visitors were unable to discern the source of these alleged vapors. More likely, it is the "emanations" of the vortex and ley lines themselves that provided her with the power to make her pronouncements. In the earliest records, the pythoness was a young girl. Later, after a beautiful young priestess was abducted from the temple, only women past menopause were employed as pythonesses.

Beside the site, open to the road, is the Castalian Spring. Castalia was said to be a nymph who drowned herself in the spring rather than submit to the embraces of Apollo. Bathing the face in the waters is said to make one beautiful and youthful, a belief that is still held by inhabitants of the town nearby. Much of the spring is now off limits to visitors, because the steep canyon walls throw down rocks and stones on the heads of the unwary. Perhaps Castalia has had enough of purely profane visitors, though the spring waters comfort and cool those who approach with reverence.

In winter, the charming modern town of Delphi assumes another guise. The ruins are capped with ice and snow as a different, but perhaps no less determined, pilgrimage takes place, and nearby ski slopes are covered with those seeking the answers to life in the form of powder snow instead of trance-possessed oracles.

TATTWAS

BY JIM GARRISON

The Tattwas are an ancient set of elemental symbols originally developed in India. Simple, yet elegant, the Tattwas were adopted by theosophists and Western occultists, who recognized their potentials as keys to unlocking and expressing the elemental forces of nature. Learning the Tattwas is a very easy, very visual way to decode the more esoteric concepts of Western ceremonial magic.

There are five elements at the core of the Tattwa system: fire/Tejas, a red triangle; water/Vayu, a silver crescent; air/Apas, a blue circle; earth/Prithivi, a yellow square; and spirit/Akasha, a black or violet egg or oval.

These five elements then are intermixed to create a set of twenty-five Tattwas. A red triangle within a silver crescent would be the fire of water, or the Tejas of Vayu, and so on. These elemental pairings all are expressions of fundamental forces and essential qualities that make up the phenomenal world. By meditation on each Tattwa, a student can discover how each element interacts with the other elements. Tattwas are distinct and powerful keys to the development and mastery of visualization.

One way to begin working with Tattwas is to build up a system of correspondences for each Tattwa by listing everything you can think of that could be an expression of each elemental combination. Make a list of all twenty-five Tattwas and keep adding entries to each Tattwa as you come up with them. You may decide to focus on a particular Tattwa each morning to think about and look for the particular things that might go with it. This list will help you to personalize your understanding of the Tattwas, but the real key to the Tattwas is in using them. Each Tattwa is like a pure, powerful, uncluttered hieroglyph. Used in place of a word, it magically transmits an entire experience.

The ideal method for starting to work with the tattwas is by exploring the ancient technique of *Tratak*—staring, unblinking, at the image so that it "burns" into the retina, and consciousness, and then

using the afterimage to unlock the secrets of the particular element. Tratak, as a means of visualization, when combined with the system of correspondences that you assembled earlier, reveals the hidden language of the symbol.

Another method of working with Tattwas is to use them for scrying—a form of magical meditation that allows the Tattwas to become doorways to the deeper, elemental realms of the universe. Pick any one of the five sets to begin. Get comfortable, relax, slow your breathing down, and let go of all tension. You might play music appropriate to the element being explored, or burn some incense. You might even want to wear clothing the same color as the element. Make the best use of the correspondences you've developed.

Whether or not you prepare sacred space, perform the Lesser Banishing Ritual of the Pentagram, or do something similar is entirely up to you. I recommend doing something, even a token gesture, to establish an atmosphere conducive to spiritual exploration—perhaps a brief prayer or a bit of yoga practice.

Take the Tattwa card you've selected and look at it. Hold it in your hands, or let it rest on the floor or table top before you—whatever is comfortable. With each intake of breath, visualize the symbols on the Tattwa expanding. With each breath, visualize the Tattwa shrinking. Synchronize this expansion and contraction with your breathing. Keep this up for a while, until you feel the Tattwa expand enough that you could fall into it. Once you reach that point, let your perceptions "fall" into the Tattwa, through it into another plane of existence.

When you return to normal consciousness, do something to ground and center yourself once again. Record your impressions and experiences in a journal. After you've gone through each of the twenty-five Tattwas, you'll want to go back over your entries and compare the various scenes/impression/experiences to see what you can discover about the various elemental sub-sets and the whole sequence of Tattwas altogether.

ANCESTRAL PATHS

BY KEN JOHNSON

All over the world, mysterious roads and paths run in perfectly straight lines—sometimes plowing through difficult terrain when easier land lies just to one side, or going up and over mesas and mountains instead of around them. What is their purpose, and why were they constructed with such utter disregard for the practicalities of road-building?

An Englishman named Alfred Watkins, who believed he had discovered straight-line paths dotting the English landscape and connecting the old stone circles in a grand design, called them "ley lines." He theorized that they were the roads of ancient merchants. Other British researchers have concluded that they are energy paths, linking the sacred sites of ancient Britain, or perhaps even serving as roadways for UFOs.

There are straight-line roads on the European continent as well, and these have given us a hint as to their ultimate meaning. In Holland, such roads were once known as "pathways of the dead," and often led to cemeteries. It was once a common European belief that the souls of the dead traveled along straight lines—as when that procession of spirits called the Wild Hunt came swooping through the villages, causing joy to some and terror to others, dancing through the sky to the North Star, as well as upon the earth. Those who followed the Wild Hunt, the medieval Witches, also traveled in straight lines—up a chimney or riding on a broomstick—to join their departed friends.

No wonder that Chinese geomancers or feng shui men prefer curved lines to straight ones! According to

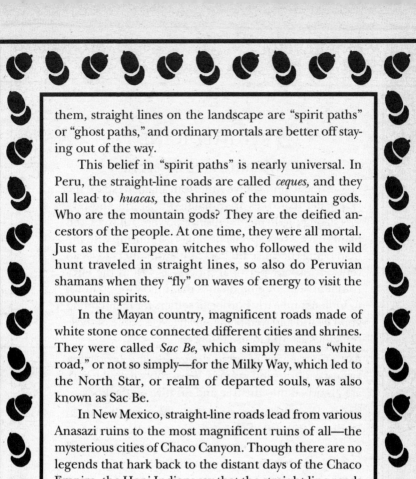

them, straight lines on the landscape are "spirit paths" or "ghost paths," and ordinary mortals are better off staying out of the way.

This belief in "spirit paths" is nearly universal. In Peru, the straight-line roads are called *ceques,* and they all lead to *huacas,* the shrines of the mountain gods. Who are the mountain gods? They are the deified ancestors of the people. At one time, they were all mortal. Just as the European witches who followed the wild hunt traveled in straight lines, so also do Peruvian shamans when they "fly" on waves of energy to visit the mountain spirits.

In the Mayan country, magnificent roads made of white stone once connected different cities and shrines. They were called *Sac Be*, which simply means "white road," or not so simply—for the Milky Way, which led to the North Star, or realm of departed souls, was also known as Sac Be.

In New Mexico, straight-line roads lead from various Anasazi ruins to the most magnificent ruins of all—the mysterious cities of Chaco Canyon. Though there are no legends that hark back to the distant days of the Chaco Empire, the Hopi Indians say that the straight-line roads are "ancestor paths," used for ritual rather than for practical purposes.

Rather than embodying the magic of a single culture or people, the straight-line roads are part of a common human heritage that resonates with some of the oldest spiritual beliefs of all—reverence for the spirits of our ancestors, and a willingness to walk with them on the North Star Road.

Tree Medicine

By Marguerite Elsbeth

Euuropean and Native American shamans share the belief that trees are inhabited by spirits and possess strong medicine or curative powers. All trees and plants have a very special healing relationship with human beings because they act as natural filters to clean refuse from our personal sphere, as well as the environment. The tree medicines that follow were known to Indians and early European settlers for maintaining good health and well-being on all levels. Some of these remedies are still in use today.

ASH brings peace of mind, longevity, and protection against ruptures and wounds. Warts rubbed on the bark are absorbed into the tree and dissolve on the body.

BEECH trees balance mental health as well as heal frostbite, skin inflammations, hives, swellings, and infertility. The future may be divined in the smoke of beech branches thrown into a fire.

BIRCH calms the mind, gives beauty, and guards crops and cattle. The bark cures wounds, burns, ringworm, and ulcers. An honored branch thrown into a stream brings rain.

CEDAR cleanses negative atmospheres. The boiled bark makes a good astringent and purgative. Cedar smoke brings good dreams.

COTTONWOOD is intelligent and provides helpful medicine in most matters. Talk and listen to cottonwood when seeking a solution to troubles.

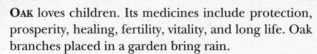

Oak loves children. Its medicines include protection, prosperity, healing, fertility, vitality, and long life. Oak branches placed in a garden bring rain.

Sassafrass medicine eases problems involving the teeth, eyes, and digestive system. Prosperity results when money is buried near the roots of this tree.

Pines are messengers to the Otherworld. The cones symbolize fertility and abundance. Sit under a pine to recharge depleted energy, especially in winter.

Willow aids in spirit communication, eases labor pains, and gives vital energy to the sick and aged. Burned alone or mixed with cedar, sage, and sweetgrass, willow smoke soothes and guides the souls of the dead.

Tree Medicine for Clearing Negativity

Find a private space out of doors where there are many trees. Select a tree from the above list or one that seems special to you. (If you do not have access to an outdoor area, use a house plant.) Speak to it and ask permission to give it all the negativity you have gathered in your physical, emotional, mental, and spiritual bodies.

Beginning at the top of your head, scrape the heel (the pinky side) of your right hand down the left side of your body, ending at your feet. Again, scrape your left hand down the right side of your body. Now, rub the heels of both hands on the trunk of the tree, thus releasing all the toxins gathered in your hands. Likewise, scrape the front and back of your body and give the toxic residue to the tree. When you are finished, thank the tree. Watch how strong and fast it grows!

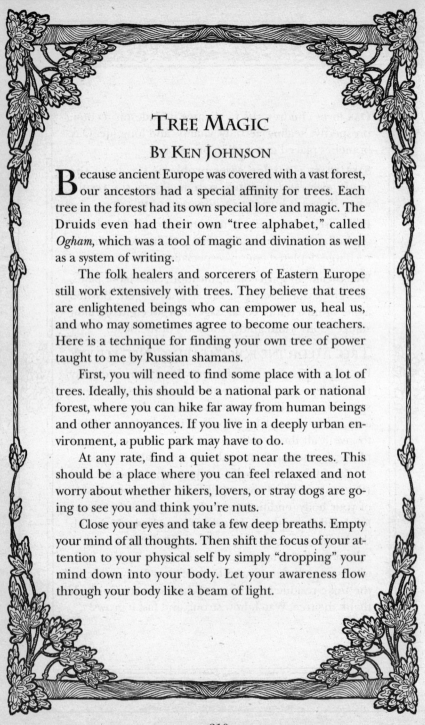

TREE MAGIC

BY KEN JOHNSON

Because ancient Europe was covered with a vast forest, our ancestors had a special affinity for trees. Each tree in the forest had its own special lore and magic. The Druids even had their own "tree alphabet," called *Ogham,* which was a tool of magic and divination as well as a system of writing.

The folk healers and sorcerers of Eastern Europe still work extensively with trees. They believe that trees are enlightened beings who can empower us, heal us, and who may sometimes agree to become our teachers. Here is a technique for finding your own tree of power taught to me by Russian shamans.

First, you will need to find some place with a lot of trees. Ideally, this should be a national park or national forest, where you can hike far away from human beings and other annoyances. If you live in a deeply urban environment, a public park may have to do.

At any rate, find a quiet spot near the trees. This should be a place where you can feel relaxed and not worry about whether hikers, lovers, or stray dogs are going to see you and think you're nuts.

Close your eyes and take a few deep breaths. Empty your mind of all thoughts. Then shift the focus of your attention to your physical self by simply "dropping" your mind down into your body. Let your awareness flow through your body like a beam of light.

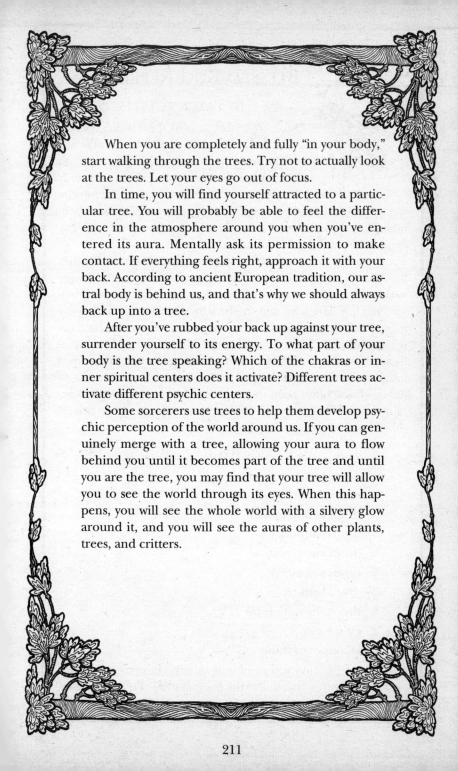

When you are completely and fully "in your body," start walking through the trees. Try not to actually look at the trees. Let your eyes go out of focus.

In time, you will find yourself attracted to a particular tree. You will probably be able to feel the difference in the atmosphere around you when you've entered its aura. Mentally ask its permission to make contact. If everything feels right, approach it with your back. According to ancient European tradition, our astral body is behind us, and that's why we should always back up into a tree.

After you've rubbed your back up against your tree, surrender yourself to its energy. To what part of your body is the tree speaking? Which of the chakras or inner spiritual centers does it activate? Different trees activate different psychic centers.

Some sorcerers use trees to help them develop psychic perception of the world around us. If you can genuinely merge with a tree, allowing your aura to flow behind you until it becomes part of the tree and until you are the tree, you may find that your tree will allow you to see the world through its eyes. When this happens, you will see the whole world with a silvery glow around it, and you will see the auras of other plants, trees, and critters.

BLESSED BUG REPELLENT

BY PATRICIA TELESCO

At the turn of the century, before the advent of chemically enhanced insect repellents, people depended on their knowledge of herbs to prevent not only bug bites, but garden infestation. Generally speaking, herbs with pungent, acrid aromas seem to work best, including thyme, lemon grass, lavender, pennyroyal, eucalyptus, yarrow, basil, and chamomile.

To create your own herbal bug repellent, begin with either fresh herbs or organic herbal extracts. Fresh herbs take longer to decant, and the extracts are stronger and tend to have a better shelf life. The advantage to the whole herb recipe is that the ingredients do not separate after blending. Recipes for both approaches follow. In both instances, alcohol is an optional ingredient, but one that allows you to keep the preparation for a longer period of time without refrigeration. If you choose to delete the alcohol, keep the bug repellent in an air-tight container in the refrigerator until it turns cloudy. After this, it should no longer be used.

OIL RECIPE

8   drops lemon grass oil
4   drops thyme oil
6   drops pennyroyal oil
3   drops lavender oil
8   drops eucalyptus oil
2   drops yarrow oil
2   drops basil oil
3   drops chamomile oil
2   cups water
2   tablespoons vodka

For this preparation you need only mix the ingredients together. Note, however, that due to the combination of oils with water, you will have to shake well before each use because the mixture will separate into its component parts.

Herb Recipe

2	teaspoons lemongrass, chopped
1	teaspoon dried thyme
2	teaspoons pennyroyal leaves
1	teaspoon lavender flower
2	teaspoons dried eucalyptus leaves
½	teaspoon yarrow flowers
½	teaspoon dried basil
¾	teaspoon chamomile flowers
1½	cups water
1	tablespoon vodka

Begin by warming the water and adding the herbs as you might for a tea. Let this simmer until it reduces by ½ cup. If you choose, you may steep the ingredients together in sunlight rather than using the stove. Cool, then add the vodka as a preservative. After cooling you may strain out the herbs, if desired. This is recommended if you do not add the vodka, as the herbs will decay.

Storage

Find a dark, air-tight container to store the blends. This should be kept in a cool area even with the vodka additive, as the longevity of the aroma is hindered by heat (as is that of any herb).

The Spiritual Dimension

For the magical flair, prepare the repellent during a waning to dark Moon (for banishing) or any traditionally "dry" astrological Moon sign (Aries, Gemini, Leo, or Sagittarius). Visualize white light pouring into the repellent as you prepare it, because white is the color of protection.

BUG MAGIC

BY RACHEL RAYMOND

Many works have explored the magical significance of the larger animals, but few discuss the lore of the insect kingdom. Insects may be small, but what they lack in size they make up for in sheer numbers. They achieve amazing feats of strength and skill and were held in high regard by our ancestors.

ANTS

Ants—pound for pound—occupy as much mass on our planets as *Homo sapiens,* which, believe it or not, is a good thing. Ants are the unsung agricultural heroes of our planet. They aerate the soil, remove debris, and do the thousand and one chores required to keep a planet's surface healthy. Their strength and communal spirit is well known.

In dreams they are said to mean activity, health, and community support. They were the only living thing the Greek Goddess Hera left on the island of Aegina after one of Hera's priestesses was betrayed there. The Greek hero Achilles married the Queen of the Myrmidons, who were a goddess-worshipping ant clan.

Ants are sacred to grain and fertility goddesses because they have matriarchal societies, and they are industrious providers of food for their communities. Their movements were often interpreted as divinitory signs and omens. It is considered to be highly unlucky to disturb a colony of ants, and those desperately wishing an antidote to love may consume ant eggs.

BEES

Bees have had a long and rich association with human beings that is reflected in the abundance of bee lore in cultures all over the world. Aphrodite's priestesses were called *mellisae* (bees). These priestesses had male counterparts, called *essenes,* or drones. Honeycombs were considered sacred to Aphrodite because they were six-sided, and Aphrodite's sacred number was six. The Greek agricultural goddess, Demeter, was called "Queen Mother Bee." Bees were revered by goddess-worshipping peoples for their matriarchal society and their key role in the fertility of plants. According to Plato, the

souls of quiet folk come back as bees. To the ancient
Celts, the bees were the birds of God, and were
said to be in communion with the holy spirit.
All societies revered the bee because they are nature's alchemists, and provide products that are impossible to live without.

Consider the importance of honey in a world
without sugar or chemical preservatives. In addition
to acting as a sweetener, honey is a natural preservative,
and could be stored for years without losing its taste or value. It was used in medicinal preparations, both internal and external.
It is one of the four sacred fluids, along with milk, olive oil, and wine.

Bee pollen has been called a "perfect" food. It tastes sweet and
contains all the nutrients needed to sustain human life. It is a proven
remedy for certain kinds of asthma, and is considered to be an overall tonic.

Propolis is a gummy substance that bees use to cement parts of
their hives. It is highly antiseptic and has many medicinal uses. I have
taken it myself for sore throats and found it to be quite helpful.

Humanity's long association with bees has created a rich mine of
bee lore. It is bad luck to buy a bee hive with cash. It is considered far
wiser to barter for your bees. If you want your bees to stay, avoid marital discord, as bees will not stay in a home filled with strife. The bees
like to be informed of any important domestic news. It was common
practice to tell the bees if anyone had been born, wed, moved in our
out, and most important, if any member of the family had died. Then
a little strip of black cloth was tied to each hive, and wine and sweet
cakes were set out so the bees could participate in the funerary rites.
If a bee buzzes over a sleeping child, it indicates that the child will be
very lucky for the rest of her life.

BEETLES

In most places, the appearance of a beetle is considered to be extremely bad luck. This is hardly surprising, since beetles ruin grain
and flour. One noted exception to this rule is the scarab beetle, which
was revered in Ancient Egypt as a symbol of rebirth. Scarab beetles roll
two-inch balls of dung along the desert sands. The dung was implant-
ed with a single scarab egg and left to hatch in a warm sunny spot. This
behavior was used to explain the movement of the Sun across the sky.
It was said to be pushed in its heavenly orbit by a giant scarab. Scarab

beetles were carved from every type of gem and molded in copper, silver, and gold. They were worn as amulets by the living and the dead in order to ensure resurrection in the afterlife. Scarab beetles decorated temples and tombs. One from the temple of Amon-Ra at Karnak was five feet long, three feet wide, and weighed more than two tons. When the Ancient Egyptians co-opted the zodiac from the Ancient Greeks, they replaced the crab in the sign of Cancer with the scarab.

BUTTERFLIES

Butterflies are so magnificent in their maturity and so mysterious in their transformation that human beings have used the butterfly as a metaphor for the rebirth of the soul since time immemorial.

The caterpillar wraps itself in a shroud and appears to be lifeless, just as human beings die and become cocooned in the earth. Finally the butterfly breaks free from its cocoon, lifts its radiant wings skyward, and flies! From this example we humans inferred the hopeful correlation that we too would shed our mortal coil, and raise unseen soul wings and fly. Celtic, Chinese, Mexican, Siberian, and Ancient Greek lore also said that butterflies were the souls of the dead looking for new bodies to enter.

FLIES

Flies are usually connected with the underworld in mythology because of their function as scavengers. The Sumerian goddess of love, Inanna, sends a fly as a messenger into the underworld to rescue Her husband, Dumuzi. In return for this favor, Inanna grants the fly the right to enter all taverns and beer houses, and to listen to music and the discourse of the wise and learned.

It was considered bad luck to kill the last housefly of winter. Yet for a fly to fall in your drink is said to be extremely good luck.

The magic of insects has been a casualty of the war on bugs waged by pesticide companies. We have learned how all species are vital to the health and well-being of our Mother the Earth. By honoring the magic of bugs we are honoring the Goddess in some of Her tiniest and most fascinating guises.

Make a Portable Altar!

By Edain McCoy

Modern life can sometimes make being a Witch very difficult. Demands of business travel, military life, and restrictions on college campuses can all present obstacles to practicing the religion of Witchcraft. You find yourself up against airline officials who view your athame as a weapon and want to confiscate it, college dorms that do not permit the lighting of candles, and hotel rooms that have both limited space and a sterile, decidedly non-spiritual atmosphere. What's a Witch to do?

One solution is to make a "portable altar," one that contains no objectionable candles or knives, and that takes up no more space than a small carry-on bag or briefcase. This kit can be stored where space is limited, be easily transported, and its contents will rarely be questioned during security checks. Use these guidelines to make your portable altar kit, or allow them to inspire your own creative ideas. First, get a small tote bag or briefcase, then start putting in the items you feel are most needed—like your elemental symbols—and then see how much space you have left over for extras.

The Altar

Drape a clean handkerchief over a corner of your dresser or over the top of your briefcase and use that as the basis of your altar. The cloth will protect your portable "ritual tools" from the mundane energies that are inherent on these surfaces due to their use for non-spiritual purposes. When not being used as an altar cloth, it can be used to wrap and protect breakable items in your altar kit.

To Represent Air/East

The most lightweight item you can use to represent air is a feather culled from your own backyard. Next time you take a walk keep your eyes open for fallen feathers. *Editor's note: Feathers*

found in the wild can contain microsopic organisms that damage the lungs of human beings. Please consider using one of the several brands of feather spray disinfectant (available at leather or craft shops) on your feathers before using them in ritual.

People who inspect baggage at airports expect to find letter openers inside briefcases, and these make the perfect substitute for your athame. Because they represent communication, they are naturally linked to the air element. They also have the same projective feel as the athame, but are much smaller and lighter, and won't get you arrested at the metal detector.

TO REPRESENT FIRE/SOUTH

Instead of using actual fire you can substitute a small "wand" made from a twig that appeals to you, or a fiery stone such as iron pyrite or a meteor. Small arrowheads or pieces of flint also make excellent fire symbols.

TO REPRESENT WATER/WEST

Nothing represents water quite like water. Rather than using a paper-wrapped hotel glass, or carrying around your own large and heavy chalice, invest in a set of one-ounce shot glasses, which are easy to find in gift shops and department stores. They are small, comparatively lightweight, and usually come in sets of six. If you break one you'll have five spares to fall back on. Fill these with a little bit of water and—presto!—you have your water problem solved.

TO REPRESENT EARTH/NORTH

A small stone always works well as a representation of the earth element. Find one you like and carry it with you to use when nothing else is readily available. Good choices here are bloodstone, obsidian, shale, or a stone from your usual worship setting.

To connect yourself either to the energy of your home, or to the area in which you are working, you can collect a small bit of local soil or grass. Take along a spare, empty prescription bottle to keep this in, then transfer it to one of your shot glasses before placing it on your altar.

CANDLE REPLACEMENTS

If you have a few spare dollars to invest, you can purchase battery powered "candles." These are fairly lightweight, usually stand six to eight inches high, and, with the exception of their marquise-shaped light bulbs that substitute for flames, they look enough like real candles to satisfy your subconscious mind. These have uses outside of traveling too. I use them to mark the four quarters of my circle whenever it is not safe to use real fire. While you are traveling, or wherever open flames are prohibited, they also make good working candles and/or candles to honor the God and Goddess.

OIL AND INCENSE REPLACEMENTS

Essential oils and incenses are highly flammable, and they are generally not safe to pack in your luggage. Oil bottles can break and stain everything else in your suitcase. Incense can also stain if it gets loose, and, if you are in a place where fires are prohibited, you will not be allowed to burn it anyway. The strong scents might also raise objections from hotel owners and roommates.

To use scent to set an atmosphere for your private devotions, try making a scented lotion you can rub on yourself prior to your ritual. Use only a drop or three of oil per eight-ounce bottle of unscented lotion. Shake well to thoroughly mix before applying. Using more oil will not only be overpowering to your sense of smell, but can seriously irritate your skin. Trust that a few drops will be enough to give you the atmosphere you need without forcing others to have to have to breathe your fumes.

ODDS AND ENDS

Depending on how much space you have in your carry-on bag, briefcase, or dorm/locker storage, you can add other items to your altar kit . Certainly a divination device like tarot cards or rune stones is useful. Personal talismans, ritual jewelry, lightweight statuettes, or portable cassette or CD players can also be included.

MOBILE MAGIC

By Cerridwen
Iris Shea

Most of us lead busy lives. Most of us tend to accumulate all kinds of tools. Most of us can't carry a bag big enough to bring our tools with us as we run around dealing with our lives. Here are some ideas for magic on the go. Most of them require items you might have in your purse or bag already.

Representing the Elements

You probably have representatives of the four elements in your bag, and don't even know it. A small spray bottle of perfume or cologne can represent both water (the perfume) and air (it is sprayed through the air and scented). A mint or candy can represent earth. A lighter represents fire. I don't smoke, but I carry a lighter in my purse anyway.

Tools

A pen can double as a wand. It is used to write something down when inspired, so there's the element of air again.

Put an extra key on your key ring—one that doesn't unlock anything you currently own. This key is both for luck and to use as a focus for meditation or thinking when you need the "key" answer to a question.

Keep a special coin (such as a Susan B. Anthony dollar or a fifty-cent piece) in your wallet that you never spend, to signify that your wallet will never be empty, and you will always have enough money.

A SPECIALLY CHARGED MIRROR can work wonders. I have a small compact mirror that is only used magically. If I need to rebound something negative, I simply pull the compact our of my purse and use it as a shield. It looks like I'm merely checking my makeup. It is also a useful way to check out what's behind you if you're feeling uneasy. Needless to say, if you feel you are being followed and in danger, get yourself out of the situation as quickly as possible. Men can also use a metal lighter in place of a mirror.

KEEP A DECK OF PLAYING CARDS in your purse. It can be used for divination, similar to the tarot, or for solitaire when you are stuck somewhere waiting. You would be surprised at how much divination information you can get out of a game of solitaire!

TRICKS WITHOUT TOOLS

INVISIBILITY

If you feel uncomfortable, pull in your energy as closely as possible to become "invisible." Sometimes I imagine myself covered in Hera's feathered cloak of invisibility. Again, use the invisibility to get out of the dangerous situation.

RENEWING VITALITY

If walking in the sunlight, concentrate on feeling the warmth of the Sun coming through your skin. Breathe deeply and feel the Sun energy fill you up, making you buoyant and energetic.

You can use a walk in the moonlight as an opportunity for a mobile Moon bath. Again, let the Moon's energy wash over you and through you. Let it fill you up and ride along its energy.

Envision the energy from the earth coming up, through the concrete and through your shoes. Let the mother's gentle, soothing, steady energy flow upward to fill your body and give you the energy you need.

When you get home, have a good meal, plenty of water, take a long, hot, scented bath, and get some sleep.

Waiting for a Train

I live in New York. Often, I need to ride the subway, and often it is the N or the R. They are not nicknamed "rarely" and "never" for nothing. Instead of getting impatient, I have found this little rhyme often helps.

N or R, please come to me
Your help I need, my friends to see.

Feel free to modify it to call to you whatever transportation you need. You do need to be relaxed when using this. If you are angry, you will just stand there feeling more frustrated. The very fact that it sounds like a silly nursery school rhyme relaxes me when I say it. I rarely have to wait for a train or a bus now.

Plane Travel

If traveling by plane makes you nervous, perhaps a visualization will help. Picture a large aerial dragon, horse, or winged being of your choice bearing the plane upon its back. It will get you safely to your destination. Make sure that once you arrive, you give thanks and a libation at the earliest available opportunity.

As your five senses become sharper, so will your sixth. All those wonderful tools you accumulate to aid in ritual are just that, objects to aid and focus. The ultimate tool is yourself, and you take yourself along wherever you go.

Working with Herbs and the Moon

By Chandra Beal

Working with herbs is one of my favorite pastimes, along with studying and working with Moon energy. To my delight, I have found that when I combine these two hobbies, a personal sense of power and pleasure results.

Just as the earth and her oceans are influenced by the Moon, so are we affected by its flowing energy. Working with herbs that are ruled astrologically by the Moon can help us learn to flow with the natural rhythms of our emotions.

Lunar rhythms are deeply connected to our subconscious. Using herbs affected by those rhythms can assist us in developing our intuition. They can increase sensitivity and vision, and broaden our imagination and understanding. These herbs are often feminine in nature and govern the uterus, ovaries, and breasts. Exploring lunar herbs can be a soothing and nurturing pastime that will enrich our lives and the lives of those around us.

The following recipes call for the use of lunar herbs either by themselves or in combination with other types of herbs.

Sea-Salt Rub

Try this sea-salt rub after your bath to increase circulation, soften skin, remove impurities and toxins, and remove dead skin cells. This treatment will make your skin feel radiant.

This bath ritual honors the Moon goddess Aphrodite, whose name means "born of the foam." A seashell would be an appropriate container for mixing the salt and oil. The sea goddess was also known to the Romans as Marianna, whose name means "the sea."

Honoring the lunar goddess should always be a celebration of love, sensuality, and the ebb and flow of life. Alignment with the cycles of the Moon can help us feel more balanced, creative, and renewed.

8 ounces sea salt

Few drops of wintergreen oil

To prepare the materials, pour the salt into a large seashell or other container and mix with the wintergreen oil. You may wish to prepare this mixture ahead of time and keep it in a tightly sealed glass jar.

Doing this ritual in the bathtub or shower allows for easy cleanup. If you have a loving partner, invite him or her to rub the salt onto your body while you relax on clean towels or sheets.

Begin with a warm bath or shower to relax your body and open your pores. While your skin is still wet, rub a small handful of salt between your palms. Add a little water, if necessary, to keep the salt about the consistency of wet sand. Vigorously rub your entire body with the salt, using circular motions. Begin with your shoulders and work toward your feet. Do not apply the salt to your face. Your skin will flush and feel warm as your blood rises to the surface. When you have covered your entire body, relax while the salt dries.

As the salt dries it will begin to fall away from your body like dry sand. Rinse your body with lukewarm water. You should feel immediate results. Your skin will feel silky and soft. You may feel like you are glowing like the Moon itself. Use a towel to gently pat your body dry. Apply your favorite lunar essential oils or moisturizer, such as rose or jasmine, to your skin. You may want to follow your bath by laying slices of cucumber on your eyelids to soothe them and reduce puffiness. Enjoy!

POTPOURRI SACHETS

Another way to enjoy lunar herbs is to make a sachet of potpourri. These sachets can be used for many purposes, such as scenting your bureau drawers and closets. Roses, especially white ones, are distinctly feminine and represent love. They are most closely associated with the goddesses Aphrodite and Venus.

> White rose petals, dried
> Few drops of rose oil
> 1 teaspoon orris powder
> Paper bag
> Fabric, cut to size
> Ribbons

Give yourself the gift of some white roses and save the petals. Dry the petals on a flat surface, which allows air to circulate around them. When the petals are completely dry, place them in a paper bag. Add the rose oil and orris powder. Shake the bag to coat the petals. Now place the petals inside a piece of fabric or lace and tie it closed with pretty ribbons. The sachet can be renewed with herbs to suit your needs.

SUN AND MOON OIL

I like to make this oil frequently. It makes a great all-purpose massage oil, and has also been effective as a treatment for dry and flaky scalps. The herbs in this recipe are governed by both the Sun and the Moon. The combination of both symbolizes balance between those energies. Almonds, chamomile, and juniper impart Sun energies, while lavender, rose geranium, and peppermint are ruled by the Moon.

> Few fresh juniper berries
> Few drops of rose geranium oil
> Few drops of peppermint oil (optional)
> 4 ounces almond oil
> Few spikes of fresh lavender
> Pinch of fresh chamomile flowers

Crush the juniper berries with a mortar and pestle. Mix the rose geranium and peppermint oils into the almond oil. Pour the oils into a sealable container, leaving room at the top. Drop the crushed juniper berries into the container. Add the lavender spikes and chamomile flowers. Seal the container tightly. Leave the container someplace where it will be in both the Sun and moonlight for two weeks. After two weeks, strain the oil through cheesecloth and remove the herbs. Re-bottle the clear oil and enjoy!

SWEET DREAMS PILLOW

The herbs used in this recipe are said to be beneficial in promoting sleep. Mugwort can help induce visions while preventing nightmares. Verbena and lavender will calm the nerves while protecting the dreamer. Lavender is associated with Hecate, the dark Moon goddess, while mugwort and verbena are sacred to the Moon goddess Diana.

- 2 equal-sized rectangles of a soft fabric of your choice, such as flannel or cotton

    Enough cotton batting to stuff the pillow

    Needle and thread to match the fabric rectangles

- 1 (6-inch square) piece of cheesecloth
- 1 zipper, the same length as one of the short sides of your fabric rectangles
- 1 cup rose petals (for women)
- 1 cup lemon verbena (for men)
- ½ cup lavender flowers
- 2–3 tablespoons mugwort
- 1 teaspoon orris root powder

Shake all the herbs together with the orris root in a paper bag. Coating the herbs with the orris root will help the scent to last longer. Remove the herbs from the bag, wrap them tightly in the cheesecloth, and tie it closed with thread.

With the right sides of the two fabric rectangles together, sew three sides of the fabric together to form the pillow. While the pillow is turned inside out, sew the zipper (unzipped) into the fourth side. Turn the pillow right side out. Stuff some of the batting inside the pillow. Place the cheese-cloth bundle in the middle of the stuffing and cover it with more batting. When the pillow is stuffed full, close the zipper and enjoy sweet dreams.

A Selection of Herbs Ruled by the Moon

Camphor	Jasmine	Rowan
Cabbage	Lettuce	Seasalt
Chickweed	Lily	Sesame seeds
Coriander	Moonwort	Star anise
Cucumbers	Orris Root	Watercress
Fleur-de-lis	Poppy	Water lily
Ginger	Pumpkin	Wintergreen
Holly	Purslane	
Iris	Rose (white)	

Taming the Wild Dandelion

By Edain McCoy

Children seem to know instinctively that if they pick up a puffball dandelion, one on which the buttery yellow flowers have withered to shades of wispy white, they may make a wish as they blow the little helicopter-like tendrils to the four winds. This simple wish magic is only one of the many uses for this otherwise annoying but hearty little weed.

Blowing away the tendrils is a magical trick that has been used successfully to call spirits. To do this, get a clear picture of the spirit you wish to have present in your mind, then blow the dandelion to the otherworld to carry your message. The same technique can be used to let a person who is on your mind know you are thinking of him or her.

The edible yellow flowers were used liberally by the American colonists as a garnish and seasoning, and also to weave love spells. Placing a yellow dandelion bud under the plate your intended will be eating from will make him or her sit up and take notice of you. Wearing one in your hair or on your lapel will cause potential partners to make their interest in you known.

The dandelion roots also possess potent magical powers. They can be dried by hanging them up in an arid place for several weeks, or by spreading them out on a cookie sheet and heating them in a warm oven, about 200° F, for ten to fifteen minutes. They can then be brewed into teas that help open the psychic centers. To make the tea, you need one root stalk for each cup of tea you wish to make. With a mortar and pestle, crush the dried roots down into as fine a pulp as you can, then place it in a cheesecloth or tea ball and boil in one cup water. *Editor's note: Make sure they have not been sprayed with pesticides.*

You can also use the roots to neutralize the power of an enemy by binding several of the root stalks together with some string, then dressing them up in a likeness of an enemy while visualizing his or her power over you being neutralized. When you have finished, bury the roots.

The dandelion has a long and noble history as a medicine. Just as the root can be used in magic to neutralize the powers of an enemy, it also works as an antacid to neutralize stomach acids. The root produces both a mildly diuretic and laxative effect without being considered a purgative, a name for a more vigorous result of the same properties when found in other plants.

The leaves of the dandelion have been used liberally as a food source. The bitter taste made them a popular seasoning when salt was not plentiful. Teas made from the leaves have shown promise as a tonic, which may help prevent cancers. They are high in vitamins A and C, natural anti-oxidants which can strengthen the immune system by preventing cell damage due to oxidization. The leaves have also been used to add nutrients to salads, to make earthy-flavored wines, and to stand as main or side dishes all on their own.

STEAMED DANDELION LEAVES

3–4 cups dandelion leaves

1 tablespoon each orange and lemon juice

1 teaspoon grated lemon rind

⅛ teaspoon powdered garlic

¼ cup finely minced onions

Safflower oil

Pinch each of nutmeg, paprika, and tarragon

Salt and pepper to taste

1 hard-boiled egg, chopped

Thoroughly clean the leaves and place them in a steamer. Allow to steam for about fifteen minutes. While leaves are steaming, combine all of the other ingredients except the hard-boiled egg and onions in a small saucepan. Cover, and allow to warm over low heat. Check periodically to make sure the mixture is not getting too dry. If it appears dry, add some safflower oil. In a medium-size skillet, brown the onions in safflower oil, then add dandelion leaves and lemon juice mixture. Stir all ingredients together in a warm skillet, but do not allow them to become dry or scorched. Add the egg and serve hot.

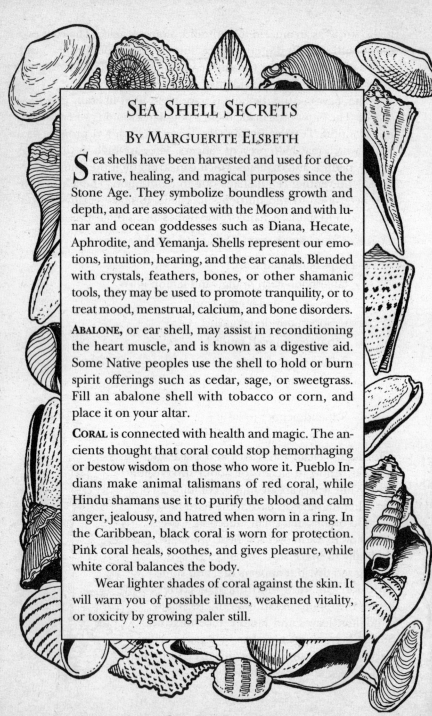

Sea Shell Secrets

By Marguerite Elsbeth

Sea shells have been harvested and used for decorative, healing, and magical purposes since the Stone Age. They symbolize boundless growth and depth, and are associated with the Moon and with lunar and ocean goddesses such as Diana, Hecate, Aphrodite, and Yemanja. Shells represent our emotions, intuition, hearing, and the ear canals. Blended with crystals, feathers, bones, or other shamanic tools, they may be used to promote tranquility, or to treat mood, menstrual, calcium, and bone disorders.

ABALONE, or ear shell, may assist in reconditioning the heart muscle, and is known as a digestive aid. Some Native peoples use the shell to hold or burn spirit offerings such as cedar, sage, or sweetgrass. Fill an abalone shell with tobacco or corn, and place it on your altar.

CORAL is connected with health and magic. The ancients thought that coral could stop hemorrhaging or bestow wisdom on those who wore it. Pueblo Indians make animal talismans of red coral, while Hindu shamans use it to purify the blood and calm anger, jealousy, and hatred when worn in a ring. In the Caribbean, black coral is worn for protection. Pink coral heals, soothes, and gives pleasure, while white coral balances the body.

Wear lighter shades of coral against the skin. It will warn you of possible illness, weakened vitality, or toxicity by growing paler still.

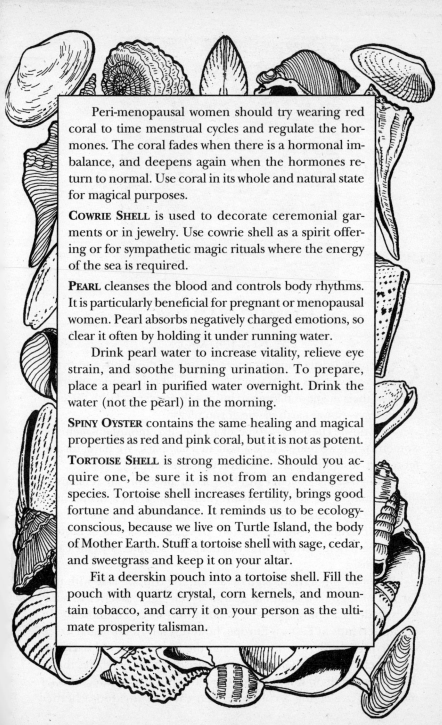

Peri-menopausal women should try wearing red coral to time menstrual cycles and regulate the hormones. The coral fades when there is a hormonal imbalance, and deepens again when the hormones return to normal. Use coral in its whole and natural state for magical purposes.

COWRIE SHELL is used to decorate ceremonial garments or in jewelry. Use cowrie shell as a spirit offering or for sympathetic magic rituals where the energy of the sea is required.

PEARL cleanses the blood and controls body rhythms. It is particularly beneficial for pregnant or menopausal women. Pearl absorbs negatively charged emotions, so clear it often by holding it under running water.

Drink pearl water to increase vitality, relieve eye strain, and soothe burning urination. To prepare, place a pearl in purified water overnight. Drink the water (not the pearl) in the morning.

SPINY OYSTER contains the same healing and magical properties as red and pink coral, but it is not as potent.

TORTOISE SHELL is strong medicine. Should you acquire one, be sure it is not from an endangered species. Tortoise shell increases fertility, brings good fortune and abundance. It reminds us to be ecology-conscious, because we live on Turtle Island, the body of Mother Earth. Stuff a tortoise shell with sage, cedar, and sweetgrass and keep it on your altar.

Fit a deerskin pouch into a tortoise shell. Fill the pouch with quartz crystal, corn kernels, and mountain tobacco, and carry it on your person as the ultimate prosperity talisman.

COSMIC CAMPING

BY KEN JOHNSON

O ur pre-Christian ancestors were people of the woods and rivers, of rocky coasts and warm fields. Like all tribal and traditional peoples, their magic and lore was intimately concerned with the land and its ways—it was earth magic, if you please.

And now? These days some of us feel like mountain men (or women) when we merely take a walk in a city park. We have, for the most part, lost our deep connection with the land.

Enough of the ancient earth-lore of our ancestors still remains so that we may, if we choose, nurture within ourselves a deeper and more magical relationship with Mother Earth. Here is a simple exercise that originates with the *kolduny*, or village sorcerers of Eastern Europe, and helps us to identify our deeper resonance with the earth beneath us.

When we modern folks go on a camping trip, we take with us a car full of high-tech camping gear, and relegate ourselves to carefully tended camping spaces in national forests or monuments. In the hinterlands of Eastern Europe, however, it is not unusual to see countryfolk wandering the roads and the forests with old packs on their backs, making their camp wherever darkness overtakes them. Those among them who practice the old magical arts have a special method for selecting a campsite. You can use this too, whether you're a serious backpacker, primitive camper, or simply seeking to choose between a number of different camping spaces in your favorite national park.

First, stand on the piece of earth you want to assess. Take a few deep breaths and relax.

Next, move your whole consciousness out of your mind and into your body. If you've practiced meditation for many years, you may find this fairly easy, but for most people this is the hard part. One way to go at it is to imagine that your head is sinking, drifting down the back of your spine until it reaches the center of your body (we all have to find our own center, but it's usually somewhere between your heart and your belly button). Imagine that your head is resting there—nose, mouth, ears, and so on. When you breathe, it's the center of your body that's breathing, not just the nose in your face. When you open your eyes and look around you, it's the center of your body that's seeing, not just the eyes in your head.

When you have moved your consciousness into your body, you will feel your whole physical being resonating with energy. Imagine that this big powerful energy source is like an umbrella. Open the umbrella underneath you, so that the dome of light and energy extends down into the earth.

Now start walking. We have a tendency to want to sit for long periods of time and just meditate whenever we're out in nature, but the sorcerers tell me that earth energies are better understood when we keep moving. How does the ground beneath you feel when you walk around on it? If it's a good place for you to camp, it should feel light, breezy, and happy. Maybe it will cause a pleasant sensation in one of your own inner centers of power—your heart, your belly, or the top of your upper diaphragm. If it's not such a good place, it will feel heavy and murky, as if you were walking through muck and mud—which, from an energy point of view, is exactly what's happening. Such negative energy zones may also cause unpleasant sensations in our inner centers.

Keep repeating this exercise until you find a spot that feels really good. This is your campsite. Enjoy.

THE SACRED PIPE

BY MARGUERITE ELSBETH

This is a famous and often-told story of how the sacred pipe came to the Indian nations. The story is meant to be shared with all people, but it belongs to the Indians of the Great Northern Plains.

Ptesan Win, White Buffalo Woman, wore her hair loose on the right and tied with buffalo hair on the left. She carried *ptehincala huhu canunpa,* the buffalo-calf-bone pipe. The pipe stem was in her left hand and the bowl was in her right. As she walked she sang her song:

> *Niya taninyan (With visible breath)*
> *Mawinaye (I am walking)*
> *Oyate le (Toward this nation)*
> *Imawani (I am walking)*

So Ptesan Win gave the great gift of visible breath, the sacred pipe, to the Painted Arrow (Cheyenne), the Little Black Eagle (Crow), and the Brother People (Lakota Sioux).

The pipe is perhaps the most sacred object in Native American spirituality, and is used by many Indian tribes for prayer. It is not merely a symbol of that which is sacred. The pipe itself is sacred. *Unci Kunshi,* the Grandmother Earth, lives in the bowl. The stem represents *Tunkashila,* the Grandfather Sky.

The pipe is carefully wrapped in fine, soft hide, such as elk or deer, and kept in a special bag. In the old days, the pipe bag was the most elaborately decorated item a warrior owned, because it protected his dearest possession, and the same holds true for pipe carriers today. The bowl and stem are separated for storage, and the pipe

stem is placed facing east when not in use. The pipe bowl may be carved in many different shapes from a variety of substances, although the traditional pipe bowl is made of catlinite from Pipestone Quarry in Pipestone, Minnesota. The stem may be made of stone or wood. Sometimes the pipe is decorated with beads, feathers, and painted symbols.

The pipe is always handled with the utmost respect. The bowl is filled with canshasha, the red willow bark tobacco, or herbs such as sage or wild cherry bark. Then the pipe is lit and the smoke offered to Grandfather Sky, Grandmother Earth, and to the four directions. As the pipe is shared among the people, the smokers become one with the earth and sky, because they are filled with Wakan Tanka, the Great Spirit, the great mystery of visible breath.

Hupa gluza. Raise one's pipe in prayer.

BIBLIOGRAPHY

Crow Dog, Leonard, and Erdoes, Richard. *Crow Dog: Four Generations of Sioux Medicine Men.* New York, HarperCollins Publishers, Inc., 1995

Making a Stang

By Jim Garrison

The stang is one of the more mysterious tools that is mentioned, but rarely described, in many of the books available on Witchcraft. A stang is a forked tree branch or stick that acts as a vertical altar. It is usually set in the north of the circle. The stang is related to the besom, or broom, that was "ridden" by Witches during fertility rites and the astral journeys to the Grand Sabbat. Originally, the stang may have been a simple staff topped with an animal skull—either that of a bull, goat, or stag. The tines of the fork resembled the animal horns, thus suggesting a connection to the old Horned God of ancient Europe.

As a tool of the "old Craft," the stang has a particular character and energy that may be attractive to modern Witches who are exploring the traditional old ways of our ancestors. Unique, and with a strong symbolic connection to primal forces, it is a fascinating addition to your usual ritual equipment.

You can make a stang from ash, rowan, or some other type of wood that's common in your part of the world. You might want to do a bit of research into what the magical properties of various trees are, and select one that suits you. If that doesn't seem practical or desirable, then you can also use a garden fork. Sometimes you can find an old fork by going to farm auctions, garage sales, or flea markets. You may just have to buy a new one from the local hardware store. However you acquire your stang, as long as you treat it like any other magical tool, it should work.

Once you have the basic stang, either a branch or a fork, you need to clean it. Strip the bark from your branch—you may want to lash the tips with rawhide, thread, or thin cord to keep them from fraying or splitting. Once you have it stripped down, you may want to sand it smooth, or at least take the rough edges off of it. After sanding, you may want to drive an iron nail into the foot of the main shaft to seal the end. According to tradition, this is done to block off energy so that it builds up in the stang. Some folks like to carve their stangs. Others may prefer to use a wood burning tool to personalize theirs. Linseed oil, stain, varnish, or paint can be used to decorate or finish the wood.

If you are working with a fork, feel free to decorate or modify it to suit your needs. You may want to refinish the shaft or repaint the fork, and certainly remove any labels or markings that you find distracting. Do what it takes to make the stang a magical tool you feel comfortable using. By all means, cleanse and consecrate the stang in whatever manner you feel best. Leaving it on a hilltop overnight during a Full Moon is one way to clear a stang, though you could also ritually purify it during an esbat, or during the waning or New Moon. Again, do whatever works best for you.

What does the stang symbolize, anyway? The symbolism behind the stang is strongly tied to the Horned God. It resembles a set of horns or antlers, and it is used as a representation of the "young" Horned God by some groups. Others see the stang as a representation of the duality of Goddess and God merging into the unity of the All, and as such the stang can be used as a focus for meditation, pathworking, or even spell-work. Since the fork is at the top, usually, one might also look on the stang as a symbol of lineage, procreation, and fertility—the separate tines or forks reaching upward from the one source at their base, like plants from the soil, or generations of offspring from a shared set of ancestors. Another way to look at the stang is to see it as the embodiment and union of the forces of creation, destruction, and balance in one weapon/tool of the God.

So, once you have a stang, how do you use it? Well, for one thing, it is usually stuck into the ground in the north of the circle when working outdoors. The stang is hung with garlands of ivy, wreaths, fresh flowers, or other decorations according to the Sabbat being celebrated. You could hang masks, wineskins, medicine pouches, amulets, charms, or tokens from the forked head of the stang as well. Stangs are sort of handy that way. When you use a stang in ritual, it is common practice to place the cakes and wine in front of it. Some groups have developed guidelines for how to arrange and decorate their stangs for each of the sabbats.

Whatever you do, stangs are handy tools for carrying supplies and holding stuff in ritual, and they make good, discreet altars for those who might not have room or access to a more conventional table-type altar. A stang is a highly portable altar that you can carry anywhere, like a staff— though if you do decide to use a pitchfork, it might not be as inconspicuous as a forked branch hung with feathers, shells, and beads.

You may decide to create a set of stangs—one for each quarter—or you may want to have personal stangs for everyone in your group. Some traditions have a coven stang that is used by the whole group, either in addition to their personal stangs, or as the only one in the group. You could also create a special one for each sabbat, or for specific purposes such as rites of passage, initiations, or for healing work. Some groups create one for the Holly King and one for the Oak King, using each only during its half of the year.

Combining the function of the altar with features of the staff, a stang is a rather unique magical tool that lends itself to a wide range of uses—many of which have yet to be discovered. One novel way to make use of a is to build spells around—and upon—a stang, which is then left in the area to be protected, or in the home of a person seeking a new job, or in the garden to bless the plants. The possibilities are as endless as your own imagination and ingenuity.

Iao Needle, Iao Valley, Maui

Iao Valley, Maui

By Bernyce Barlow

Located on the Hawaiian island of Maui is a valley called Iao (Hawaiian spelling), sacred to all Hawaiians. Iao is the valley of kings. Within the lush green boundaries of the valley, sacred Hawaii has been buried in caves, behind waterfalls, under boulders, and scattered from ledges. Iao Valley was the royal burial grounds of the ancient kings, mois, and ruling chiefs of the islands. To fully appreciate the power behind this site, we look to the kahunas (Hawaiian specialists) for enlightenment.

First, it is important to understand the Hawaiians believed a certain "mana," or magic, was given to all their rulers via the gods. This mana was stored in the bones and teeth of a body after its death. The more powerful the ruler, the more powerful the mana. Mana could be called on for many things such as protection, victory in battle, illness, and interpreting dreams and prophecy.

Burial mana was considered extremely powerful and god-given to few, so it was fiercely protected. If the bones of a ruling mois fell into the hands of his enemy, the results could be humiliating and disastrous. The enemy would take the bones and make them into ordinary and

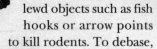

lewd objects such as fish hooks or arrow points to kill rodents. To debase, reduce, and flaunt an enemy's mana was considered an exploitation of his family and gods, an act of war. There were two places on the Hawaiian Islands where royal mana was kept and protected. These were The City of Refuge, at Honaunau on the island of Hawaii, and the Iao Valley. The kahunas kept a close eye on both sites because they gathered some of their personal power there.

There were many ways the kahunas protected burial mana from enemy debasement. The rituals were long and complicated, sometimes lasting for weeks. During a royal mourning period the islanders were allowed to act crazy, breaking every tabu in the book without penalty. After the mourning period was officially over island life returned to normal. By this time, the kahunas had disposed of the royal bones appropriately. Some of the ways the bones were hidden were quite ingenious. One king had his bones powdered and put into the poi at his burial feast.

There are also burial caves located in the middle of sheer cliffs, with camouflaged entrances blocked by boulders. Once in a while, an earthquake will shake loose a hidden cliff cave and give us a peek at royal skeletal remains, sometimes accompanied by a guardian entourage. Early Hawaiians would scale the cliffs to reach the caves with their strong fiber ropes in tow. Accordingly, they would take a log and bore holes in one end, hoist it up the cliff, secure the other end of the log in the cave and use it as a boom to haul up the sacred remains. The cave would then be closed off with gigantic boulders, soil, or vegetation.

Complete destruction of a ruler's bones was unheard of. Although most of the bones were hidden at the bottom of the sea, ground to powder and scattered, or concealed in a cave, some talisman of mana had to remain intact. Temples called *heiau*(s) were built to protect these skeletons of power. The more royalty a heiau represented the more powerful the temple, and in the islands, he who has the most power wins! One talisman belonging to the Kamehameha line is called the *Kiha-pu*, a shell trumpet embedded with the teeth of the great warrior chiefs. Legend tells of its power to summon up the spirits of the war gods and ancestors to favor the owner of the clarion. This was the type of mana charm used by the kahunas and kings that would be kept at a heiau.

The Iao Valley is filled with the mana of the ancients. It is a Garden of Eden, a paradise where waterfalls tumble over volcanic cliffs covered with lush tropical vegetation and magical rainbows are the backdrop for exotic flowers and birds. The air is always sweet in the valley—scented by a heady plumaria and orchid mix. The sacred grounds are overwhelmed by color, and accented by a river of crystal water

Ki bundle offering to the spirit of place of the Iao Valley

that occasionally gathers in enchanted pools. The West Maui Mountains rise above the valley floor like a fortress, protecting Iao on all sides with steep slopes. The mountains also keep the mana safe, as if they were a temple in their own right.

What is popularly called the Needle (*Nanahoa*), a phallic volcanic upthrust found in the Iao Valley, was once used by women as a sacred fertility site. Women would make pilgrimages to this site overnight to petition the gods for blessings and favor. Ceremony, ritual, and rite were performed regularly in the Iao Valley by both men and women. During some chiefly reigns, however, women were tabu from specific sites in Iao, including Nanahoa, so not to anger certain gods.

As you can see, there is more to the Iao Valley than meets the eye. It is truly a site of mystical empowerment representing centuries of Hawaiian history and magic. There are many mysterious legends surrounding the Iao Valley that have been handed down for generations through royal family lines. It has been said that the spirits connected to the valley can be seen through a veil of awe-inspiring beauty, sometimes behind the mist of a waterfall, silhouetted behind a rainbow, or in a sacred cave. To spend any time alone in the Iao Valley becomes a personal journey of many dimensions.

REMOTE VIEWING

BY SILVER RAVENWOLF

Have you ever had to make a choice between one unknown path or another, or has someone expected you to make a decision when many of the elements of the situation remain mysteries to you? "Of course I have," you say, "and I normally use my divination tool to assist me in making the right choice." That's terrific, but what if you don't have your divination tool tucked into the waistband of your pantyhose twenty-four hours a day? Then it's time to try your hand at a technique called "remote viewing." This process has a few rules.

1. Register your feelings first.

2. Use the first impression that comes to mind.

3. Don't force impressions or feelings.

4. Don't analyze your impressions until after you've finished the process. If the issue encompasses several facets, take each facet at a time, rather than try to get what you need all at once.

Although practice will bring you more information, you should be able to get enough to assist you the first time you try the technique. To keep a record of your remote viewing experiences, you may wish to purchase a ninety-minute tape to collect your various impressions.

Here's how you can use the remote viewing process. Let's take a mythical situation first. Harold is an acquaintance of yours. He wants you to throw your time and energy into a project, and he's been bugging you about it because you haven't made a decision. You're fairly busy, and don't know if you can spare the time. Here's how you do it:

STEP ONE: Sit comfortably. Turn on the tape recorder and record a front-liner. For example, "Today's date is August 6, 1997. Time: 3:00 P.M. Remote view: The Harold Issue."

STEP TWO: Close your eyes. Bring up a mental image of the problem—a person's face, a document, a place, etc. Remember that if the problem has many facets, you need to deal with each section individually. In this case, you would focus on Harold. Try to see his face, or at least an outline of him.

STEP THREE: How do you feel? Ascertain the emotions that occur when you think of the image. Use your first impression. If there's more than one impression fighting to get out, then relax and experience them one at a time. You may say, "When I think of Harold I feel sad." Or, "I feel cold inside," or "When I think of Harold I feel confused."

STEP FOUR: Let mental pictures form. Allow the pictures to come—don't block anything out or think that the picture is silly or doesn't pertain. It does; trust me. For example, "I see Harold. He's drowning in a pool and he's trying to pull me in with him." Or, "Harold is covered with some sort of black slime. I don't know what it is."

STEP FIVE: When you've covered all the facets of the issue, open your eyes, take a deep breath, and say, "End session." Turn off the tape recorder, rewind, and play back what you said. Now is your chance to analyze. With the example given, your remote viewing experience plainly tells you that you should bow out of the venture with Harold. What were your keys? You didn't feel good when you first examined your emotions. The words "sad," "confused," and "cold inside" acted as emotional alarms for you. Secondly, the images that came to you in this example, "drowning," leading you astray, and "black slime," should let you know that this venture carries negative connotations for you.

STEP SIX: End analysis. Taking your emotional barometer and pictorial images into consideration, your solution will take shape in your mind. In this example, the decision would be to stay away from Harold and his project.

What if, given your remote viewing experience, you still can't make up your mind? Before you go to bed, write a specific question relating to the issue on a piece of paper, and put the paper under your pillow. Play the tape again, then ask divinity to help you come to a solution in your dreams. When you waken, write down any feelings, impressions, or dreams you can remember. Often, you don't need a full dreamscape to come to a conclusion. If you don't feel well when you open your eyes, then that would serve as an emotional indicator, even though you may not remember any dreams.

Once you begin to practice remote viewing, the technique will expand. You will get more information, and you will begin to add nuances to the technique, tailoring it specifically for you. When you open your logical mind to the existence and practice of remote viewing, your intuition will help you when you aren't settled in that chair, with tape recorder in hand. What may be difficult for you (I know it was for me) is accepting what you receive. For example, before I wrote this article, I had three experiences reminding me of the value of my remote viewing practices, which led me to choose this topic for inclusion in the *Almanac.*

Three weeks ago I asked my friend Brett about a mutual acquaintance. Brett said, "He's just fine. His group is growing. He's doing well." I smiled at Brett, but inside I knew Brett wasn't telling me the truth. I also knew that Brett wasn't lying to me. What he told me he thought was true, but what I was getting in my head played out an entirely different scenario. Normally, I would have passed off the warning bell, except the impression I received carried a feeling of total dead calm. I was not angry, sad, happy, etc. There was just a silent, placid realization that what I was hearing wasn't so. Rather than debate the issue with Brett, I smiled and let the whole thing go. Shortly thereafter, I ran into the wife of the acquaintance and discovered that she'd left him, and that his group had walked out on him. All was not happy and doing well in the life of my acquaintance, just as my perceptions had told me.

About a week later, the mother of a friend of mine called me in hysterics. She wanted an appointment immediately. Things weren't going well in her life, and she wanted help, or so she said. Unfortunately, I had a house full of people when she called, and my schedule was packed. I told her I couldn't see her for a few days. She finally acquiesced, and made an appointment. I also told her that the slot I'd given her was the only one available in the next two weeks. My initial impression during the phone conversation bordered on uncomfortable, because the woman tried to force me to see her immediately, and insisted on talking for fifteen minutes, even though I indicated that I had a class in progress.

As we got closer to the appointment, I felt a sensation of irritation. I decided to do remote viewing. I saw her in her home, walking around and around, debating on whether she should come to visit me or not. Two days had passed, and now she wasn't so sure she wanted to talk to me. The house was lonely, deserted—that feeling you get when you go into an old person's home where all family activity has ceased long ago, and only vague memories rustle among the faded doilies. At the end of the remote viewing session, I realized that she wasn't going to keep her appointment, nor would she call me to cancel. As 7:00 P.M. came and went, I sat alone in my dining room. She never showed, and she never called.

Remember that remote viewing practices may not tell you precisely what is happening. For example, the lady in the last example may not have been pacing the room when I tuned in on her, but my intuition formed the best picture it could to show me the answer to my question. Just like Harold drowning in our first example. Harold may not like to swim, and may never put one pinky-toe into a pool; however, this impression gave you the appropriate answer. Sometimes you will be able to tune in on what another person is actually doing. That's called clairvoyance.

Practicing remote viewing techniques allows you to utilize the natural and important part of you—your intuition.

WORRY BEAD SPELLS

BY DAVID HARRINGTON

When in Greece, you quickly become accustomed to the sound of worry beads clicking together. On street corners, in parks, and in the local tavernas you see Greek men deftly work the beads from finger to finger. In the hands of an expert this enterprise can take on the artistry of a juggler. After landing at the airport in Athens, one of the first gifts presented to me was a set of worry beads. It was surprising how soon I found myself, in my inept way, working the beads. The experience, when mastered, is soothing and relaxing.

The beads themselves are made of many diverse materials, anything from glass, metal, or ceramic to faceted jewels. While much of the Greek use of worry beads is unconscious habit, the spinning motion of the sacred circle of beads generates an energy field that can be easily adapted to magical purposes. You can easily make your own set of worry beads to use in magic.

TO MAKE WORRY BEADS

Cut a length of cord thirteen inches long. You can also use a length of necklace chain if you prefer, particularly if you are using metal beads. Gather twenty beads, about one-fourth by one-fourth inch gauge. Beads that are somewhat heavy work best. Whatever type you choose, they should be fairly durable, since the beads click against each other as you rotate the strand. The beads and string color should represent your magical desire—pink or red for love, green or gold for money and prosperity, and so on. If you have access to gemstone beads, use ones that are appropriate for your need.

String the beads loosely onto the cord. The more space left for the beads, the more easily they move. Tie the end the of cord securely.

The strand should take on the appearance of a short rosary. You can leave a short tassel on the end below the knot.

Take the beads and consecrate them to your purpose by passing them through the smoke of an appropriate incense, such as cinnamon for money, rose for love, or sage or copal for health. Say these words or something similar:

Blessed be these worry beads
May my worry flee from me.

Loop the the beads around your middle and pointing finger and start spinning clockwise, imagining your magical intent while doing so. If you like, with each rotation of the beads, you can restate your magical intent, though the consecration with the incense smoke should have imbued your intent into the strand itself, so each rotation sends that energy out.

As the beads come toward you, imagine what you want coming to you. As the beads move away from you, imagine the lack of what you want leaving you.

For example, in a prosperity spell, imagine money flowing to you as the beads come to you. When the beads are moving away from you, imagine your money worries or poverty leaving you.

Bring me money! Banish need!
Bring abundance on every bead!
Heal my heart! Let loneliness depart!
Hello prosperity, goodbye to poverty!
Healing comes from head to toes,
Pain departs, sickness goes!

Take the beads with you and continue working with them until your need is met and the new reality has manifested itself. Wrap the beads in silk cloth and put them away until you need to use them for the same purpose again. With regular use of the worry beads, you may have very few worries left!

THE ROCKING CHAIR MEDITATION FOR SUCCESS

BY SILVER RAVENWOLF

We all want to be happy and successful. By using meditations, visualizations, and guided imagery, we can program our minds toward our treasured goals and desires. Over the past several years I have written several induction techniques for myself. the Rocking Chair is one of my favorites, as it brings back memories of a time when I would visit my Aunt Mamie and Uncle Homer on their farm. My aunt and uncle are long dead and the farm sold to Goddess knows whom, but those lazy summer afternoons will always stay with me.

Using pleasant memories to create induction tapes speeds the programming process. Feel free to substitute your own special memories or use this induction as written.

You will need a ninety-minute tape and cassette tape recorder. Practice reading the induction aloud several times before committing it to tape. Remember to take your time and relax while taping the induction. You may wish to play soft music in the background so that when you pause, the tape won't record unwanted sounds. As you read, you will notice that the grammar, sentence structure, and syntax in an induction are lousy. They are supposed to be. You will also notice that certain words are repeated often, such as *now, relax, sensation, feeling, safe, secure,* etc. These are key words and are meant to be repeated.

THE INDUCTION

Before we begin, I would like you to take three deep breaths. (Pause) Now, let's take a good stretch. That's right, stretch those arms and legs, get the kinks out of your back. Doesn't that feel good? Now settle yourself in a relaxing position. Just relax and let yourself sink into a nice comfortable position. Good. Close your eyes, feel your eyelids drifting slowly down, down, down. Relax your eyes. Feel any tension around your eyes flow out of your body. As you begin to relax, your immune system will begin and continue to function in perfect order for your body.

Take a nice deep breath. (Pause) Good. And another one. (Pause) And one more. Good. Just feel your muscles begin to relax throughout your body. Let all the muscles in your face relax. Feel the muscles in your forehead relax, now the muscles around your eyes and nose, relax and let it go. Safe and secure. Feel the muscles around your mouth relax, feel this relaxing sensation flow into your neck, and your shoulders. (Pause). Now the muscles in your arms relax. Feel your hands and fingers go loose and limp.

Good. Let yourself begin to float now as the muscles in your chest and back relax. Feel this relaxing sensation travel down your back like a soft spring rain. Down, down, down. Down your back. Relaxing all the muscles. Safe and secure, loose and limp. Now feel this relaxed feeling travel into your stomach and your hips, traveling down your upper legs and into your calves. Loose and limp. Safe and secure, as this relaxing sensation travels down into your ankles and your feet, into your arches and toes, and out the bottom of your feet. Now take another deep breath and relax.

Now I would like you to imagine that it is a glorious summer day. Not too hot. Simply pleasant. You are sitting on the wide front porch of a yellow farm house. The porch boards are painted a soft, soothing gray color. You are in your bare feet and you can feel the smooth floor boards as you walk on the cool porch. With every step you take, you will feel more relaxed. You will feel safe and secure, loose and limp. From this moment on, any outside sounds you may hear will help to enhance your state of deep relaxation.

I am going to count down from ten to one, and when I reach the number one, you will be in a deeper state of mind, deeper than you have ever been before. As I count down from ten to one you will walk across the porch toward a magical rocking chair. This is a very special chair, for as soon as you sit in the chair you will go ten times deeper than before, ten times deeper, into a deeper level of mind. This is a beautiful cane chair, a chair made just for you.

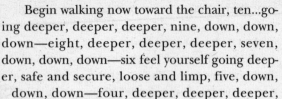

Begin walking now toward the chair, ten...going deeper, deeper, deeper, nine, down, down, down—eight, deeper, deeper, deeper, seven, down, down, down—six feel yourself going deeper, safe and secure, loose and limp, five, down, down, down—four, deeper, deeper, deeper, three, down, down, down into a deeper level of mind—two, deeper and deeper, down, and down, one, deeper and deeper, into a deeper level of mind. (Pause). Now sit slowly in the chair. Feel the heavy weights lift from your shoulders, feel yourself float up and up. You are in a deeper level of mind, deeper than before. A pleasant state, a safe place. That's right, just relax and let it go. Let it go. Yes, that's right. All gone. (Pause thirty seconds.)

Breathe deeply and relax. Drift and float into a deeper level of mind. Just float into total relaxation. Feel yourself getting lighter and lighter. You are filled with harmony and peace. Now, begin to rock the chair. That's right, nice and easy, and as you rock the chair you will become more relaxed. Back and forth, back and forth, back and forth, back and forth. Yes, just enjoy the summer day. Hear the soft breeze blowing in the trees. The sky is a beautiful azure blue. You can smell the rich earth around you. You can hear birds in the trees and see the sunlight streaming down, kissing the world gently with golden rays. Just enjoy this beautiful day, rocking back and forth, back and forth, back and forth. (Pause two minutes.)

Each time your magic chair rocks it is gently rocking success toward you. Yes, that's right. As the chair goes back and forth, success becomes a part of you. You are a successful person. Each time the chair rocks back and forth it breaks down the barriers you've created. You are expanding your horizons, feel success center on you, settle into your mind, that wonderful feeling of accomplishment. Nothing will stop you from achieving your goals. Each time the chair rocks you are getting closer and closer to your goals. Closer and closer to ultimate success. That's right, you will achieve your most fervent dreams. You will achieve success. You will complete your intended goals. (Pause two minutes.)

Feel these goals come toward you and wash over you. You are adding to your future. You are becoming more confident, more alive, more passionate about your goals. You will succeed. You will bring ultimate success into your life. You are worthy of the success you seek. You are worthy of abundance. Succeeding and reaching your goals is very beneficial to you and to those around you. You are comfortable with your success. Your success helps others. See yourself as a successful person. Feel yourself as a successful and deserving person. You will emerge into a successful, happy, and harmonious individual. You will always know the right thing to say in any given situation. (Pause thirty seconds.)

Feel yourself growing centered and strong. You will now move in the direction that is most successful and beneficial to you. Your success will assist those around you. You are protected and comfortable with your success. Now, take a few moments and visualize yourself in the future. See yourself obtaining your goals. See yourself as a leader. Experience the feeling of accomplishment. Visualize your rewards. (Pause four minutes.)

Good. Each time you listen to this tape you will draw closer and closer to your goals. You will reach your goals and become a confident, caring individual. You are a successful, harmonious person. You are centered and strong. You always say the right thing at the right time.

It is time to come back now. I'm going to count from one to five, and when I reach the number five, you will be wide awake and fully alert, feeling better than you did before. If you would like to go to sleep after listening to this tape, you will slip into a deep, restful sleep with beautiful dreams. When you awaken, you will feel refreshed and confident to begin a new day. Your immune system will continue to work in perfect order.

One, coming up now, two...remember you will feel refreshed and confident as a result of this session and will not feel any negative side effects from this session. Three, almost there. Four. Five. Wide awake and fully alert, feeling better than you did before the session.

SACRED MOUNTAINS

BY KEN JOHNSON

The world is a powerful and sacred place. Ancient buildings, straight-line roads, and mysterious monuments, as well as magical landscapes, attest to the energies hidden within the earth.

Of all the powerful places around the globe, sacred mountains are perhaps the most awesome and revered. Hindu and Tibetan adepts say that great masters, and even deities, may sometimes make themselves manifest as mountains. On the boundary of India and Tibet stands one of the most sacred mountains of all, Mt. Kailas, which carries the power of the great god Shiva himself.

In China, no less than five sacred mountains were recognized, one for each of the four directions, as well as one for the center. This same tradition is found in the American Southwest as well, where both Pueblo and Navajo peoples think of their land as surrounded by four sacred mountains. The eastern mountain is Mt. Blanca, near Crestone, Colorado, while the southern mountain is Mt. Taylor, near Grants, New Mexico. The western mountain, where the kachina spirits live, is Humphreys Peak near Flagstaff, Arizona. The northern mountain is a bit more obscure, but may well be one of the peaks in the San Juan Rockies of southern Colorado. The mountain in the center of it all is said to be a butte or mesa near the ruins of Chaco Canyon.

There are other sacred mountains of great power in the United States. Mt. Shasta is perhaps one of the best known, associated with UFO activity and the legends of the lost continent of Lemuria. Mt. Rainier in Washington state is said by the Native people to be a goddess. In the eastern part of the country, the Great Smokies have been held sacred for generations.

Wherever you live, there is very likely to be some mountain or hill that has been held sacred by Native Americans. A little research will tell you where it is.

Mixing Pantheons

By Cerridwen Iris Shea

In the past year, I have read an amazing number of articles
regarding the need to pick a pantheon and
stick to it. While I have an enormous amount
of respect for the writers of these articles and
their beliefs, I do have a slight problem with
what I've read.

I disagree.

Disagreement is one of the best tangibles
of our work; it allows us to celebrate our diversity. I respect the publicly published positions on the importance of same-pantheon
work, but I do disagree, and I will explain
why I disagree.

I am a practical, eclectic kitchen
witch. I've been trained in several of the more formal traditions,
but my actual daily work and spiritual life is based on beliefs, ideas,
and tools I can use. I believe in living the magician card in the
tarot—take the idea formulated in the astral, pass it through your
body (action) and create it as a reality. Ideas, inspirations, and beliefs are wonderful, but to me they have very little meaning unless
they are tangible.

Deities in various pantheons have similar meanings: for instance,
Hestia and Vesta. This, however, does not mean that they are inter-
changeable. Hestia is Grecian, Vesta is Roman. Both are connected
with fire, household affairs, mothering, and guardianship. Hestia also
handles families and tribes, earth and nature. Vesta handles ceremonies. Hestia is one of the Hesperides. Gaia gave Hera golden apples on her wedding day, and the Hesperides, aided by the dragon
Ladon, are the guardians of those apples. Vesta is one of the Appi-
ades, who are the nymphs of the Appian Spring, located in Rome.

As a fire-challenged Witch (my astrological chart has almost no
fire in it), I tend to have problems with fire, and therefore work with

fire goddesses to balance out. As a kitchen witch who does a great deal of home, hearth, and earth magic, Hestia is one of the goddesses I work with the most. Her connection to Gaia, apples, and dragons is more in keeping with my daily spiritual practices. For a large, public ceremony, especially one with feasting, I would call on Vesta.

The very name I write under is an example of mixing pantheons. "Cerridwen" is from the Celtic pantheon. She is a crone goddess, the keeper of the cauldron of wisdom. I am drawn to her because I know I can learn from her throughout my life, and share knowledge with those who seek it. I will never know everything, but I will keep learning

Athena

every day. "Iris" is from the Greek pantheon. She is a messenger between the gods and the underworld (Cerridwen's realm), and can move from the heavens to the underworld freely, the goddess of the rainbow, and a goddess of balance. I learn from her about balance, communication, and joy in the small details of daily life.

I work with Hera a great deal (Greek), Medusa (Greek), Bast, Anubis and Sekhmet (Egyptian), Ishtar (Mesopotamian), Lakshmi and Saravasti (Indian), and the Valkyries (Norse). Sometimes I work with several of them in the same ritual.

How do I make it work? I do my research. I decide what the purpose of the ritual is, and I research to see which goddess has the closest shade of meaning to what I seek. If I feel a combination of deities are useful, I make sure I learn as much about each of them as possible. Lakshmi and Saravasti are from the same pantheon, but it is reputed that they don't get along. I need both of them in my life. Therefore, I created a ritual where I invoked both Lakshmi

Ishtar

and Saravasti and explained why I needed both of them in my life, and asked them if all three of us could work together. I also pointed out that it was quite probable that somehow some scribe somewhere either got it wrong or purposely misinformed people. For all I knew, the two goddesses got along perfectly well for all these centuries and are just getting bad press. Both of them were extremely generous and supportive of me in the past year, and I will continue to work with and honor them.

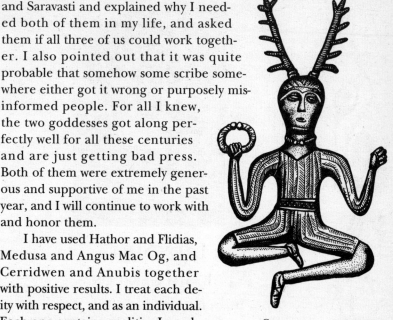

Cernunnos

I have used Hathor and Flidias, Medusa and Angus Mac Og, and Cerridwen and Anubis together with positive results. I treat each deity with respect, and as an individual. Each one contains qualities I need in my work and my life. I don't go in unprepared, and I am careful to make gratitude and joy part of the ritual.

"As in heaven so on earth" is one of the catch phrases in our work. If we expect to live as individuals in tolerance and support diversity here on earth, I don't think it is unreasonable to look for the same in the heavens.

I keep careful notes on my rituals and the deities I work with. At least once a year (usually around Samhain), I have a ritual of thanks for all the deities I have worked with throughout the year. There are libations and music and feasting and a list of thanks. This ritual is only about thanks and honor. I do not ask for anything. The entire house feels light and joyful for weeks afterwards.

Take the time to do your research and focus your ritual needs. That is necessary to create the full potential of a ritual anyway, but even more so in mixing and matching pantheons. One can never learn anything, but each deity, each legend, each myth out there has something in it that can enrich our lives. Part of our journey's fun is discovering it.

LADY SHEBA

BY JIM GARRISON

I, Jesse Wicker Bell, daughter of Della, daughter of Margarett, daughter of Nancy (Nanshee) the Cherokee, have kept the Wisdom that came from the Watchers so that all who come after me may find joy and peace in the worship of the old Gods and the Gracious Goddess of the ancient Wicca.

—The Grimoire of Lady Sheba

America's own Witch-Queen, Lady Sheba provided the first Book of Shadows to be made available to the public in 1970. Controversial, outspoken, and down to earth, Lady Sheba revealed the principles and practices of her family tradition in the hopes that the times of persecution were over and the need for secrecy adopted by the British traditions was no longer necessary.

American Traditional Witchcraft is a living mix of all the ancient pathways that have come together here in the land of freedom. Pilgrims who came to America brought their own customs and their own brands of Witchcraft with them. These Witch Traditions have intermarried and borne fruit for many generations. I believe this is why the gracious Goddess chose to release the book of shadows in America, by an American, for the whole world.

Born July 18, 1920, in Kentucky, Lady Sheba—Jessie Wicker Bell–was a naturalist, a poet, and a Witch born into a family tradition that preserved the Old Ways of Europe as well as the practices of the Native American traditions of her great grandmother. Her family originally objected to the publication of the Book of Shadows, but after several of them attended some of the lectures Lady Sheba gave at various colleges, they relented. Lady Sheba's family agreed that there was a great need in the world for the knowledge they guarded, and even though they were reluctant, they allowed Sheba to publish it.

As a mother of eight with fifteen grandchildren, Lady Sheba's life was filled with all the joys and all the sorrows of raising a family. A very earthy person, she always had land of her own, and loved her garden. Lady Sheba felt that it was especially rewarding to walk the earth, to gather salad greens or herbs for tea—it was important to her that there be no chemical sprays or insecticides on her herbs or produce.

Outspoken and honest, Lady Sheba genuinely cared about people, and was extremely popular among high school and college students. She listened, and answered people's questions regardless of their age. Both admired and hated by other Witches for making the secrets of the Craft available to the world, she was motivated by her devotion to the Goddess and the desire to prevent the Old Religion from dying out. It was her fondest hope that the wisdom of the ancient Witches would go on and that anyone who wanted to follow the old teachings would be able to do so.

During the late sixties, while in London, Lady Sheba met with Dr. Gerald Gardner, and in light of the many similarities of her family's Book of Shadows and his own, Lady Sheba became an honorary Gardnerian Witch. Reportedly, Dr. Gardner and Lady Sheba shared the view that in the far distant past, Sheba's family tradition and Gardner's version of the Craft may have come from the same source—though they had some major differences.

According to Lady Sheba, her family's tradition originally had no degrees, no oaths, and no vows of any sort. They practiced the Old Ways without making a fuss, and they never gave their word without meaning to keep it unto death. The rite of three degrees came from the English covens, and with the publication of her Book of Shadows, Sheba established a similar rite of three degrees for the American Celtic Tradition.

She openly acknowledged that she had adopted aspects of the Gardnerian tradition into her own, which led to many initiates into the American Celtic Tradition of Lady Sheba to consider themselves a branch of the Gardnerian tradition. As she was accepted by Gardner, so her followers thought, they might be accepted, likewise. Obviously this is not sound logic, nor did it work out that way.

In 1971 Lady Sheba officially registered The American Order of the Brotherhood of Wicca with the state of Michigan. It was her dream that this organization would serve as a rallying point for the various branches of the Craft in America, and act as a shield against religious discrimination. It was an idea ahead of its time, and has been replaced by such organizations as Covenant of the Goddess and Circle Sanctuary.

One always hears about Gerald Gardner, Alex Sanders, Raymond Buckland, and so forth, but somehow Lady Sheba is usually forgotten. Lady Sheba played a highly significant role in establishing Wicca as a legitimate religion, and by publishing her Book of Shadows, she opened the doors for thousands who otherwise had no way to train with a traditional teacher or coven. Lady Sheba brought the magic to the masses, and made it possible for whomever wanted to pursue the matter to gain access to the Old Religion. Such, she believed, was the will of the gracious Goddess.

Lady Sheba was quite a contrast to the academic and scholarly personas of Gardner, Alex Sanders, Raymond Buckland, or the Farrars. She was more akin to Sybil Leek, speaking her mind. Lady Sheba made no bones about her feelings or her opinions. She made appearances at some of the earliest Pagan festivals, such as the Gnostic Aquarian Festivals in Minneapolis where she performed public demonstrations of Wiccan rituals. During a time of intense interest and a lack of any real information, she made it possible for people to empower themselves and to reclaim the Old Religion from a legitimate source.

> *Never close the door of your mind to a new concept or a different pathway of knowledge. This can cause mental congestion, which is the opposite of the cosmic law of circulation, the law of motion, which exists everywhere, at all times, on all planes. There is a cosmic law that nothing can deny its own nature; and in this life no one can retain what does not belong to him by divine right of consciousness, nor can we be deprived of that which is truly ours by divine inheritance. The great secret of life is to cooperate with nature. If we could know and understand all of the divine, universal laws of nature, and could apply them to our daily lives, we could live long, vigorous lives, and when it comes our time to leave this plane of existence, we could transcend consciously.*

> —*Witch*, Lady Sheba

For all we know about her, Lady Sheba remains a mystery. Preferring to live in seclusion, maintaining a simple life, she came to greatly regret the attention and notoriety that came with her fame. At one point, when pressed for biographical information during an interview to promote her third book, Lady Sheba refused to add anything more to what she had already revealed. She wanted to go back to living a quiet life as a modern Witch. One of her last letters to her publisher ended with "I am that, that I am. It is enough."

Though her books have gone out of print and she eventually withdrew from the Pagan scene, Lady Sheba's tradition still exists, in a variety of forms, all across the country. Her early efforts at establishing Wicca have yielded a rich harvest. She may be gone, but she is not forgotten.

CASPARI

ABCs of Pagan Parenting

By Kirin Lee

Pagan parents have a unique task—that of teaching pagan values to their children in a world hostile to alternative religions. The following pagan child-raising ideas and values will be helpful when considering your children's Pagan learning experiences, no matter what tradition you practice.

A IS FOR ACTIONS. Your own actions and deeds speak loudest of all. If you want them to learn your chosen path, teach them about it with actions, not just words.

B IS FOR BEAUTY. Show your children the beauty in nature and the other life on this planet. Teach them to preserve that beauty for the future.

C IS FOR CONSISTENCY. Hold to the same principles and practices. Keep your actions consistent with your words.

D IS FOR DOING. Teach your children the old ways by doing pagan projects and crafts with them. Projects such as recycling show them that doing what they can to help the earth is essential.

E IS FOR ENTHUSIASM. Let your children see your enthusiasm for the old ways, and they will develop it, too. Take them on nature walks, and other places where they can learn to understand the Goddess and her creations first hand.

F IS FOR FAITH. Faith in themselves and their abilities helps children to handle any situation they may find themselves in. Give them suitable tasks to perform. Their completion will boost self-esteem.

G IS FOR GODDESS AND GOD. Teach your children the deities of your tradition. Explain who they are and what function they have in your life and rituals. Instruct them in simple chants they can use on their own.

H IS FOR HOLIDAYS. Celebrate your tradition's holidays with rituals and appropriate decorations. Sabbats and

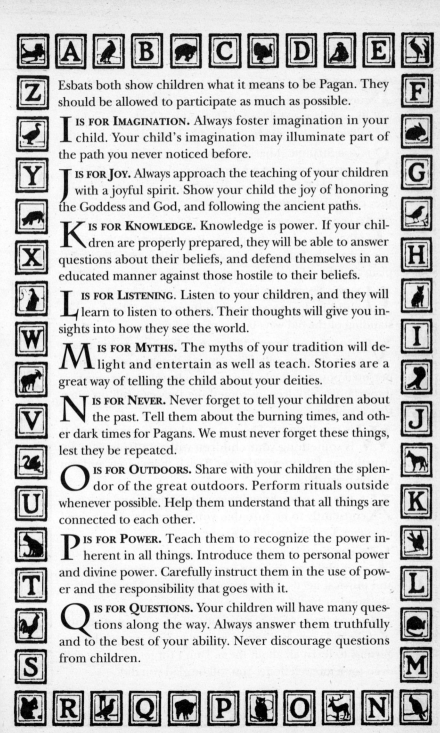

Esbats both show children what it means to be Pagan. They should be allowed to participate as much as possible.

I IS FOR IMAGINATION. Always foster imagination in your child. Your child's imagination may illuminate part of the path you never noticed before.

J IS FOR JOY. Always approach the teaching of your children with a joyful spirit. Show your child the joy of honoring the Goddess and God, and following the ancient paths.

K IS FOR KNOWLEDGE. Knowledge is power. If your children are properly prepared, they will be able to answer questions about their beliefs, and defend themselves in an educated manner against those hostile to their beliefs.

L IS FOR LISTENING. Listen to your children, and they will learn to listen to others. Their thoughts will give you insights into how they see the world.

M IS FOR MYTHS. The myths of your tradition will delight and entertain as well as teach. Stories are a great way of telling the child about your deities.

N IS FOR NEVER. Never forget to tell your children about the past. Tell them about the burning times, and other dark times for Pagans. We must never forget these things, lest they be repeated.

O IS FOR OUTDOORS. Share with your children the splendor of the great outdoors. Perform rituals outside whenever possible. Help them understand that all things are connected to each other.

P IS FOR POWER. Teach them to recognize the power inherent in all things. Introduce them to personal power and divine power. Carefully instruct them in the use of power and the responsibility that goes with it.

Q IS FOR QUESTIONS. Your children will have many questions along the way. Always answer them truthfully and to the best of your ability. Never discourage questions from children.

R IS FOR **RITUAL.** Rituals are an important part of all traditions. Let your children participate as much as their age will allow. A young child may only be able to help set up the altar. Older ones can join in the chants, drumming, or dancing.

S IS FOR **SHARING.** Sharing is an important lesson. Here is where you must set a prime example for your child. By sharing the old ways, you are giving them an honorable path they can follow all their lives.

T IS FOR **TOLERANCE.** Teach your child tolerance for all the others who share this planet. Remember that there is no one right path. Tolerance, however, should have its limits. Explain that they should never tolerate abuse for their beliefs.

U IS FOR **UNDERSTANDING.** Be understanding when your child is slow to grasp something new. Their understanding of the old ways takes time and patience.

V IS FOR **VISION QUEST.** Vision questing is something most older children will enjoy, especially when seeking their personal power animals. Power animals usually become very important to children, as something they can call on when they are alone.

W IS FOR **WISDOM.** There is no substitute for wisdom. It is something your children will gain from your instruction and their experiences. Teach them wisely and you will be rewarded.

X IS FOR **EXAMINE.** Examine your principles and practices constantly to be sure that you are not sending mixed messages. Confusion helps no one.

Y IS FOR **YOU.** Don't spend so much time worrying about your children that you forget about your own spiritual and physical needs. The way you treat yourself sets an example, good or bad.

Z IS FOR **ZEAL.** Always share your zeal for life, nature, and the old ways. You will be rewarded with your child's eagerness to learn all about them. Don't forget to praise children for a job well done. You will be glad you did.

Rainy Days Crafts for Kids

By D. J. Conway

Magnetic Holders

Children like to make things that, when given as gifts, other people will use and appreciate. Clothespin magnets are easy and fun for children; they can stretch their imaginations when creating the critter to go on them. You will need: spring-type wooden clothespins; magnetic tape or small magnets with adhesive backing; glue; tiny wiggly eyes; colored pipe cleaners; small pieces of felt; and small pre-made pompom balls in assorted colors. To make a caterpillar magnet, glue one-inch black and orange pompom balls onto a clothespin, alternating the colors. On the pompom to be the head, glue a pair of wiggly eyes. Attach a small magnet on the reverse side of the clothespin. For a bumblebee magnet, glue a half-inch black pompom ball for the head near the "snapping" end of a clothespin. Behind this, glue a one-inch yellow pompom followed by a one-inch black pompom. Glue a pair of wiggly eyes on the head. Attach short pieces of black pipe cleaner behind the head for the antenna. Cut out wings from yellow or black felt and glue them to the yellow pompom for the wings. Attach a magnet to the reverse side of the clothespin. Small black pompoms can make a butterfly's body; attach felt wings. A big green pompom with a smaller one

Magnetic Holders

glued on top of it and felt feet at the bottom can become a frog. Children's ideas for this project can be endless and can easily fill a rainy afternoon with fun and imagination.

CRAYON CAN

Being short of funds one year at Yule, I made my children crayon cans by painting scenes on salvaged coffee cans. I felt bad presenting them with such gifts and wasn't prepared for the enthusiasm with which they were received. No one else had such a special crayon can. This project is for slightly older children you can trust to use acrylic paints. If the children are young and you wish to include them in this activity, substitute paper cut to fit the outside of the can and let them color a design on that; then attach it to the can. You will need small coffee cans with plastic lids; any small metal container with a lid will work. Prepare the cans in advance by spraying the outside with a flat, light-colored paint. Let the children plan out their designs and paint them on the can with small brushes and acrylic paints. By

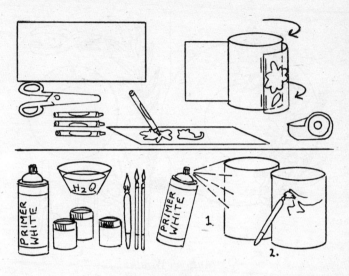

Crayon Can

the time they work their way around a can, they will have a
whole story in the design. This project can also be used to
make pencil cups (without the lid), containers for small sewing
things, or even cookie tins (using larger coffee cans).

A WREATH FOR THE AUTUMN EQUINOX

This is a project even three-year-olds can do with a little help.
Probably the most exciting part is gathering the natural materials needed. You will need: autumn leaves, small acorns, small
pine cones, dried flowers (in fact almost any plant material);
glue; scissors; a paper punch; and paper plates. Gather and let
dry the leaves, pine cones, and other plant material. Take this
opportunity to explain to the children what plant or tree each
leaf and nut comes from. Take a paper plate and, using a glass or
small bowl, mark out and cut a hole in the center of the plate.
Let the children glue the leaves and other dried flat material
around the wreath-shaped plate. Fill the wreath from edge to
edge. Let them add a few acorns and pine cones to the last layer.
Punch a small hole in the top of the plate for hanging.

Autumn Wreath

SPATTER-PAINT DESIGNS

Ever wonder what to do with old toothbrushes? I always have a few handy to clean around faucets and other hard to reach spots, but when my children were little, old toothbrushes were often saved for art projects. This project is for slightly older children you can trust with water colors. Still, you should choose a working space other than the living room carpet and protect the working area with lots of newspapers, or you will be scrubbing paint off floors and walls.

You will need: large sheets of drawing paper; old tooth-brushes; popsicle sticks; water color paints; cut-out figures and/or large dried leaves. Place the leaves or cut-outs on the drawing paper in a pleasing design. Use a flat surface where the child can kneel beside the paper. Dip a toothbrush lightly into the water color paint. Aim the toothbrush at the paper and, with the popsickle stick, spatter the paint on the paper. This is done by gently pulling the stick along the bristles to-ward you. If the stick is pushed away from you, you will get the paint in your face and all over your clothes. The trick is to not

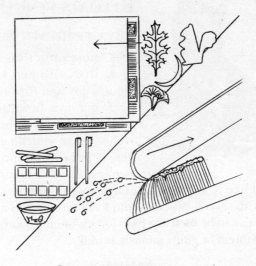

Splatter-Paint Designs

use too much paint at a time. If you wish to change colors, wash out the toothbrush and simply dip it into another color, repeating the process.

POLKA-DOT CARDS

This is a fun project for older children and even adults. These cards are personal greetings on special occasions, or if you are really ambitious, you can make stationery. You will need: different colors of construction paper; glue; a paper punch; ready-made plain folded cards and envelopes, or cut out your own cards from drawing paper; and a black pen. First, decide what design you are going to make. Using the paper punch, punch out the colors you want from the construction paper and glue them onto the card. With the black pen, draw in the rest of the design. The designs are more fun if you try to have one animal or plant in the design doing something opposite of all the rest. Let your imagination soar, and have fun!

Rituals for Pets

By Cerridwen Iris Shea

Those of us who share our lives with pets know how much joy and love they bring into our lives. In appreciation, I like to bless my pets at least once a year, sometimes more often, depending on the need and what is going on with our various lives. I would like to share some of my favorite rituals. I share my home with several cats, to whom I will refer in this article, but the rituals can be used as a basis for any animal. Don't forget to include totem or guide animals as well!

Samhain

This ritual is dedicated to Hecate, Cerridwen, and Bast. Cast a circle in your usual tradition, but make sure your pets are within the circle. Holding each animal facing you, draw an invoking pentagram on their heads with clove oil, saying:

> *I bless and consecrate* (name of pet) *in the names of Hecate, Cerridwen, and Bast, that s/he may have a year of love and good health, and may continue his/her companionship and loving relationship with me.*

After all the pets have been anointed, say:

> *I ask that blessings rain down upon* (names) *for happy homelife, companionship among each other, the elementals, and me. May their coats be shiny, their health fantastic, their tummies full, their water bowls clean, their catbox tidy, their tummies and ears scratched whenever desired, and may they have many toys, plenty of catnip and love, love, love.*

> *I thank my totem and guardian animals* (name them) *for their friendship and guidance this year. May we continue in good health and happiness into the next.*

> *Bless all creatures in happy homes. Bless all homeless and sick creatures that they may find comfort in loving homes. May*

there be no frightened, abused, starving or homeless creatures in the coming year. This I, your earth daughter ask, in the names of Hecate, Cerridwen, and Bast.

Give thanks, give the animals their treats, and feast. Note: Make sure that the oil is not harmful to the pets before putting it on them. You don't want to burn skin. If in doubt, use blessed water.

HATHOR'S DAY/BLESSING OF THE PETS

Sometimes, instead of blessing the pets on Samhain, I will do so on Hathor's Day (around October 4), in a ritual dedicated to Hathor. Again, cast a circle in your tradition, with your pets in the circle. Say:

Great Mother Hathor, who combines the elements of light and dark, mother, guardian, heaven, hell, sky, heavens, domesticated animals, happiness, Sun, day, justice, and destroyer of life, tonight your priestess/priest asks your blessings on (name animals), *blessings to be bestowed on these loving creatures.*

Again, draw a pentagram on each little head, saying:

(Pet's name), may the blessings of Hathor keep you safe from all harm; healthy, happy, and joyful. May you be secure in the love of the Great Goddess Hathor and her priestess/priest.

Then take the time to thank each of the animal guides or totem animals you work with, specifying why each one is important to you. Make a libation, give the pets a snack, and feast.

TRAVEL

When I travel and/or my pets travel, I take the time to bless them. To do this, cast a circle in your usual tradition, with the pets inside. I call on Bast, Flidias, and Hera. Draw a pentagram on each of them, saying:

I bless and consecrate (name) *in the names of Bast, Flidias, and Hera. May* (pet's name) *be healthy, safe, and happy while I am gone. May they know I love them and am eager to return to them. Blessed be.*

WELCOMING A NEW PET

I usually have a simple ceremony to welcome the new pet to the household. It seems to cut down on the spitting, hissing, and adjustment time between the pets.

To do this, cast a circle in your usual tradition, with your pets inside it, including the new one. Have the new one in a travel case if things are a bit tense. Dedicate the circle to Flidias. Play with and pet each of the original housemates, saying:

My dear housemates, I love and adore you and thank you for sharing my life. We live in a home filled with joy and love, and now it is time to share that joy and love.

Give each pet a treat. Remove the new animal from its carrying case, and say:

Welcome (name) to this happy home. We have joy and love to spare, and share it with you. Thank you for joining us.

Give the new pet a treat. If possible, play with all the pets together in the circle before making your libation and opening the circle.

DEATH OF A PET

The unfortunate truth is that most people outlive their pets. If you love animals, you will have to say farewell, probably more than once. Sometimes it is a welcome relief after a long illness. Other times it is sudden, sometimes violent. The pain and rage and loss are still there. I lost my beloved little Maude unexpectedly this past year. I won't get over the loss, but I have learned to live with it.

In my ritual to Hathor for the blessing of the pets this year, I added a section to bless Maude:

Hathor, I ask that you take care of Maude, who died in July and is so sorely missed.

I drew a pentagram over her photograph, saying:

My darling little Maude, you are loved, adored, and missed. May you be happy where you are for all eternity. Blessed be.

I kissed the photograph and lit a green jar candle, saying:

I light this candle in your memory. You always have a home in my heart, and this candle represents the light and joy you brought into my life.

Keep burning the candle (extinguishing and re-lighting as necessary) until it burns out.

There is no easy way to lose a loved one, but ritual helps. My cats, in general, enjoy rituals, and seem especially pleased when, once in awhile, a ritual is all about them! Blessings on all your pets!

INCENSE FOR CATS

BY BERNYCE BARLOW

Cats and magic have enjoyed a natural partnership throughout history. The Egyptians relied on feline cunning to destroy the rodents that plagued the Nile Valley granaries. Cats saved the population from starvation. Thereafter, cats were given a place of honor in Egypt.

The black jaguar of the Mayan people represented their most powerful deity and was the driving force behind their magic. This is still true today.

Giant ground pictures called *intaglios,* which are etched in to the Colorado basin of California, depict two mountain lions, each over a hundred feet long. According to the Mojave tribe, these are the tribal creator's helpers.

Of course, no cat story would be complete without mentioning all the wonderful tales of Witches and their feline familiars. One gem that has been handed down through English history is an incense recipe for cats:

3   teaspoons catnip, dried and crushed

1   teaspoon frankincense

3   teaspoons pine needles, dried and crushed

½–¾ teaspoon gum Arabic

Rain water to bind gum Arabic to other ingredients

Mix all ingredients together in glass bowl. Burn on self-igniting charcoal. For your cat's safety, burn this recipe before he or she comes in to play, or place the burner out of reach.

10/31/96

By Susan Sheppard

Outside, the sky drops like a lavender hem.

This is the night dusty souls
languish in their sewers,
watched over by granite lambs.

It is the night saints wear kilted skirts
spattered with coffin dirt, when skull-faced children
carry lanterns of skinned and grinning heads.

This is the night trees release
leaves of red witchery, when angels
in flimsy gowns ride their fiery discs.

Tonight is the night a dark wood swoons
around us like the rings of Saturn, when death
beautifully polishes things, leaves them there.

It is the night blackness
drives away the indigo light
and slaps us back inside our caves

Tonight is the night I can nail a board
over the face of anyone
I have ever loved.

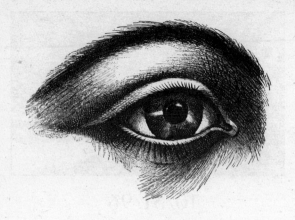

THE EVIL EYE

BY MARGUERITE ELSBETH

Mal occhio, the evil eye, is considered a very serious business in Italy, where the practice of *Stregissima,* or Witchcraft, abounds. However, Italian *Strege,* Witches, swear by the following sure-fire ways to avoid getting hexed, ward off evil spells, and to protect yourself from harm:

- Beware should someone give you a blackened lemon stuck with black pins. Even one black pin among a host of colorful ones indicates that someone wishes you harm. The lemon is a fruit of Diana, Queen of the Fairies and the Goddess of Witchcraft, so to undo the evil charm hold the lemon in your hand and chant this incantation to her while looking at the sky:

> *I call Diana, queen of the Sun and Moon and stars*
> *And, with what power I have, I conjure her*
> *To grant me a favor.*
> *I have gathered a lemon to bring me luck;*
> *I hold it in my hand.*

Then remove the black pins and bury them near running water. Stick the lemon with as many colorful pins as is necessary to replace the black pins. Now the lemon will bring you good fortune.

- If you see someone staring and pointing at you with arm and index finger extended in your direction, it is possible that he or she is putting you under an enchantment. Ward off the evil by turning the spell around. Face the person and stand on your left foot with your right leg held off the ground, knee bent close to the chest. Close your left eye and then extend your right arm and index finger in their direction.

- Anoint your forehead with three drops of olive oil, applied three times in the sign of the crossroads, to remain out of harm's way throughout your day.

- Burn your loose hairs or throw them into a place where no one is likely to look for them in order to save the hair from falling into the hands of evil sorcerers.

- Say this charm to Saint Anthony, patron saint of magic, when fairies, goblins, or other mischievous beings have spirited away your valuables, or even if you have simply misplaced your keys. Repeat three times:

  Dear Saint Anthony,
  Please come around;
  Something is lost
  And cannot be found.

- Protect yourself by placing a clove of garlic in a scapular (made from two small pieces of silk, wool, or cotton cloth joined by strings), along with an icon of your favorite saint or deity. Wear it around your neck, concealed under your clothing.

- Call to Saint Michael, a Christianized version of Mars, the Roman god of war, when you are in danger. Say his name boldly three times and you will be safe from harm.

A Folk Cure for the Evil Eye

By Jim Weaver

In the countries surrounding the Mediterranean Sea, the belief in the evil eye has been a part of daily life for centuries.

In this region of the world, when someone has a run of bad luck or comes down with a sudden illness, the evil eye is frequently suspected as the cause.

Although the evil eye is one of the world's oldest magical beliefs, no one knows for sure how the evil eye is "put on" someone. It is believed to be caused by a jealous stare or an envious look. Most persons who have the ability to cast the evil eye don't even know that they possess this unfortunate power.

The people of the Mediterranean have always relied on many folk magic cures, spells, charms, and remedies to break the power of the evil eye. Many of these cures are family secrets, passed down from generation to generation.

If you feel someone has put the evil eye on you, due to their feelings of envy or jealousy toward you, the following folk cure from the eastern Mediterranean may help destroy the negative energy directed at you. This particular remedy originated on a remote Greek island over a century ago. It is easy for anyone to perform, regardless of the spiritual path of the person performing it.

The two desired goals of this ritual are to find out how many people may be working against you, and to destroy the negative forces aimed at you. This ritual is not intended to direct negative magic toward someone or to get even with anyone. The basic purpose of this cure is to protect you and cleanse away any negativity that might be hanging around. Here are the materials you'll need:

1   new white candle

¼   cup water

½   teaspoon olive oil

1   small bowl

9   whole cloves

The white candle represents healing and protection. Water and olive oil have been associated with cleansing and blessing since ancient times; they appear in many cures used to break the spell of the evil eye. The purpose of using nine cloves is significant. The number nine, long associated with magic, here also represents the seeking of knowledge or answers. The cloves symbolize healing, protection, and help to purify.

The procedure for this cure is simple. Select a time when you won't be disturbed. Assemble all the materials listed above on a table, altar, or even a kitchen counter.

Combine the water and olive oil in a small bowl; set aside. Next, light the candle and gaze into the flame as you say a prayer or affirmation for protection. Visualize yourself surrounded by a circle of protective energy.

Pick up one of the cloves and ask aloud or silently, "Has anyone put the evil eye on me?" Then, holding up the first clove by the stem end (or use a pair of tweezers if that's easier), raise the clove so the bud end is barely above the tip of the candle's flame. Be careful—it will ignite instantly. Immediately drop the burning clove into the water/oil mixture to extinguish it. Repeat this procedure with each of the remaining cloves—this will only take a minute or two.

Pay attention as each clove is ignited. If a clove makes a popping or cracking sound as it bursts into flame or when it touches the oil and water, that means one person has put the evil eye on you. The popping noise you hear symbolizes the negative power of the evil eye being destroyed. Also, the smoke and scent released by the smoldering cloves has a purifying effect, which increases the power of this cure. If none of the cloves "pops" when burning, that's good; it means any evil directed at you has passed you by, and you've weathered the storm.

To finish the ritual, first snuff out the candle. Then you must conclude the cure by disposing of the water, oil, and cloves in a respectful manner.

Take the bowl containing the water, oil, and cloves, and with your fingers, lightly sprinkle the mixture around the room, or your entire home. Sprinkle in the corners, and in front of windows, doors, fireplaces—any opening where negativity might enter. Again, this is a good time to say a prayer of thanks for having your home free of hostile energy.

If you have any of the mixture left, you may take it outside and pour it onto the ground around your home. Visualize the negative power draining back into the Earth, where it will be purified. For apartment dwellers, use the same visualization while pouring it down a drain.

I like to put the candle and bowl away in a safe place so I can use them again, just for this ritual.

Now relax. You have just used a bit of old folk magic in a positive way: to remove the curse of the evil eye from your life and your home.

THE VRYKOLAKES OF SANTORINI

BY deTRACI REGULA

Santorini is the most mysterious of the Greek islands. Enigmas cling to the layered volcanic rocks. Approaching by sea, an eerie silence settles over travelers as they stare at the sharp-banded cliffs of black and red, crowned in some places by a snowy white layer not of ice, but of tufa, a bright, soft volcanic stone. It's a place easy to believe in spirits, and that may be why Santorini has another name: The Island of the Vampires (*Vrykolakes*). Perhaps because of the island's terrible history, Santorini has acquired a new claim to fame in modern times. It is the home of the Aegean's most experienced vampire vanquishers. If Van Helsing, the vampire hunter of Bram Stoker's *Dracula,* could have his choice of vacation retreats, he probably would select Santorini. A Greek phrase for an unnecessary effort is "To send vampires to Santorini," a useless endeavor, since they already have plenty.

In the seventeenth century, there was a great plague of vampires on Santorini, and in the Greek world in general. Because of this, the inhabitants developed a specialty in dealing properly with the disposal of them, and this actually developed into a financial opportunity for the island. Other islands afflicted with active or suspected vampires would disinterr their bodies and ship them to Santorini experts for proper disposal. In this sense, Santorini became something of a toxic waste dump for the undead. This persisted until at least 1902.

Greek practices for eliminating vampires rarely employed the stake through the heart method found in Slavonic tales, though this may have occurred occasionally in districts where the influence of the Slavs was strong. The preferred method was to burn the corpse, ideally on an island, since it was believed that the vrykolakes could not cross salt water. Sometimes, however, the body would be chopped into pieces and reburied, but there was a sense that this was not entirely sufficient. During this dismemberment, which sometimes was accomplished by a mob of terrified villagers, the heart was given special treatment. It was torn out and then boiled in vinegar.

Vampires in Greece seem capable of feats that vampires of other nationalities are not. They are often seen in daylight, and sometimes eat normal food. On the island of Corfu, one incident was recorded where no fewer than fifty witnesses attested to having seen the vampire at large, resulting in an official pronouncement of exhumation and destruction of the body. Occasionally, vampires were said to gorge themselves on green beans, though vegetarian vampires seem to be something of a contradiction.

It was believed that vampires were often created as the result of excommunication from the church. Part of the excommunication, which is essentially a liturgical cursing, contains the words "and after death you shall remain indissoluble." The incorruptibility of such cursed corpses was apparently so common that a little guide was produced to help identify the reason the remains had not decomposed. If only the front parts of the body were preserved, the victim had left a command from his parents unfulfilled or was under their curse. If the corpse looked yellow and its fingers were wrinkled, the victim was under an anathema (a curse). If the corpse looked white, the victim had been excommunicated by divine laws, and if the corpse looked black it had been excommunicated by a bishop.

The Greeks recognized two types of vampires, one group of the truly undead, who animated their own corpses and came out of the grave to do their damage, and another group of the still-living, who fell into trancelike states and sought out their victims. Originally, the Greeks also accepted a more benevolent type of returning spirit, similar to a ghost, who nonetheless could appear and do farm work or other helpful labor, and in one instance, give another child to his widow. After the seventeenth century, during the great plague of vampires, tolerance of these benign returning spirits vanished, and any undead were dealt with harshly.

Today, in modern Santorini, mention of a vampire is likely to bring a dismissive laugh, until you turn down one of the narrow, whitewashed alleys just as the Full Moon is rising. In the glimmering light, an emaciated gray face with wild yellow eyes appears next to yours. You step back, stumbling, then realize it's just a poster glued to a post, announcing a vampire-themed evening's entertainment. Someone on Santorini still knows the island's history.

But surely no real vampires would be bold enough to visit this island of expert vampire-vanquishers...or would they?

THE WATCHERS

BY BERNYCE BARLOW

Along the coast of Central California is a mountain range called the Santa Lucia. The seventy-
mile stretch of the infamous Big Sur coast is a part
of this range. Big Sur is known for its pristine beauty, healing springs, crystal blue-green coves, waterfalls, and majestic redwood forests. Big Sur is also
known as the home of the Watchers. John Stein-
beck, who grew up in Salinas, California (near Big
Sur), wrote about his experiences with the Watchers in
his short story called *Flight*. Most of the locals have at least
one story to tell about the dark, shadowy figures with trans-
parent human form, and many visitors to this area do too!

It has been said if you are being watched, you will instinctively know it, and the first glimpse of a Watcher will
come from the corner of your eye at night. In the dark of the
massive redwood groves one would think an ebony shadow
would be impossible to discern, but our eyes can adjust to
darkness, allowing shadows to take on life, and so it is with
the Watchers. The Watchers' presence can be felt during the
day, but it seems as if they can stand in the light without casting a shadow. Perhaps light is their camouflage. After all, a
shadow cannot be cast without light. The Watchers do not
disturb, they watch. The more you are aware of them, the
more they are aware of you. Their intent is not curiosity.
When you turn to face them eye to eye, their shadow form
dissolves, yet their presence lingers. Have I ever met a
Watcher? One does not meet a Watcher.

There are many theories about the Watchers. Some folks
say they are Star People sent here from the Pleiades, other
folks feel they are disassociated spirits left on earth as a pun-
ishment for their greed and selfishness and that they cannot

interact or fully materialize until the human family becomes one, once again. Other stories illustrate the Watchers as beings from another dimension, the conscious protectors of the Santa Lucias, if you will. The most ancient tale describes the Watchers as shy spirits of nature who prefer to live among the rugged coastal caves or in the shadows of the redwood forests, and who are here to assist those crossing over to another realm of being. No one knows for sure who the Watchers really are or why they reside in Big Sur. They only agree that the Watchers are watching.

If you ever find yourself in Big Sur or the interior of the Santa Lucia mountain range, take some time to explore the locale. I would suggest you take a hike through the redwood groves or stroll along the beach, submerge yourself in hot springs, allowing the Pacific salt mist to cool your body after bathing. You can sit along a river or by a cove hosting sea otter. The point is that if you allow Big Sur to embrace you, it will. Oh, by the way, during your visit if you happen to catch a glimpse of a shadowy form out of the corner of your eye, at the same time as you get the feeling you are being watched, you probably are.

Redwood grove considered to be inhabited by the watchers

THE RAVEN

BY MARGUERITE ELSBETH

Ravens belong to the bird family called *corvidae:* large, omnivorous, gregarious, and obnoxious. These black birds can't sing worth a lick, though their raucous language is quite communicative and extensive. Live food doesn't interest ravens; they prefer dead things, like roadkill and other birds' eggs. In fact, ravens hold funerals for their dead. One bird will guard the body and rattle a death song, letting the other ravens know what has occurred. They form a circle around the corpse, and dance round and round, croaking softly from deep within their throats. For this reason, the ancient Celts and other tribal peoples associated the raven with death goddesses. Considering the habits of this bird, it is easy to derive other attributions also.

- The black-feathered raven calls to mind the beginning, the maternal night, the primordial darkness, and vital primal earth.

- Soaring through the sky in graceful, rag-winged flight, the raven is a messenger heralding transformation and change.

- Some North American Indian tribes believe the raven to have the powers of attention, observation, swiftness, and ambivalence, as well as the ability to find lost objects.

- Celtic and Germanic tribes, as well as American Indians and Siberian peoples, once believed the raven to be the creator of the visible world.

- Contemporary tribal people the world over still associate the raven with magic, believing that through its spirit one can divine the future.

- In Celtic myth, the raven was one of the most important symbols of the Terrible Mother, for the raven is a scavenger that devours corpses on the battlefield. Fighting Celts would find ravens eating the rotting flesh of the dead warriors, adding to the bird's mystique as guardian spirit of the dead.

- The raven eating the dessicated remains of the body is an earthy symbol of the Celtic goddesses Badb and the Morrigan, who, like the Aztec goddess called Filth-eater the Witch, consume all misconceptions lingering in our souls.

- The Celtic goddess Blodeuwedd, Freya and Holda of Norse myth, and Rhea and Artemis in the Mediterranean are often depicted as sorceresses—black-faced and long-haired, with a raven flying above them.

- The Scottish witch Isobel Gowdie testified that she often left her body and traveled in the shape of a raven to Otherworldly realms.

- The Irish banshee, or "woman of the hills," is often imaged as a raven, for she is heard moaning and keening whenever death is near.

- Sometimes the raven is a White Goddess of death and rebirth: the ancient European Queen of the Dead. The White Lady, as she is sometimes called, may be seen dressed in black when she comes forth as a raven to gather the souls of the dead. The Celtic love goddess Branwen's name means "White Raven."

- The Pueblo Indians of New Mexico say that one day, a long way back, ravens had white feathers and could speak like humans. E-yet-e-co, the mother of life, told the ravens to stop picking the eyes out of dead people or they would be punished. One raven couldn't resist this tasty treat, and picked out the eye of a dead person anyway. At that moment, all the ravens turned black and lost their ability to speak.

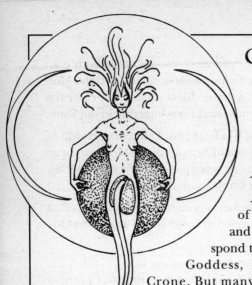

GREEN HECATE, THE DARK PHASE OF THE MOON

BY ESTELLE DANIELS

Everyone is familiar with the three phases of the Moon, waxing, Full, and waning. These also correspond to the three aspects of the Goddess, Maiden, Mother, and Crone. But many cultures recognized a fourth phase or face of the Moon, the dark phase. This corresponds to the three days when the Moon is invisible, between the last waning crescent, through the astrological new Moon, and up to the first waxing crescent.

In my mystical studies and meditations I have become acquainted with a deity that I call Green Hecate, and she corresponds to that dark Moon phase. She is symbolized by the seed that has germinated and sent down a root, yet has not sent up a shoot above the ground. Her colors are black, pale green, white, and neutral, gray, or tan, the colors of a germinated seed and the fertile earth it grows in. She rules the possibilities of germination and fertilization, which are infinite. She is the potentiality between death and decay and the new young things that emerge from the compost. Her time is the gray spring, when the snow has melted and yet nothing has started to poke out of the earth. Things are growing, but they are invisible as yet.

In astrology she also is symbolized by the twelfth house, the traditional house of self-undoing and merging with the infinite. This house holds the culmination of all the lessons and experiences of the other eleven houses, and the potentiality of the new incarnation, shown by the first house. This house can be read to indicate karma, issues brought from past lives, and possibilities for reincarnation.

Green Hecate is both a Maiden and a Crone. She is slim, but it is both the slimness of youth and the withered flesh of age. She is old and wise, and also young, naive, and innocent, holding all possibilities out to those who would seek her. She is the chaos of formlessness and pure potential, before any form or possibilities have manifest. She is also the chaos and dissolution of death and decay, the breaking down into the primal elements that follows death. She resides in that instant before the big bang and after the collapse of the universe. She rules the limitless possibilities in genetics and evolution. Old species die out so as to make room for new ones, or to allow new ones to develop where they would not have before. Sometimes these ends are accomplished by sudden cataclysm, like a comet hitting the earth and wiping out all the dinosaurs. Sometimes they are more deliberately accomplished, like when humans kill whole species outright, or introduce new species into environments where they take over, killing the native plants and/or animals.

She can bestow inspiration, bringing ideas and thoughts out of nothing. She can give invisibility, the ability to act and create without having your actions become known. She can also allow the final, behind-the-scenes clearing out after something has ended. She can show a person infinite possibilities if that person is open to anything.

Green Hecate's time is short, sometimes no more than the blink of an eye, and sometimes just three little days between last crescent and first crescent. She is easy to overlook or ignore because she doesn't appear to the world. Her realm is imagination and the inner planes. She rules the place where a person who has lost touch with reality goes. Where does your mind go when you are daydreaming, asleep, blacked out, unconscious, under sedation, catatonic, autistic, or insane? She is in those moments before sleep and before waking when you are not in this world, but not in the dream world either. She cannot be concretely grasped, not held or captured. You can only perceive her in passing, understanding intuitively who she is and what she is about.

You can see her in an eclipse, but how often do you see eclipses? Some find her scary, but only because she is so elusive, yet so powerful. Some are afraid of her limitless potential, preferring to keep their possibilities numbered and concrete. Some are afraid because she cannot be seen, and therefore you cannot always tell what she is up to. Is she working on decay and dissolution, or is she building limitless growth potential? Only time will tell, and often one turns into the other. Death and decay can be frightening, but we forget that rot turns into compost, which nourishes the soil, making a fertile environment for new growth. Even as things break down they provide the building blocks for the next generation of growth.

Green Hecate also rules that time between lives, when the soul evaluates the past life and other previous lives, determines what new lessons need to be learned, and participates in choosing the next life—the new vessel for growth and evolution.

We have to be careful when we invoke Green Hecate, for she is never truly predictable. We have to be open to any and all possibilities. She can also provide us with ideas and possibilities heretofore undreamt of. Her time is short, but that is appropriate, for we cannot exist in formless chaos for long. In this universe, potentials soon take form and then are no longer limitless. Her time is magic, and fleeting, and to be treasured. Next time you are at the end of your rope with nowhere to go, think of Green Hecate. She may provide a way out that is impossible, yet wonderful. When all has collapsed around you and you have nothing left, think of the possibilities. Just close your eyes and take that first step. You may be surprised where it leads.
Blessed Be.

THE CHARGE OF THE CRONE

BY JIM GARRISON

Hear the words of the Dark Goddess who stands within the crossroads, whose torch illuminates the Underworld:

I am the Queen of Magic and the dark of the Moon, hidden in the deepest night. I am the mystery of the Otherworld and the fear that coils about your heart in the time of your trials. I am the soul of nature that gives form to the universe; it is I who await you at the end of the spiral dance. Most ancient among gods and mortals, let my worship be within the heart that has truly tasted life, for behold all acts of magic and art are my pleasure and my greatest ritual is love itself. Therefore let there be beauty in your strength, compassion in your wrath, power in your humility, and discipline balanced through mirth and reverence. You who seek to remove my veil and behold my true face, know that all your questing and efforts are for nothing, and all your lust and desires shall avail you not at all. For unless you know my mystery, look wherever you will, it will elude you, for it is within you and nowhere else. For behold, I have ever been with you, from the very beginning, the comforting hand that nurtured you in the dawn of life, and the loving embrace that awaits you at the end of each life, for I am that which is attained at the end of the dance, and I am the womb of new beginnings, as yet unimagined and unknown.

ACCEPTING THE PASSAGE

BY ROBIN GREENWILLOW

Cerridwen, the Celtic goddess of transformation, has a cauldron where the changes she creates occur. Everyone is touched by the goddess and her cauldron, and so we each change, but the real story lies in accepting the transformation.

When Gwion, Cerridwen's servant, became wise, it was a simple thing. He just put his finger in the cauldron he was stirring and tasted it. Wham-o! All of a sudden he was wise. It was accepting the changes that wisdom brought to his life that Gwion fought with. He did not want to face Cerridwin's wrath when she discovered that her brew, a special concoction for her son that took over a year to prepare, had been eaten by Gwion. Although Gwion left plenty of the brew in the cauldron, he took all of the wisdom out of it with his little taste. This meant that only the useless dregs were left for Cerridwen's son, and that her plans were ruined. To avoid Cerridwen's wrath, Gwion fled by changing his appearance. He shifted into the shapes of many animals, and Cerridwen followed him, shifting shape as she chased him. It was only when Gwion shifted into the shape of the hard-to-find but helpless grain that Cerridwen caught him. She could see past his outer appearance and ate him. Taking him into her, she also set him free of his old life by giving birth to him. When he finally accepted his new life he became the great bard Taliesin.

For most of us, life is like this tale. Initial change may be easy, but it is the consequences that we dread. Even when a change is a good one or a happy one, we sometimes hesitate because of the consequences that a change will bring to our lives.

A new job or a new relationship may be a wonderful thing, but it may also mean less time for good friends. Coming out of a closet (broom, or otherwise) is painful, but for many a necessary part of being who and what they are. Like Taliesin, we may try many guises to cope with the stress of wanting both the old and the new.

When Gwion changed by becoming wise, he did not try to undo the change by becoming unwise. He tried to find ways to be the same old Gwion and be wise at the same time. He shifted from shape to shape in an effort to remain Gwion. We do this as well. When a change comes into our lives we sometimes tell ourselves, "I'll still find time for all of the old commitments too."

We try to put everything together—this is the first shape shift. Then we try to negotiate between the parts of our lives that don't mesh well, which is the second shape shift. Then perhaps we try to keep separate parts of our lives separate—the third shift—and so on. This is the painful part of change. Even when the change is a good one, it may lead to the realization that another part of one's life is not working anymore. This can mean changing in ways that we would rather not, like giving up bad habits that, while comforting us, also harm us.

The trick is to change anyway—to accept the growing pains for what they are—a necessary part of becoming the person we want to love, the person we want to be. While most people don't want to cause unnecessary pain, sometimes we use that as an excuse for not causing growing pains. We can grow in a caring way. We can grow in ways that ensure that we harm none. We may not be able to grow in ways that prevent others from harming themselves. We can try to help them cope, we can offer them love and understanding, but ultimately we must accept our own changes, and allow ourselves to grow.

SHAPESHIFTING:
REFLECTIONS OF OURSELVES

BY SIRONA KNIGHT

From my bed I feel myself slipping into lucid dreaming, where my mind skirts the fine line between being awake and dreaming, and being aware of both states simultaneously. I give myself the suggestion to begin shapeshifting, and within moments my flesh sprouts golden feathers, changing my arms into wings that carry me to the sky. The stars are like stepping stones lighting a path through the cosmos. As the eagle, my wings are one with the breeze, and from my place at the top of the world, I see an overview of the world, and how the web of light connects together. Earth, wind, fire, and water, I soar with the light to a place where all is oneness.

Several writers have recently spoken about a change occurring from an old world view, which saw the world in mechanistic terms, to a new view, deriving from a more natural and spiritual approach to life. Shapeshifting is a method for becoming more in touch with nature, ourselves and oneness. As we shapeshift and change our awareness, we also change our personal dream, and in turn change the consensus dream, and with it, the overall view and direction of society. Using shapeshifting to harmonize with the natural patterns of the Earth and connect to a higher energy has been a common practice down through the ages, exercised by many cultures throughout the world.

The adolescence ceremonies of many Native American and South American traditions included the vision quest, where the importance of dreams and visions was stressed. Through awareness of these dreams and visions, the initiates discovered the guardian spirit that was to walk with them throughout their lives. Discovering their guardian spirits and communicating with divinity often meant bonding with a particular animal,

and thus taking some of the characteristics of that animal into the person's personal myth or dream. Essentially, this bonding with animal energy to connect with one's guardian spirit is a form of shapeshifting. By shifting into the form of an animal, the individual gains another view into the divine.

In the book *Once and Future King* by T. H. White, Merlin the wizard deliberately changes young Arthur's form, shapeshifting him into a fish, squirrel, and bird as part of Arthur's training, thus giving the boy certain insights into both animal and human behavior. This technique of using shapeshifting as a learning device ties back into an ancient Celtic rite, where Druid initiates enhanced their knowledge and craft by shapeshifting into various animals in order to understand the essence of that animal, and how this essence reflected the natural faces of the Goddess.

Legend describes the art of t'ai chi as originally scripted from Chang San-feng, who watched the movements of a snake and a crane. t'ai chi taps sources of energy known only to the wild animal and the young child. Students are taught to be fully conscious in their dreams, eliminating the barrier between conscious and subconscious. Doing slow, flowing, meditative movements called "the form," t'ai chi practitioners let go of their self-images and, as an example, replace them with a tiger's image, while making an effort to embody tiger-ness within specific movements of the form. Simply acting like a tiger does not work. The practitioner must let go and become one with the animal. The use of imagery in t'ai chi brings the person into harmony with the nature, and it is a form of shapeshifting.

Shapeshifting, as a whole, is a way of putting us back in touch with the animals, the earthly cycles, and ultimately ourselves. As each one of us is a part of oneness, each of our personal dreams are part of the consensus dream. By using shapeshifting with dreaming, we each begin incorporating this new awareness of the natural patterns into our personal dream, thus effecting the consensus dream.

The Renaissance essentially began with Columbus' rediscovery of the New World, and was characterized by the ideas of Rene Descartes and Sir Isaac Newton, who subscribed to the belief that everything, including life, could be ultimately understood within the terms of reason and science. The spirit, which cannot be measured in scientific terms, was left in the domain of mystics and magicians, and given no place of residence within the realm of science as built and sculpted by "the age of reason." The consensus dream is now moving away from this idea of science being the answer to everything, to one that now integrates human spirituality with a new scientific view that sees everything as interconnected systems. This view is not far from the spiritual concept that everything is a pattern in the web of oneness. Because everything is a pattern connected by oneness, everything is essentially a mirror for all other aspects of oneness, no matter how large or small.

The concept of the mirror and everything being a reflection is an essential element in shapeshifting. It is often said that you bring the aspect of the animal back into yourself, but in actuality you simultaneously recognize an aspect of yourself in the animal.

In this recognition, you become more knowledgeable about yourself as a human being, and as a part of nature and the divine whole. Your view of what is possible also expands.

Eastern, Western, Old World, New World; many cultures have used shapeshifting as a means of increasing self-awareness and spiritual growth. The idea of the animal totem is beautifully described in the Native American Algonquian word *nto'tem*, meaning "my kin," and alluding to the special relationship and very real kinship between animal and human energy. By virtue of our connection to oneness, we are reflections of one another. We are the animals; the animals are us; we are one. The many shapes we shift into are the many faces of ourselves and oneness.

Ritual and Magical Masks

By Patricia Telesco

While the function of masks changes depending on the cultural setting and time period in which they are found, there are some themes that are common to many mask-making cultures. The use of masks as a religious tool is very old, and is documented in ancient Greece and Egypt, with some evidence to suggest mask use as far back as paleolithic times.

Masks were worn predominantly by healers and participants in rituals. The healers donned them for two reasons. The first was to commune with the spirit being called upon for aid. Second, the mask provided a psychological advantage for the patient, both hiding and heightening the healer's personality. It was much easier to anticipate a miraculous cure from a costumed figure than from "Joe" who might have lived in the next hut!

For ritual purposes, masks allowed participants to throw off the mundane world in favor of another visage one presumably pleasing to the animal, spirit, ancestor, or deity they were worshipping. One good example comes from tribal societies, where during planting festivals, people would regularly dress in masks depicting vegetation gods, then perform high-jumping dances so the grain would grow tall.

It should be noted that masks and costumes regularly appeared as counterparts to one another, and as an accent to sacred dance and music. Together these adornments improved the symbolic impact for the worshipper, and were believed to be a potent tool in communicating with the divine. From such combinations of mask, costume, music, and movement, it is but one short step to the development of ritual theater, like the Hill Camora Pageant still seen today.

Priests and participants alike also donned ritual masks at various rites of passage. In some African tribes, the circumcision mask got discarded after use at a boy's coming-of-age ritual, marking the end to the old life and the beginning of adulthood. The gold funerary masks of Egypt, however, not only escorted the ruler from this life to the next, but lasted long enough should the spirit return to the body. As John Mack said in *Masks and the Art of Expression,* "(the mask) is used at those times when human experience is transforming."

Traditionally, people made masks out of a variety of materials, including precious metal, stone, wood, clay, basketry materials, corn husks, and more recently, paper maché. They were (and are) then decorated with rope fibers, furs, shells, bark, feathers, hair, leaves, stones, sand, or other suitable materials, according to the goal of the ritual.

By using the historical contexts for masks as a starting point, one may update, adapt, and apply the concept fairly easily for metaphysical goals. The idea in creating a mask is to allow yourself, for one moment, to harmonize with a specific energy. Exactly how that energy is used afterward changes according to the mask created and the goal of the ritual. Here are some examples.

Someone wanting to overcome a bad habit may make an ugly mask and don it momentarily to understand the self-destructive nature of that habit. At the end of the meditative ritual, the mask gets torn off (to indicate that person's readiness for change) and destroyed to help banish the negativity.

When you're having trouble adjusting to a specific situation, make a mask and costume through which you can positively act out success in that situation. Afterward, keep the mask where you can see it regularly to help manifest change in the situation.

For children, masks are terrific fun, allowing them to learn simple magical ideas through a creative medium. Let them make representations of animals or the elements,

then act out those things. Afterward, discuss how they felt during the exercise. You will be surprised by their insights.

If there is a fear that seems difficult to overcome, make a mask representation of that fearful thing, put it on, then look in a mirror. By facing our fears head-on, we can often overcome them.

While you might feel awkward at first about making and wearing a mask for such purposes, remember that all of us wear figurative masks from time to time. Additionally, mask-wearing has a strong precedence in our civilization from the time-honored heroes of the Lone Ranger to Superman (whose mask is actually only a pair of glasses), and the surgeon's mask that protects both doctor and patient.

To make a mask yourself, first think of one simple goal that you can depict pictorially. Cut out the mask so it has an appropriate shape for that goal. For example, people seeking more balance in their lives might create a large triangle representing the body-mind-spirit symmetry. Next, paint it an appropriate color or colors and add decorations. I have found that the following common items work well for improving the visual impact of your mask: string, wrapping paper, ribbons, felt-tip markers, paint, crayons, scrap fabric, feathers, cork, powdered herbs (chosen for aroma, magical affiliation, and visual appeal), cut-outs from magazines, flower petals, and leaves (chosen for symbolism and color).

Masks help us to reconnect with our imaginative self, something very important to effective magical procedures. When one can visualize goals in realized form, very often those goals get achieved. So, by delving into our creative nature to put an image on our fears, hopes, and goals, we encourage external manifestation on internal change, and learn much about ourselves in the process.

Mysterious, Magical Masks

By Silver RavenWolf

The need-fire rages. The drumbeat pounds a pattern in your soul. Breath comes quick. The night air pulses with enchantment. Your eyes fill with the sight of masked dancers, challenging, enticing, feeding the energy of the fire....

From primitive times, shamans and tribal peoples used masks to identify themselves with the powers and energies of animals, supernatural entities, or divine beings. From ancient societies to Greek and European theater, humans used masks, costume, or face paint to convey emotion and add to the imaginations of their audience.

In Pagan cultures, the construction of the mask concentrated on bringing the benevolent energies of the chosen subject to assist the wearer and the tribe. Often constructed in secret, then empowered through ritual, these masks played an important function in community life. Ancient belief systems felt that the wearer of the mask could achieve possession by the energies that the mask represented.

Masks fall into four categories: realistic masks, animal masks, stylized masks, and forceful/dynamic masks. Realistic masks show natural, human, or god-like images. Animal masks bring forth the representation of a particular animal. Stylized or abstract masks and forceful/dynamic masks can represent a compendium of images, such as a human, god, plant, animal, mythical, or natural force.

In the twentieth century, Witches and Pagans work with masks to enhance ritual, drawing forth benevolent energies to affect both the wearer of the mask and those participating within the magic circle. These energies may represent god and goddess forms, animals, mythical creatures, or natural forces. As in times past, ritual players usually enact some type of legendary occurrence. Favorite mythos include the descent of the goddess, the battle of the Oak and Holly Kings, the courtship of the God and Goddess, the divine marriage, seasonal representations such as planting or harvest, and of course, various initiation rites.

In ancient times, masks were fashioned with natural materials found indigenous to the area of the tribe. Today, with the advent of synthetics, the ritual mask-maker finds no end to the materials he or she can use to represent his or her creative genius. All materials for the mask need to be cleansed, consecrated, and subsequently empowered for a specific purpose. If the mask-maker constructed a mask to represent an animal totem, he or she would concentrate on the specifics of the energies of that totem while making the mask. For example, an animal mask made in the likeness of a wolf would draw loyalty, teaching, and kinship. A mask fashioned to represent the Oak King would call for strength, stability, and depending on the ritual in which the mask will function, victory or death.

The magic of the mask does not end with the completion of the image. A good ritual, or choreography of that ritual, can make or break the final intent. Rituals involving masks and costumes need not be long, but do require the appropriate focus of the player. Many magical practitioners use meditation or trance work to draw themselves into the desired state of mind before the ritual begins, and may not fully remember the specifics of the entire performed ritual as a result of that altered state.

When a player places the mask on his or her face, he or she can allow the real world to fade into the mists of memory, pulling energies, talents, skills, and emotions normally blocked by logic or personal inhibition into his or herself. One becomes the God, or melds his or her energies with the element of water, the emotion of transformation, or the strength of a totem animal. The magic of the mask frees the wearer, permitting him or her to walk into another time, another place, another form of existence. When two or more players allow the enchantment to manifest within the magic circle, extraordinary rituals and events of memorable proportion ensue for all present, including spectators.

The use of sound, particularly the drum, helps to create, move, and control the energies of the masks and the players who wear them. Other instruments, such as rattles, bells, and flutes, add nuance and clarity to any performance, because the sound affects the chemistry of the players as well as the audience. When a drum speaks, humans listen.

Firelight also promotes the magic of masks, through their inception to their use. Dim lighting or flickering light enhances the player's art of illusion. As the light caresses the costumes, the mask, and the performer, the magic comes alive in the hearts of the spectators—the battle of the Oak and Holly King comes alive, the touch of the Goddess as She moves around the circle sparks the heart and mind, the joy of the water-nymph as she plays at the west quarter rests forever in the memory.

Use your gift of creative genius to make a mask, and watch the magic and mystery come alive in your hands.

CRAFTING CHINESE LANTERNS TO HONOR THE DEAD

BY EDAIN MCCOY

The last major festival of the Chinese year falls on its final Full Moon. At this time the spirits of the dead are honored in the three-day Lantern Festival. Delicate paper lanterns in a rainbow of colors decorate every possible surface: in and around homes, at gravesites, in the streets, in shops, on trees, etc. The eye-catching, multi-colored paper of which they are made represents the beauty of the soul, and the light within symbolizes the eternal nature of the soul, while serving as a beacon to guide those who have died during the previous year safely to the land of the dead.

Lantern making in China is a cherished art form, and many of these offerings are awe inspiring in their elaborate and intricate designs. You can make similar lanterns with materials easily found in craft and hardware stores. They can be used to honor your beloved dead, or be incorporated into any other lunar celebration you observe during the year.

MATERIALS

The materials you will need include a warm iron, sheets of different colored craft-weight tissue paper, some inexpensive penlights (one for each lantern you wish to make), batteries for each light, plenty of fishing line or lightweight craft wire, a glue stick, and a bag of popsicle sticks. The sticks and the paper are easy to find in craft stores. The penlights can usually be found in office supply, hardware, or novelty shops.

INSTRUCTIONS

Begin by gluing the sticks in groups of four to form squares. You will need two sets of these for each lantern you will be constructing. To all four corners of one of these sets of four, attach lengths of fishing line approximately one and a half feet long. Gather up these ends and hold them up, adjusting them until the square below hangs level. Tie these off together, leaving about one foot of their length. These will be used to hang the finished lantern.

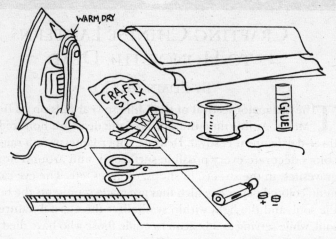

Chinese Lantern Materials

To any two opposite corners of this same square of four, attach two more lengths of fishing line, each about ten inches long. Allow these to hang loose down in the center of the square. These will be used to hold your penlight when the rest of the lantern is completed.

Cut four pieces of the colored tissue paper in sizes twelve inches wide by one-half inch longer than the length of the popsicle stick you are using. For example, if your sticks are five inches long, you will cut your pieces into twelve by five and a half-inch rectangles. It will work even better if you first cut a template out of a piece of poster board in the size you need and trace around the paper so that the papers will all be identical in size.

Gathering up the four sheets, place them one on top of each other. Keeping them together as much as possible, begin folding them accordion-style with each fold about a half inch from the next. When you are finished, use a warm iron to lock these folds into place.

Glue the pieces together by the long (twelve-inch) sides, making sure they overlap by no more than a quarter inch (see illustration). If you overlap more than this you will have trouble fitting the lantern to the space allowed by the popsicle stick squares. Permit these to thoroughly dry before going on to the next step.

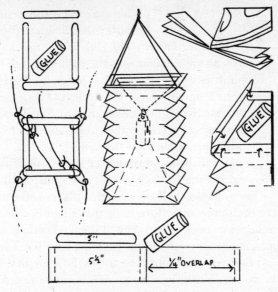

Constructing the Lanterns

Next, take the square of popsicle sticks without any fishing lines attached to it, and insert it into the first inner-fold at one end of the tube of tissue paper. Fold the bottom flap over the sticks. You have just attached the bottom half of the lantern. Glue it securely in place and allow it to dry thoroughly before continuing with the next step.

Take the square with the fishing line and, keeping the four longest lines on the outside, fit this piece into the top fold of the lantern. Glue it in place the same way you did the bottom and allow it to dry thoroughly.

Carefully reaching inside the delicate lantern, take the two ten-inch lines and tie them to the top of the penlight (so the end with the light in it is pointing down). It may be easier to pull the two lines out through the top for this operation. Make sure when you are done that the light remains fully inside the lantern as high up as possible. This will give you the best distribution of light through the colored paper, and will assure that the penlight will not be hanging out the bottom.

Hang the lantern up by the top fishing lines and enjoy!

OTHERWORLD MIST

BY KEN JOHNSON

There are many different ways to enter that magical dimension called the Otherworld. Here is yet one more. Readers who are familiar with the myth and lore of Celtic countries will remember that heroes and magical pilgrims frequently enter the Realm of Faerie by walking into the heart of a dense mist or fog. Though this particular exercise comes from Eastern Europe, the principle behind it is the same.

Lie down on your back with your arms at your sides. Breathe deeply, until your entire body relaxes. Try to let go of all the thoughts that crowd your mind. This may take both time and effort, so be patient and be persistent.

When at last your body is in a state of deep relaxation and your mind is empty, envision a wall of mist covering your feet. As the fog creeps up and over your feet and your ankles, imagine that this part of your body has simply vanished: no more feet, no more ankles. The Otherworld Mist has swallowed them.

Then the mist rises to your knees, then to your thighs. Finally, your whole lower body is invisible, swallowed by the fog. You may perceive this in one of two different ways: some people lose all feeling and sensation in those parts of the body that have vanished, while others become aware of a tingling, a special "aliveness" in those areas. Either way, it means that part of your body has entered the Otherworld.

Let the mist rise to your chest, your shoulders. Then the Otherworld Mist swallows your head, and you have completely entered the Realm of Faerie.

What happens now? Those who have been trained in Wicca or other contemporary magical disciplines may allow themselves to experience images, pictures, visions, if you will. When this exercise is employed by the esoteric Christian mystics of Eastern Europe, they allow themselves simply to float in the ecstatic state of consciousness induced by their entry into this other realm. When the exercise is used by the *kolduny,* or traditional Slavic sorcerers, they take advantage of the situation to explore their Otherworld body with spiritual eyes, hunting for imbalances or "dark spots." They collect the darkness and breathe it out through their tailbones (the root chakra of Hindu yoga).

Mr. Crowley

By Jim Garrison

Every man and every woman is a star.

—*Liber Al vel Legis I:3*

Poet, mountain climber, world traveler, cross-dresser, magician, heroin addict, big game hunter, prophet of the Aeon of Horus—Edward Alexander Crowley was all of these things, and more. It is impossible to do the man justice in less than a million words. He was a complicated, paradoxical, and greatly misunderstood man who changed the world in ways we have yet to fully realize.

Assuming the Gaelic form of his middle name, Aleister, he came to be reviled in the scandal sheets of his day as "The Wickedest Man in the World." Aleister Crowley was a man of passion and lust who gave the world a new religion, a new perspective on magic, and a new eon.

Raised in a strict, fundamentalist Christian household, Crowley began life as a dedicated student of the Bible. After the death of his father, however, things went progressively sour between Aleister and his mother, who dubbed him "The Beast," a title he quickly adopted and relished throughout his colorful life. Although he was sickly and often bullied as a child, Crowley proved to be very intelligent for his age. As he developed intellectually, he determined to overcome his weakness, and so took up rock climbing because it was regarded the most dangerous of sports. The self-confidence and physical vitality that came with his new-found athleticism, coupled with the eruption of his sex drive, led him to thoroughly reject Christianity because he saw it as the embodiment of all the cruelty, meanness, and fanaticism he had endured in the course of what he described as a "boyhood in hell."

Free of the stifling oppression of the Plymouth Brethren, Crowley pursued mountaineering, poetry, and sexual conquests. Reading voraciously, he filled his rooms with books, but he graduated without a degree. He practiced at chess up to four hours a day, became the president of his chess club, and yet never went on to become the world champion he had once planned on becoming. His inheritance gave him the means to indulge his emerging hedonistic tendencies, something he did with a wild abandon—love without guilt and sex without shame were his way. Casting off his parents' morality, Crowley explored every facet of human sexuality with gusto, having affairs with men and women alike. Ultimately, it would be his free-wheeling bisexual liaisons that would be used to deny him initiation, sparking the downfall of the Golden Dawn.

Through all his escapades and adventures, Crowley remained fascinated with the teachings of magic, alchemy, and of Eastern philosophies. In his search for answers he eventually met George Cecil Jones, who initiated young Mr. Crowley into the Hermetic Order of the Golden Dawn in 1898. Crowley adopted the magical name of Frater Perdurabo, Latin for "I will endure to the end." Of all the great Adepts of the Golden Dawn, he has indeed endured. Crowley has more disciples today than at any time when he was alive.

The Golden Dawn collapsed in the midst of bickering and petty politics, with Crowley right in the thick of things. From out of the ashes emerged a number of off-shoots and descendent magical lodges and orders, including Crowley's own order, the Astrum Argentium. Five years later, in 1912, Theodor Reuss initiated Crowley into the O.T.O.—the Ordo Templi Orientis, or Order of the Temple of the East, a radical lodge of German Masons who practiced sexual magic. Crowley immediately embraced the O.T.O and re-made it in his image, becoming the International Head of the order in 1925. It is perhaps his involvement with the O.T.O. that most influenced Crowley's work. A great deal of his writings and records have been maintained and published by the O.T.O., who have worked to keep the magic of the master alive.

Reckoned by many to be the foremost magician of the twentieth century, Crowley has had a tremendous impact on the world through his various publications, public ritual performances, and shocking behavior that opened the door for the sexual revolution and the occult renaissance of the sixties.

Crowley lived a grand life of passion and élan, traveling across the world, exploring the mysteries of every esoteric discipline he could find, including Shaivism, Tantra, Yoga, Taoism, and Sufism. The ancient teachings of the East captured his imagination and left their mark upon everything he did. He applied the analytical techniques of modern science to everything from sex, to drugs, to yoga, to magic. Crowley kept meticulous records of every experiment, leaving behind an invaluable treasure trove of personal research into the effects of various drugs, mind-states, and ritual techniques. A bold pioneer and trail-blazer into ambiguous and subtle regions of human consciousness and spirituality, Crowley opened the doors for those who would come after him. He saw clearly that others would follow, and that he was just the beginning of something greater than himself.

Past Lives Meditation

By Ann Moura (Aoumiel)

The powers of the Dark Lady and Dark Lord can be utilized to reveal the secrets of the past through a black mirror meditation. This type of meditation may be used on its own or in conjunction with a dark aspect ritual such as a dark Moon esbat or a Sidhe Moon esbat (second dark Moon in a solar month).

With all meditations, it is a good idea to incorporate your own ideas for a more rewarding experience. Another person's visualization is not the same as your own. It is fine to alter and personalize a published meditation to make the experience more meaningful to you. If music is used during the meditation, it should be chosen to supplement, and not overpower, the mood being set. It helps to keep music very low so as not to interfere with the mental focus.

A dark Moon esbat ritual may be used in conjunction with a black mirror meditation, although the meditation may be done without the esbat ritual. It is a matter of preference. The meditation may be used alone by creating a circle using dark Moon esbat imagery and calling on the Elementals to guard the sacred space.

A black mirror may be purchased at most occult stores, mail ordered, or made by the individual. Prior to use, wash it in water infused with mugwort, dry it, and consecrate it at both the Full Moon and the Dark Moon so it can be used for a variety of meditations.

Smoothed and polished obsidian also makes an excellent meditation tool. If a tool will be used for Otherworld meditations, it should be consecrated with burdock root rather than salt.

MEDITATION

Be seated either before the altar, or at a table that can be used for this meditation.

Light a black candle in its holder using the center altar candle, and say:

This candle glows to light the path into darkness.

Place the candle in front of the propped-up black mirror. You may want to drum or shake a gourd rattle against the palm of your hand as you chant:

I call upon the dark and the past;
The ancient of days in the Realm of Repast.
Unleash to my sight the paths I have roamed;
And show me the forms of lives I have known.

Look past the candle and into the mirror to gaze into your own eyes. Continue to shake the gourd and chant the rhyme, without really listening to it or paying attention to the motion. Focus on the mirror and watch as the face changes into those of past lives. Do not be surprised to see faces of the opposite sex or even of beings not guessed at or known. The soul's journey encompasses the universe, and where one has resided may be other than Earth. In some cases you may even see a progression of lives into other life forms of Earth. Not all lives need be considered from the "past," as some may be yet to come, or are on other planes, for the location of the past depends on one's location on the spiral at any given moment.

When done, if still shaking the gourd, stop and say:

The memories of past and future are shown;
The faces of me in time are now known.
Blessings I give to the Veiled One of Night;
For through this mask am I given the sight.

Cover the mirror with a black cloth and snuff the candle.

Proceed with the esbat ritual or take some refreshment and move back into a normal routine.

A Wizard's Prayer

By Ken Johnson

This simple ritual, practiced by traditional Slavic sorcerers, is an excellent way to cleanse your room or workplace of all undesirable influences and, at the same time, to prepare yourself for magical work.

Take a kneeling position, your thighs resting on your heels, and your hands placed loosely on your knees. This may be uncomfortable at first, but hang in there, and any soreness will soon vanish. Face any direction you like; although the four directions were important to Slavic sorcery during Pagan times, they are no longer taken into account for practical work.

Take a few deep breaths, until you are relaxed but still perfectly aware. Focus your attention on your chest. Try to move your consciousness inside your chest, so that you think, breathe, and feel from a place deep within you.

Now, turn on a light inside your chest, and imagine that it beams forth ahead of you into infinite space.

Whether silently or aloud, call out this blessing:

May all beings be peaceful!
May all beings be quiet and calm!
May all beings be filled with bliss!

Repeat this three times, each time imagining that your own consciousness is becoming more peaceful, calm, quiet, and blissful.

Now move your inner beam like a searchlight so that it shines out into infinite space on your right. Once again, repeat the blessing three times and feel how it works upon you as well as upon the spirit world all around you.

Now move the beam of light so that it shines out in back of you and repeat the blessing three more times.

Move the beam of light to your left and repeat the blessing three more times.

Now shift your beam of inner light so that it shines directly above you, awakening your upper spine along the way and illuminating your face, your eyes, and your head as it travels into the infinite sky. Repeat the blessing three more times.

Finally, move the light so that it shines below you, awakening your lower spine, traveling beneath the earth to the very center of things, blessing the ancestors who dwell below. Repeat the blessing three more times.

Now simply become quiet and listen to your body. Are you peaceful, calm, and filled with bliss? If so, you are ready to meditate or begin magical work.

Dressing Kabbalistically

By Estelle Daniels

Kabbalah is an old system, originally transmitted orally and then written down in the 1300s by the Jews in Spain. The system has been further refined and codified by both Jews and Christians ever since, and it is a wonderful guide and teacher.

The Tree of Life, a diagram of ten spheres connected in various ways, is the central focus of Kabbalah. Each sphere corresponds to a planet, a day of the week, a color, and many other things. The Tree of Life is a diagram that can be used to explain the workings of the universe, the path to God, a plan for spiritual development, and more.

You can adapt the Kabbalah to your personal lifestyle by adopting the color/day system. Using Kabbalah can enhance your psychic and magical abilities. You probably won't see any results immediately, but over time you might find yourself more "in tune" with the ebb and flow of the energies of life. You might find your psychic faculties are more effective and sensitive. Your intuition may become more acute and accurate. You could become more effective in presenting yourself, and gain self-assurance.

Nowadays, we have many options as to what we wear for clothing. In the past it was usual for a person to have only two or three sets of clothes, one or two for everyday wear, and possibly one for special occasions. All eventually ended up grayish (dirt colored). In the past, a Kabbalistic magician was expected to have seven separate outfits, or perhaps seven robes of different colors, which were worn over a basic garment. To be a Kabbalistic magician was an expensive endeavor, requiring you have some independent means of living, or a wealthy patron.

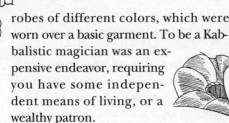

The modern magical practitioner can use these energies and correspondences the same way the Kabbalists of the past did, but because of our modern fashion options, we have many more ways to accomplish this end.

The colors and correspondences are those taken from Kabbalah, and are known as the "King's List." There are other lists, but primarily the King's List is used in the Kabbalistic correspondences.

Sunday corresponds to the Sun, Leo, yellow, and gold. Monday corresponds to the Moon, Cancer, purple, and silver. Tuesday corresponds to Mars, Aries and Scorpio, red (more cranberry red than the common fire-engine red), iron, and steel. Wednesday corresponds with Mercury, Gemini and Virgo, orange, and mercury (quicksilver). Thursday corresponds to Jupiter, Sagittarius and Pisces, blue, and tin. Friday corresponds to Venus, Taurus and Libra, green (or pink), and copper. Saturday corresponds to Saturn, Aquarius and Capricorn, black, and lead.

Using this list of correspondences, we can dress Kabbalistically by wearing the colors of each day, on that day. Or we can wear a medallion of the metal or color corresponding to the planet of the day, worn inside or outside the clothing. (How one wears a medallion of mercury, which is liquid at room temperature, is to get a medallion made of red

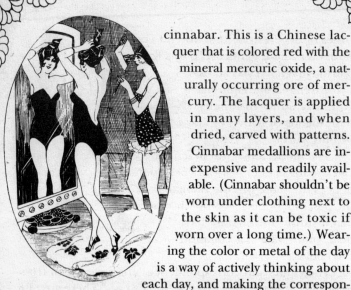

cinnabar. This is a Chinese lacquer that is colored red with the mineral mercuric oxide, a naturally occurring ore of mercury. The lacquer is applied in many layers, and when dried, carved with patterns. Cinnabar medallions are inexpensive and readily available. (Cinnabar shouldn't be worn under clothing next to the skin as it can be toxic if worn over a long time.) Wearing the color or metal of the day is a way of actively thinking about each day, and making the correspondences to the planet, color, and attributes that the energy of each day of the week possesses. Once you are dressed, the color or metal becomes a subconscious reminder of what the energies of the day are.

How a person can choose to dress is adaptable. Some people go whole hog and dress in only the one color, from underwear on out. However, you get little mix-and-match capability in a wardrobe of seven distinct colors.

Some people use the colors in their underwear and/or socks. It is easy, relatively inexpensive, and doesn't require you revamp your entire wardrobe.

The business set can use ties and/or decorative handkerchiefs. Women can use scarves as accents. You could also have colored shirts. This way a person can have a basic gray, black, navy, or brown suit, and add the accent for the day color. It allows one to be conservative, yet Kabbalistic, in dress, and as only the accessories are colored, you still get the mix-and-match adaptability of the modern business wardrobe.

If you wear a uniform, you can go with underwear and socks, or one person I know uses a different color hair tie (the elastic ones) for each day of the week. A bandana or colored handkerchief may also work.

As so many people wear blue jeans today, having different colored shirts, sweaters, sweatshirts or t-shirts is an easy way of working with Kabbalistic correspondences. Personally I consider denim color (blue jeans color, light or dark) to be a neutral color, since that is the default uniform of people who don't have to dress up for work. Gray and brown (tan) are also neutrals.

When you haven't done laundry for a while, it helps to have several different clothing options available.

Some magicians have seven different sets of ritual robes or colored cords, one for each day of the week. Using Kabbalistic color correspondences in magic can add effectiveness to your workings, especially if you are high magic or you use some of the high magic rituals.

In the end, the rewards from this system are subtle. It takes time, but you find the color-day correspondences become a habit. In the never-ending work of the magical practitioner, this is a relatively easy yet effective method of helping attune yourself to the subtle energies all around. Knowledge and will combined can accomplish much. Blessed Be.

TEACHING A CIRCLE

BY CERRIDWEN IRIS SHEA

One of the most fulfilling, difficult, exhausting, and exhilarating activities I do is teach a circle. I consider myself a solitary, yet I belong to Sisters of the Singing Stone coven, one of the joys of my life. We are a strong, joyful, and artistic bunch, to say the least. My coven sisters enhance my work and my life no matter how far apart we are sometimes scattered.

Around Mabon in 1995, I started teaching The Circle of Muses. Enough women came to me seeking to learn about the Craft, and wanting to learn from me, that I decided it was time to teach. At times, we have been as large as thirteen; now that we are closed and have begun initiations, we are a regular working group of nine. By the time you read this, I will be teaching a second circle, The Circle of Bards, comprised of men (set to begin around the Spring Equinox 1997).

Guidelines and boundaries are essential for a working circle to not only get together, but stay together. Guidelines must be set and stuck to. My students are my responsibility—they are trusting me with their psyches, and that is an enormous honor and responsibility to bear. Part of my job is to create an atmosphere of safety, and also make sure that they do not take advantage of each other or of me. As High Priestess, it is my responsibility to make sure that the atmosphere created is appropriate. That doesn't mean we won't help and support someone who is having a bad day or going through a difficult time, but we are not a therapy group, and we cannot do our work evenly and joyfully if one or two people become a drain. It can be a painful decision, but if one member of the group is not living up to his/her commitment, or draining the energy of the group, that person needs to leave.

I have found that the following guidelines helped set up an atmosphere of love and trust for The Circle of Muses.

PURPOSE

The purpose of this work is to align you, physically and spiritually, with the world around you so you can function at full capacity. This way, you can find and fulfill your purpose with a combination of balance, responsibility, and self-reliance. This is not set up as many traditional circles are, nor does it follow one particular tradition. We are here to learn how to have the best of both—to work well within a group, and get enough inspiration to work on our own whenever and wherever we need or want to.

COMMITMENT

Not everyone will be able to attend every meeting. That is only natural. However, you are responsible for completing the homework tasks between meetings and getting them to the HPS in time to be incorporated into the ritual. We will meet approximately once a month, sometimes more frequently for celebrations. Please try not to miss more than three circles in a row. It will be quite loose for the first year, with people entering and leaving, and the group will feel quite elastic. Then, due to the nature, intensity, and trust level of the work, the circle will be closed. We will reassess where we are and where we want to go, and discuss initiation and dedications.

Rules

1. Respect and honor the members of the group.

2. Fulfill your responsibilities regarding commitments, tasks, and homework. It is bad for morale if you do not have your work done on time.

3. It is okay to disagree, but do so with respect.

4. We are here to celebrate our differences and encourage individuality. Be thoughtful of other members' feelings when discussing the group; some may not be comfortable being discussed in connection with this work.

5. Do not discuss ritual work for 24 hours after it has been done, even with other members of the group. It dissipates the energy.

6. Do not use the group for therapy. We are here to support and guide each other, but not to replace a psychological professional. Also, circle as therapy dilutes the power of the work and twists it unfairly.

7. Do not interfere with another's free will.

8. If it feels wrong, don't do it.

9. You receive a schedule of the circles at least six months in advance. It is your responsibility to call the High Priestess one week prior to the circle and find out what you need to do, bring, etc. that might not be in the notes from the previous circle.

Ways to Avoid Burnout

Monthly Meetings. I found that meeting once a month works very well. I know of circles that insist on meeting once a week for at least a year. I have watched not only the HPS burn out, but the students fry as well. Once a month gives students time to process what was done in the circle, do the homework, and get curious and excited about new discoveries. The students remain eager to be there every month. I encourage them to work on their own, and they do; sometimes two or three of them get together and work on their own and then share the rituals they performed with the rest of us. I had the flu once on a ritual day; I called my students and told them to go ahead and meet without me. They whipped together a ritual and had a wonderful time. It gave them added confidence—they knew more than they thought they did.

BE THOROUGH. For the first year, we met three times on the New Moon; then three times on the Full Moon; then three times on the waning Moon; then once on the dark Moon. Now we rotate: New Moon, Full Moon, waning or dark Moon, plus holidays. This way, the students can get a feel for what each phase means. They all also keep journals and we take the time to write in them at every circle, and especially after mediations. I keep detailed notes and also hand out copies of the ritual to each of them whenever we meet. I send copies of the rituals to anyone who missed a circle so they can keep up with the work. When they work on their own, they bring in copies of their rituals and hand them out. This way, all our books of shadows keep growing, and we learn from each other.

KEEP THE STUDENTS INVOLVED. As soon as possible, I make them active in the rituals and assign bits of the rituals to them. I make different people do different parts of the ritual each time, so that no one does the same thing all the time, and everyone has the chance to learn and actively work on different parts of the ritual. The only portion of the ritual I keep for the initiated is the actual casting of the circle. I realize that everyone will have different feelings on this, based on working traditions. I am merely sharing what works for us.

Teaching is a wonderful experience. I learn a lot from my students. They enrich my life beyond belief. In spite of some frightening political right-wing movement in the United States right now, I think we are entering an era of tolerance and individuality. Looking at the people who are drawn to and learning the craft right now, my heart fills with hope, and I do believe that a positive, beautiful future is possible. It won't be without a heck of a lot of hard work and personal, individual responsibility, but the Earth has a future and it is up to us to believe it and create it.

Jewitchery

By Edain McCoy

One of the names that the growing number of Pagans of Jewish heritage go by is "Jewitch." Like Pagans of all cultural backgrounds, they seek to reclaim their Pagan past from the centuries of religious teaching under which it has been buried. Many of the festivals of modern Judaism display Pagan roots, and have been adapted into the Jewitches' wheel of the year.

Sukkot: A Celebration of the Harvest

Sukkot usually falls in October, and is the festival of the harvest. It corresponds to Lughnasadh or Mabon on the Wiccan calendar, and is a time to give thanks for the fruits of mother earth and to pray for sufficient rain during the year to come. Meals are eaten outdoors in a structure known as a *sukkah.* The sukkah is a hut made from sticks and branches, and decorated with the fruits of the harvest. These structures were used by the ancient Hebrews when they traveled from Egypt back to their homeland after escaping from slavery, so it is also a festival that celebrates freedom.

One telling aspect of the sukkah structure that shows its Pagan links is the fact that it must include four specific types of foliage that are said to represent all growing things ever to have been placed on earth. Like the elemental tools that rest on our altars—and represent all creation—each type of foliage has an elemental correspondence. These are the *lulav,* or young shoot from a palm tree (air), the willow branch (water), the myrtle branch (earth), and the *etrog,* a fruit resembling a lemon (fire).

SUKKOT HARVEST SOUP

2   yellow squash

1   zucchini

1   cup unsweetened applesauce

¼   cup puréed currants or raisins

2   tablespoons dried, minced onions

5   cups chicken broth

1   cup water

⅛   teaspoon sage

⅛   teaspoon allspice

     Salt to taste

Cut the squash and zucchini into bite-size pieces. Place all ingredients in a large kettle or stock pot and simmer on low heat until squash is tender and liquid is hot. Serves four.

HANUKKAH: THE FESTIVAL OF LIGHT

Jewitches feel that Hanukkah corresponds to Yule or Imbolg on the Wiccan calendar. It falls during the Yuletide season, and many people are already familiar with it as a holiday in which candles are featured. Modern Judaism celebrates it as a the commemoration of battle victory, after which their temple flames burned for eight days on oil only sufficient for one, but, like other festivals of this season, it also celebrates the light of the newborn Sun.

Jewitches light their nine-branched candelabrum, called the *hannukkia,* in honor of the newly waxing Sun. The center candle from which all the others is lit is called the *shamash,* or server, and this has been adopted as the name for the working candles on Jewitch altars.

NINE CANDLE INVOCATION

As you light each of the nine candles of the season, offer
your praise to the newborn Sun and his waiting bride, the
virgin Goddess. With each candle you light, visualize the
heat of the Sun growing stronger as it returns to warm the
sleeping winter earth.

TU B'SHEVAT: A CELEBRATION OF TREES

This "New Year of the Trees" falls in late winter or early
spring. The popular paths of Teutonic and Celtic Pagan-
ism provide ample evidence that trees play a significant
role in the spiritual life of many cultures, and the old Pagan societies of the Middle East were no exception. Trees
link the underworld, middleworld, and upperworld; they
provide food, shelter, and shade; and serve as our concep-
tual model for the universe.

Celebrate this festival as modern Jewitches by planting
trees and worshipping their creators. Decorate them with
bells, eggs, and birdhouses, and provide food for their
roots and for the animals that dwell within them.

MAKING A BELL DECORATION TO BLESS A TREE

For each bell decoration you want to make you will need
three small jingle bells (look in craft stores or seasonal decoration shops for these), and thin satin ribbon (about a
quarter inch wide) in a variety of spring colors. Cut the ribbons into sections approximately one inch in length. Evenly space the jingle bells, three to each piece of ribbon, and
tie them with a simple square knot to hold them in place.

Take these around to the trees you wish to bless and
hang then on the lowest branches with a blessing.

PESACH: THE FEAST OF FREEDOM

The spring holiday of Pesach is more commonly known as
Passover, and it is one of the most cherished festivals of

both the Jewish and Jewitch year. It celebrates the preservation of life and freedom. Jewitches have adapted it as a celebration of thanks for having the freedom to worship as they choose. There is no known correspondence for this festival on the Wiccan calendar, but the lavish feasting is reminiscent of the autumn sabbats. It is also a good holiday model for Pagans of other traditions to adapt in order to celebrate their own freedom to worship or as a date to memorialize the martyrs who were executed as Witches.

FREEDOM OF WORSHIP RITUAL OUTLINE

Have individual candles on your altar for each of the world's major religions, and as many minor ones as you can find out about. Place a symbol of that religion, drawn on paper, at the base of the candle. You will also need one larger candle to represent the eternal flame of the spirit of creation—the primal deity that is both and neither God and Goddess. Place this in the center of your altar and place the other candles around it in a ring.

Leave all the candles but your working one unlit. Call on your deities and light the center candle. Begin talking about the unity of the divine creator, one being with many faces. Link this image to the many religions who all seek the same end—union with that creator. Begin lighting each of the outside candles from the inside one, seeing the growing light as one of truth and tolerance, an awakening to the knowledge that we are all one under the creator. When they are all lit, pick up the paper symbols of those religions and place them all together underneath the creator's candle. Move all the candles closer to the creator's flame while uttering your wish that all can see this unity of purpose. Acknowledge that all positive paths lead to the creator, and pray that we may all have the freedom to worship as we choose.

SHEILA-NA-GIG

BY EDAIN MCCOY

She squats frozen in time on ancient stone carvings over the threshold of many a sacred space. Is she a woman or a goddess? A mythic image or imagination? Why has she had the power to intrigue us throughout the centuries, and why do we still seek out her mysteries? At first look she seems a crude figure; roughly rendered, even coarse. Her long arms reach down between her spread legs as she grasps her vulva, parting it wide in a vaguely triangular pattern. The chasm she opens is dark, and it both beckons and repels.

This is the Sheila-na-Gig, a figure of ancient and unknown origin, whose image has been discovered all over Ireland near the sacred spaces of both the old and the new religions. One of these figures graced the entrance to the Goddess Brighid's shrine at Kildare. When that sacred site was taken over by the nuns of the new religion, they continued to keep their Sheila as a guardian of the threshold of the convent. The Kildare nuns were not the only new religion women to accept that the Sheila should remain right where they found her. In the late nineteenth century an archaeologist found a pile of them buried near the ruins of an old Irish convent in County Sligo.

When the carvings were discovered by horrified churchmen, they were vigorously hacked off the walls and doorways they adorned, and destroyed or buried. This was an image of evil, they cried. Ugly. Obscene. An image so blatantly sexual had no business in a convent whose inhabitants were under vows of chastity.

But is the Sheila offering sex, or a gift much greater?

The Sheila-na-Gig offers us an invitation into the feminine mysteries. The triangular pattern of her open vulva evokes the sacred number three of the Celts. This number represents many spiritual aspects, including the Triple Goddess, the cycle of birth, death, and rebirth, and the three levels of the Otherworld: upperworld, middleworld, and underworld. The Sheila-na-Gig's body is an open gateway to the otherworlds for those brave enough to accept her challenges and become initiated into her mysteries. The fact that the Sheila was often found over doorways to chapels and other sacred space underscores this aspect of her, since doors archetypally represent portals between worlds. Those who enter her mysteries are never the same again. They symbolically die, and are reborn back through her body, back through the same chasm that consumed them.

In this respect the Sheila embodies the insatiable, devouring energy long attributed to the feminine sex organs. This fearful image of a female who could not control her bodily urges is one of the reasons many of the old goddesses have been diabolized into vampiric demons and ugly faery hags. When stripped of their human-like qualities, when demoted from divinity, they somehow became less threatening, less real.

Sheila is not hungry to devour just to satisfy a physical appetite. She is the goddess from whom all were born, and to whom all must return to be reborn. In order to keep the eternal wheel of birth, death, and regeneration turning, the Goddess must devour us if she is to birth us anew. Rebirth in this instance is not just a physical action, but refers to a spiritual rebirth from which we emerge with knowledge of the greater mysteries of the Otherworld, our way-station between incarnations.

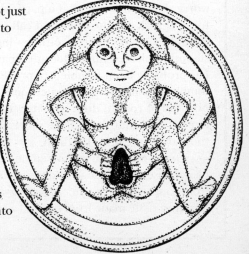

The next time you look upon the Sheila-na-Gig, note her enigmatic smile. Then close your eyes and accept her invitation into the otherworlds.

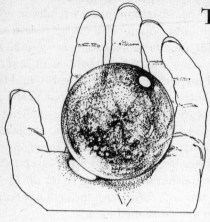

THE BASICS OF STONE WORK

BY MORGAN STARDANCER

There is a bounty of powerful gifts from our Earth that many people never recognize. Some are shiny or glittery, attracting the attention of all who behold them. Some are nondescript, maybe a dull black or brown. It matters little what they look like—they all hold natural energies that we can work with. They are stones.

I've spoken with people who swear they'll never be able to work with stones. "I'm not sensitive enough," they say. Or, "I just don't have the time to learn." Bah! It takes very little time to attune yourself with these treasures. In addition, it doesn't take special talents or abilities. Anyone can work with stones.

You can obtain stones from shops or you can go on a nature walk and search for your personal "power stones." Allow your higher self to guide you as you choose your stones. Don't worry about knowing what a particular stone should be used for; just pick out the ones that call to you. Their appearance shouldn't be of concern, either—just because a stone has a smooth, polished finish doesn't mean anything other than it has probably been tumbled (a process using an electric rock tumbler). Some of my favorite stones have been picked out of bins full of rough, dirty treasures direct from the Earth. Indeed, I feel that these have more beneficial energies than those that have been tumbled.

Once you've gotten your stones home, clean them up. It's okay to use regular soap and water to wash away dirt or grime from your stones. To shine quartz crystals and remove resistant dirt, try a paste made from salt and a small amount of water. An old toothbrush is good for scrubbing purposes. If there is grit stuck in cracks and crevices that refuses to budge, leave it be. After all, your stone may be thousands of years old, and might have spent its entire life with that dirt!

Now take a look at the stones you've chosen. Chances are you'll find some common links between them. Perhaps many of them are in the same basic color family, or similar shapes. If so, your higher self has called your attention to a particular energy that is needed in your life. For example, square stones in shades of brown symbolize earth—you may have chosen these if your life needs stability and grounding.

The next step will be cleansing on a deeper level than just physical, also referred to as "clearing." This more or less gives you a "blank slate" to work with as it disperses any non-inherent energies the stones might have picked up from being handled by other people, stored in a negative atmosphere, etc. Although many people have different methods for doing this, I recommend using the following technique until you can experiment and find out what works best for you. Submerge stones in salt (preferably sea salt, but purified table salt will also work) for at least twenty-four hours. Next, place them on a white or black surface and put them outside to bask in the Sun and moonlight. Allow the stones to sit outside for approximately forty-eight hours, more or less according to your own natural instincts.

Once they are cleansed, bring them inside. When you are ready to begin working with them, light a candle and burn a clear, purifying incense such as frankincense. Choose an especially appealing stone and hold it in your band. Here are a few things to try.

Close your eyes and meditate. Either project yourself into the stone or allow its energies to wash over you. Let your mind go where the stone takes it.

Another technique you might try with larger stones is to hold the stone in both hands, gazing into it. Again, go where the stone takes you. You may see visions. This is called scrying.

Choose a stone the color of one of the chakras, preferably one that you feel needs work. You can either hold the stone in your hand or over the chakra area. Go inside yourself to that chakra. See its color swirling and meshing with that of the stone; feel their energies combine to make the chakra stronger and healthier.

Keep a journal of what happens when you use different stones. Some might facilitate astral travel or past-life remembrances, while others relieve your stress and calm angry emotions. An important note: if you continually have negative experiences with a stone, return it to the Earth. I once had a milky quartz crystal that made me feel sad and depressed when I held it. Such a stone has been through terrible turmoil that has not yet healed, and it must be returned to the Mother so She can transform the pain.

When you've attuned more fully with stones, you can use them in every facet of your life, from amplifying your magic to boosting your energy level or even soothing minor injuries. The more you work with stones, the more natural it will seem to you. So go ahead—pick up those rocks. You might just be amazed at what they have to teach you.

MAGICAL CORRESPONDENCES? WHAT DO I USE THEM FOR?

By Silver RavenWolf

Almost every how-to magical book on the market gives you listings called magical correspondences. These lovely tables and columns brim with neat and nifty information that may include the subjects of herbs, planetary influences, candle colors, angels, gods and goddesses, metals, moon phases, magical alphabets, incesnses, stones, etc. You'll find daily correspondences, weekly correspondences, and monthly correspondences. With all this information, every single spell or magical application should work perfectly, right? Wrong.

The word *correspondence* (in magical applications) means stuff that goes together, things that match, symbols whose energies blend well with each other, or ideas that carry historical representations. These symbols enhance the practitioner's planned application. For example, the color red vibrates close to the same energy frequency as the emotion of passion. Historically, the color red conjures an association with the element of fire, and is associated with the root chakra. The heart shape travels through the collective unconscious as a symbol for love. Mythos, created by the human mind, tells us that Aphrodite stands for that elusive energy known as love. The soft scent and vibrational pattern of a rose blends easily with thoughts of love. Make that rose red, cut out a red paper heart to depict the fires of passion, call on Aphrodite, and you have the makings of a simple spell for conjuring love with the help of the correspondences you chose: Red, fire, heart shape, and Aphrodite. Through these symbols the magical practitioner uses sight, smell, touch, and emotion to focus on a chosen desire—love. If we throw in a Full Moon or a waxing Moon, we've added a planetary body whose energies affect the chemistry in our human bodies, and again, the Full or waxing Moon finds historical association—

lovers trysting under a Full Moon, and the waxing Moon's association with growth.

Correspondences don't make the magic—you do. Consider correspondences as fine-tuning devices, or that special ingredient in your favorite dish that gives the food an extra zing. Although correspondences carry energies of their own, their function relies on your focus. Throwing a bunch of stuff together (as in our previous example), a red candle, a red paper heart, rose petals, calling on Aphrodite on Friday in the hour of Venus during a waxing Moon, won't secure the love you need by itself. Correspondences help you to focus on your desire initially. Correspondences have energies that you can manipulate. The more correspondences you use in your magic, the better chances for success if you remain focused on the application, and if the universe has determined that your goal should manifest. Since not all goals and desires would be good for you, the universe may not dispense the energy in the way you wish, or in the time frame you desire, no matter how many correspondences you use.

Must you use correspondences in your magical and ritual applications? No. Some factors do override the energies of a correspondence. Emotion, for example, plays a big part in magical workings. If your need carries a high emotional level, such as how you feel during an emergency, and waiting for the right correspondence (the Moon phase or the correct planetary hour) isn't possible, your energy level may override the need for the use of those types of magical correspondences.

Magical training will also enhance the use of correspondences. If you have learned to focus, practice routine meditational exercises, work with energy flow in the body and in other areas, have a good relationship with spirit, etc., then these aspects of your training will enhance the use of correspondences.

Magical correspondences work well in our times of fallow, when our energy level feels low. Every individual experiences slow periods, and sometimes these vacant stretches can last six months or more, depending on the various issues and entanglements in our lives. In these times, the more correspondences you use, the better your chances of success in a magical or ritual application.

Must you use only the correspondences listed in magical books? Nope, although I'd work with these correspondences first to get the hang of what I'm doing. After you find your comfort zone with already published material, learn to create your own correspondences, but do so carefully. Experiment on a small scale and work up to bigger projects. Any spell book you buy represents someone's (usually the author's) experimentation with various correspondences.

Some correspondences will work better for you than others. Magical practitioners have found this particularly evident in color magic. Certain colors vibrate better, or can be massaged easier by one person than another. Again, this circumstance depends on magical training, experience, social background, personal history, and individual energy flow—all the factors that make you an individual.

Don't let those lists and columns of magical correspondences confuse you any more. Take your time, experiment, and build your skill level with the tried-and-true methods, as well as your own. You won't regret it!

COMMON SCENTS INCENSE

By Ronald Rhodes

This article is dedicated to Emma and all of the other goddesses in my life.

I've been working with herbs for more than twenty-five years. About seven years ago I started making incense. I found some of the ingredients listed in incense recipes very difficult, if not impossible, to obtain. Recently I've formulated some recipes using herbs, spices, extracts, and flowers available in any department, craft, or even grocery store. Follow these easy steps for all of my recipes.

1. Be sure all herbs, spices, peels, and flowers are completely dry.

2. All dry ingredients must be ground into a fine powder.

3. Mix all ingredients in a small glass container with a clean stick or your fingers.

4. Let the incense stand overnight to dry.

5. Store any unused incense in a tightly capped glass jar, away from light.

6. These incenses need self-igniting charcoal. Check the classified ads in this publication for this. Or, in a pinch, you might try to smolder some in a small, heavy pan on top of your stove.

7. Most important, for best results, try to blend your energies with the incense as you prepare and use it.

ALL PURPOSE INCENSE

1	tablespoon rosemary
1	tablespoon cinnamon
	Dry peel of one lemon
1	teaspoon thyme
1	teaspoon almond extract
1	teaspoon lemon extract
5	drops of your favorite scent

PAGAN POWER INCENSE

(For ritual energy)

1 tablespoon cinnamon
1 tablespoon anise seed
1 teaspoon nutmeg
1 teaspoon ginger
1 teaspoon lemon peel (dry)
1 teaspoon lemon extract
1 teaspoon peppermint extract
Dry petals of 3 white roses

DIVINE DELIGHT

(To honor your personal deity)

Dry peel of one orange
1 teaspoon nutmeg
1 teaspoon vanilla extract
1 teaspoon almond extract
Petals of one carnation
Petals of one rose

SACRED SPACE

(To clear and make pure an area)

4 tablespoons cedar chips
1 tablespoon thyme
1 tablespoon sage
2 teaspoons rosemary
1 teaspoon cinnamon
1 pinch of salt
1 pinch tobacco

WHITE LIGHT DELIGHT

(Use when invoking the white light of protection)

1 tablespoon rosemary
1 tablespoon ginger

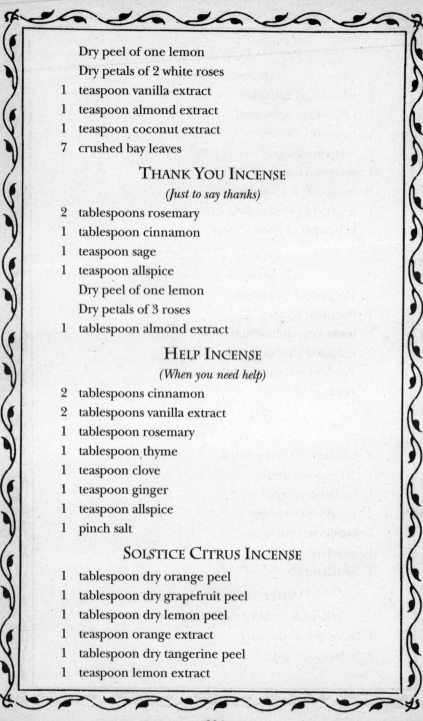

Dry peel of one lemon

Dry petals of 2 white roses

1 teaspoon vanilla extract

1 teaspoon almond extract

1 teaspoon coconut extract

7 crushed bay leaves

THANK YOU INCENSE
(Just to say thanks)

2 tablespoons rosemary

1 tablespoon cinnamon

1 teaspoon sage

1 teaspoon allspice

Dry peel of one lemon

Dry petals of 3 roses

1 tablespoon almond extract

HELP INCENSE
(When you need help)

2 tablespoons cinnamon

2 tablespoons vanilla extract

1 tablespoon rosemary

1 tablespoon thyme

1 teaspoon clove

1 teaspoon ginger

1 teaspoon allspice

1 pinch salt

SOLSTICE CITRUS INCENSE

1 tablespoon dry orange peel

1 tablespoon dry grapefruit peel

1 tablespoon dry lemon peel

1 teaspoon orange extract

1 tablespoon dry tangerine peel

1 teaspoon lemon extract

KITCHEN WITCHEN

(House blessing incense)

2 tablespoons dry lemon peel
1 tablespoon rosemary
1   tablespoon almond extract
1 teaspoon cinnamon
1 pinch garlic skins
1 teaspoon anise seed
1 teaspoon allspice
1 teaspoon coconut extract
1 pinch salt

ANCIENT ANCESTORS INCENSE

(To honor those who have passed on)

1 tablespoon anise seed
1 tablespoon ground pine needles
1 teaspoon sage
1 teaspoon thyme
1 teaspoon rosemary
1 teaspoon fennel seed
1 teaspoon basil
1 teaspoon almond extract

VERY FAIRY INCENSE

(Use to invoke the "little people" and natural spirits)

2 tablespoons dry tangerine peel
1 tablespoon anise seed
1 teaspoon thyme
1 teaspoon ginger
1 teaspoon cinnamon
1 teaspoon strawberry extract
   Dry petals of 1 pink rose

St. Nicholas the Pilgrim

By Ken Johnson

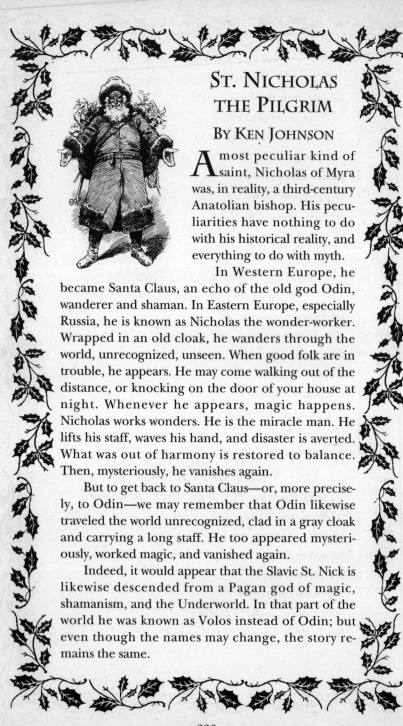

A most peculiar kind of saint, Nicholas of Myra was, in reality, a third-century Anatolian bishop. His peculiarities have nothing to do with his historical reality, and everything to do with myth.

In Western Europe, he became Santa Claus, an echo of the old god Odin, wanderer and shaman. In Eastern Europe, especially Russia, he is known as Nicholas the wonder-worker. Wrapped in an old cloak, he wanders through the world, unrecognized, unseen. When good folk are in trouble, he appears. He may come walking out of the distance, or knocking on the door of your house at night. Whenever he appears, magic happens. Nicholas works wonders. He is the miracle man. He lifts his staff, waves his hand, and disaster is averted. What was out of harmony is restored to balance. Then, mysteriously, he vanishes again.

But to get back to Santa Claus—or, more precisely, to Odin—we may remember that Odin likewise traveled the world unrecognized, clad in a gray cloak and carrying a long staff. He too appeared mysteriously, worked magic, and vanished again.

Indeed, it would appear that the Slavic St. Nick is likewise descended from a Pagan god of magic, shamanism, and the Underworld. In that part of the world he was known as Volos instead of Odin; but even though the names may change, the story remains the same.

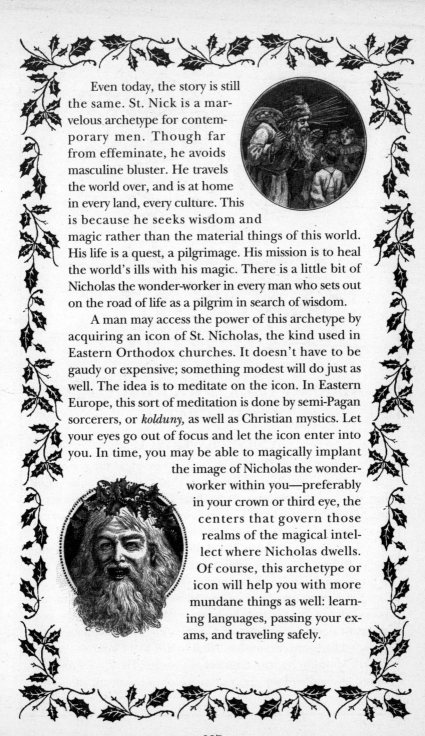

Even today, the story is still the same. St. Nick is a marvelous archetype for contemporary men. Though far from effeminate, he avoids masculine bluster. He travels the world over, and is at home in every land, every culture. This is because he seeks wisdom and magic rather than the material things of this world. His life is a quest, a pilgrimage. His mission is to heal the world's ills with his magic. There is a little bit of Nicholas the wonder-worker in every man who sets out on the road of life as a pilgrim in search of wisdom.

A man may access the power of this archetype by acquiring an icon of St. Nicholas, the kind used in Eastern Orthodox churches. It doesn't have to be gaudy or expensive; something modest will do just as well. The idea is to meditate on the icon. In Eastern Europe, this sort of meditation is done by semi-Pagan sorcerers, or *kolduny,* as well as Christian mystics. Let your eyes go out of focus and let the icon enter into you. In time, you may be able to magically implant the image of Nicholas the wonder-worker within you—preferably in your crown or third eye, the centers that govern those realms of the magical intellect where Nicholas dwells. Of course, this archetype or icon will help you with more mundane things as well: learning languages, passing your exams, and traveling safely.

Making Your Own Magic Kits from Scratch

By Silver RavenWolf

The ad at the back of your favorite magical magazine announces, "Spell kit of the Century! Just send fifty million dollars and we will send you..." and there follows a list of all sorts of magical goodies that gets your imagination rolling on the variety of things you could possibly do with such a kit. There's only one problem: you don't have fifty million dollars right at this moment. In fact, you may need fifty million dollars, which is why you want to purchase the kit in the first place.

For solving emergencies, the "allow four to six weeks for delivery" clause that protects both your rights and those of the vendor isn't a point in your favor. Goddess help you if you meet the dreaded back-order monster. What to do? Make your own magical kit. Most kits contain a variety of goodies. Here are some I've found: A candle of the appropriate color of the need; an oil with a tricky name matching the need; an herb or two; something to be empowered, such as a poppet, a crystal, or jewelry of some sort; parchment paper; colored thread or cord; and instructions.

Of course, there are spell kits that have pretty altar cloths, eye-catching trinkets, bath salts, clay braziers and charcoal blocks or unusual items that may be difficult for you to find. Although all these items can be lovely and interesting, they aren't necessary for good magic unless you think they are.

Making your own spell kit should be fun as well as eventually rewarding. Find a neat box, or decorate one yourself, to begin your kit. Consider what the kit is for—your need. Dedicate your box in the name of your need. For example, "This is my healing box, fashioned by the positive energies of the universe to fulfill the need of healing for my Aunt Pandora."

Next we establish sympathy. That means we look for something specific that connects our magic to the object of the need— a picture of Aunt Pandora in good health would work here. If you don't have a photo, ask for something that belongs to her. If that isn't possible, simply write her name on a piece of paper and put it in the box.

That was pretty easy. Now what do we do? With the establishment of need, we now go by the correspondences—you know, that list of what goes with what that your High Priestess drilled into your head, of if you are solitary, you spent hours studying by the light of your sixty-watt bulb. Get out a plain piece of paper and write down both the need and those correspondences. For example, since healing is the name of the box here, we would determine if the healing was a spiritual one or a physical one. Maybe Aunt Pandora needs both. Choose one need as the primary and the other as the secondary.

Before we go any further, let's think about when this spell has to be done. Right away? Can it wait a few days, a week or two? If it needs to be done right away, you are dealing primarily with planetary hours for your timing. If it can wait a few days then look to astrological correspondences associated with the day. If it can wait a few weeks, you can plan through the proper phase of the moon. On your paper, write down the best possible time to perform your spell. This is your target date, and you have until this day to collect the goodies to go in your spell box.

Would you like your spell box to revolve around a particular color that is associated with the need? For our healing box, we could choose blue or purple for spiritual healing, or green for physical healing. Of course, if neither is available, white works just fine. You can come up with lots of interesting items to match your color scheme. A candle, cord or string, gems and stones, jewelry, etc. If you are artistic, make a poppet, embroider a little picture, or decorate a stone with runes or other magical writing. Keep the need in mind as you create. As you collect each item, place it in the box.

Choose herbs that are "in sympathy" with the need. Groups of three work well. For physical healing you could use vervain (to make it go); rosemary (to banish negativity); dragons' blood (to give it more power). Frankincense and Myrrh are standard fare for money matters.

Now that you've collected all these wonderful items, what are you going to do with them? First, cleanse, consecrate, and empower—standard procedure for any application. Not sure what spell to cast? Don't worry about it as long as you remember to be specific. Spell kits work on the engine of sympathetic magic. The only way you can make a mistake is if you don't believe in what you are doing. With sympathetic magic, it is the intent and the belief that must be strong. The key to the spell kit is to mix the energies of everything in it to produce the desired outcome.

Once you've made and used your own spell kits, consider creating custom kits for special friends, and don't stop at the magical ones. Use your magic and creative genius to design unique kits for every occasion including birthdays, anniversaries, rites of passage, holy days, and just because you want to help a friend.

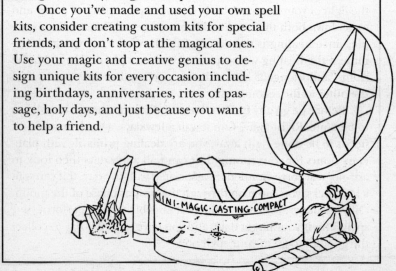

MINI·MAGIC·CASTING·COMPACT

DIRECTORY OF
PRODUCTS
AND
SERVICES

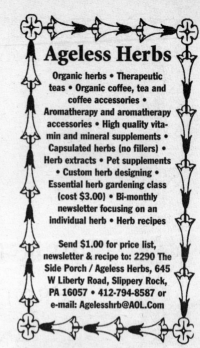
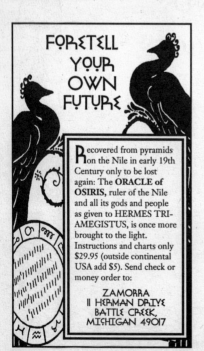

A CATALOG

A collection of hard-to-find, quality items sure to be of interest
to the serious practitioner. To obtain your copy of this full-color
catalog, send $2 along with your name and address to:

Witchery Company
Post Office Box 4067
Department L
Middletown, Rhode Island, 02842

THE WITCHES' ALMANAC

Established in 1971 and published in
the spring of each year, *The Witches'
Almanac* is an indispensible guide
and companion for adept, occultist,
witch and mortal alike. An annual
which offers insight and inspiration
through the passage of seasons with
herbal secrets, mystic incantations
and many a curious tale of good and
evil. 96 pages. To order send your
name and address along with $6.95
plus $2.50 s&h in U.S. funds.

For information on our other titles
(which include such gems as: *Love
Charms*, *Celtic Tree Magic*, and
Moon Lore to name but a few), send
us your name and
address and
we'll send you
our brochure.

THE
COMPLETE GUIDE
TO LUNAR HARMONY

$6.95

The
Witches'
Almanac

SPRING 1998 to SPRING 1999

BEING a compendium of ancient lore and
legend — the indispensible guide and delightful companion for adept, occultist, witch and
mortal alike ...

shows at a glance the phases of the moon,
notes the aspects of the planets and foretells
their influence on each sun sign in the astrological year to come ...

contains herbal secrets, advice about animals,
mystic incantations, sacred rituals and many a
curious tale of good and evil.

The Witches' Almanac
Post Office Box 4067
Department L
Middletown, RI 02842

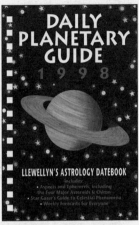

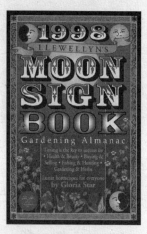

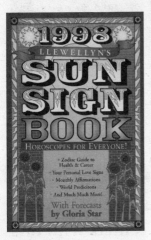

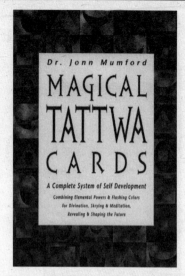

What the insiders know ...

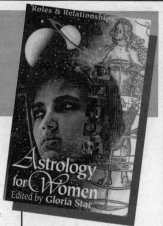

Llewellyn's Computerized Astrological Services

Llewellyn has been a leading authority in astrological chart readings for more than 30 years. We feature a wide variety of readings with the intent to satisfy the needs of any astrological enthusiast. Our goal is to give you the best possible service so that you can achieve your goals and live your life successfully. **Be sure to give accurate and complete birth data on the order form. This includes exact time (A.M. or P.M.), date, year, city, county and country of birth. Note: Noon will be used as your birthtime if you don't provide an exact time. Check your birth certificate for this information! Llewellyn will not be responsible for mistakes from inaccurate information.** An order form follows these listings.

SIMPLE NATAL CHART
Learn the locations of your midpoints and aspects, elements, and more. Discover your planets and house cusps, retrogrades, and other valuable data necessary to make a complete interpretation. Matrix Software programs and designs The Simple Natal Chart printout.
APS03-119 .... **$5.00**

PERSONALITY PROFILE
Our most popular reading also makes the perfect gift! This 10-part profile depicts your "natal imprint" and how the planets mark your destiny. Examine emotional needs and inner feelings. Explore your imagination and read about your general characteristics and life patterns.
APS03-503 .... **$20.00**

LIFE PROGRESSION
Progressions are a special system astrologers use to map how the "natal you" develops through specified periods of your present and future life. With this report you can discover the "now you!" This incredible reading covers a year's time and is designed to complement the Personality Profile Reading. **Specify present residence. APS03-507** **$20.00**

COMPATIBILITY PROFILE
Are you compatible with your lover, spouse, friend, or business partner? Find out with this in-depth look at each person's approach to the relationship. Evaluate goals, values, potential conflicts. This service includes planetary placements for both individuals, so send birth data for both. **Indicate each person's gender and the type of relationship involved** (romance, business, etc.).
APS03-504 .... **$30.00**

PERSONAL RELATIONSHIP INTERPRETATION

If you've just called it quits on one relationship and know you need to understand more about yourself before testing the waters again, then this is the report for you! This reading will tell you how you approach relationships in general, what kind of people you look for and what kind of people might rub you the wrong way. Important for anyone!

APS03-506 ....$20.00

TRANSIT REPORT

Keep abreast of positive trends and challenging periods in your life. Transits are the relationships between the planets today and their positions at your birth. They are an invaluable timing and decision-making aid. This report starts on the first day of the month, devotes a paragraph to each of your transit aspects and their effective dates. *Be sure to specify your present residence.*

APS03-500 – 3-month report $12.00
APS03-501 – 6-month report $20.00
APS03-502 – 1-year report $30.00

BIORHYTHM REPORT

Some days you have unlimited energy, then the next day you feel sluggish and awkward. These cycles are called biorhythms. This individual report accurately maps your daily biorhythms and thoroughly discusses each day. Now you can plan your days to the fullest!

APS03-515 – 3-month report $12.00
APS03-516 – 6-month report $18.00
APS03-517 – 1-year report $25.00

TAROT READING

Find out what the cards have in store for you with this 12-page report that features a 10-card "Celtic Cross" spread shuffled and selected especially for you. For every card that turns up there is a detailed corresponding explanation of what each means for you. Order this tarot reading today! *Indicate the number of shuffles you want.*

APS03-120 ....$10.00

LUCKY LOTTO REPORT (State Lottery Report)

Do you play the state lotteries? This report will determine your luckiest sequence of numbers for each day based on specific planets, degrees, and other indicators in your own chart. Give your full birth data and middle name. *Tell us how many numbers your state lottery requires in sequence, and the highest possible numeral. Indicate the month you want to start.*

APS03-512 – 3-month report $10.00
APS03-513 – 6-month report $15.00
APS03-514 – 1-year report $25.00

NUMEROLOGY REPORT

Find out which numbers are right for you with this insightful report. This report uses an ancient form of numerology invented by Pythagoras to determine the significant numbers in your life. Using both your name and date of birth, this report will calculate those numbers that stand out as yours. With these numbers, you can tell when the important periods of your life will occur. *Please indicate your full birth name.*

APS03-508 – 3-month report $12.00
APS03-509 – 6-month report $18.00
APS03-510 – 1-year report $25.00

ULTIMATE ASTRO-PROFILE

More than 40 pages of insightful descriptions of your qualities and talents. Read about your burn rate (thirst for change). Explore your personal patterns (inside and outside). The Astro-Profile doesn't repeat what you've already learned from other personality profiles, but considers the natal influence of the lunar nodes, plus much more.

APS03-505 ....$40.00

Special Combo Offer!

Personality Profile & Life Progression

This powerful combination of readings will help you understand what challenges lie ahead for you and what resources you have to achieve the success you want.

Special Combo Price!

APS03-216 $30.00

ASTROLOGICAL SERVICES ORDER FORM

SERVICE NAME & NUMBER_____

_____

Provide the following data on all persons receiving a service:

1ST PERSON'S FULL NAME, including current middle & last name(s)

_____

Birthplace (city, county, state, country) _____

_____

Birthtime _____ ❏ A.M. ❏ P.M. Month _____ Day _____ Year _____

2ND PERSON'S FULL NAME (if ordering for more than one person)

_____

Birthplace (city, county, state, country) _____

_____

Birthtime _____ ❏ A.M. ❏ P.M. Month _____ Day _____ Year _____

BILLING INFORMATION

Name _____

Address _____

_____

City _____ State _____ Zip _____

Country _____ Day phone: _____

Make check or money order payable to Llewellyn Publications, or charge it!
Check one: ❏ Visa ❏ MasterCard ❏ American Express

Acct. No. _____ Exp. Date _____

Cardholder Signature _____

Mail this form and payment to:

LLEWELLYN'S PERSONAL SERVICES
P.O. BOX 64383-K935 • ST. PAUL, MN 55164-0383

Allow 4-6 weeks for delivery.